Pierce County Courthouse
Tacoma Public Library

Thomas M. Chambers was one of the first Americans to settle in Pierce County. This was his mill located near Steilacoom on the creek that now bears his name.
Washington State Historical Society

Table of Contents

Washington State Historical Society

Old Town Photo Studio

Foreword

We make history every moment of every day. The now becomes the past in the blink of an eye. We are enriched and empowered when the realization that we are, in fact, the makers and caretakers of a "moment in history" strikes our consciousness. When this awareness happens the moment is ours.

That is why it is so important that historians like Caroline Gallacci help us cherish the memory of all those who have made history before us in Tacoma, this place we now call home. Many have left us with only a remnant of the "moment in history" that was theirs. It is the task of historians to preserve those moments.

The native people who inhabited this place passed along their oral traditions for many centuries. Then, from the latter half of the 19th century, when our contemporary city was built in the shadow of the great mountain Tahoma, illustrious writers recorded the events that shaped the history of the people of our region. Dr. Gallacci joins the ranks of historians Herbert Hunt, Murray Morgan and Ron Magden.

She has grasped the essence of history in this wonderful book. She knows the importance of remembering and recording and then sharing the history of this place with those of us who have the privilege of living the present moment of Tacoma's history.

Caroline writes of the rich cultural diversity of our city and county. The Puyallups, the foundation builders of this place, were joined by people of such diverse ancestry as the English, Swedes, Norwegians, Croatians, Swiss, African Americans, Germans, Japanese, Irish, Chinese, South Pacific Islanders and Italians, among others. History being written in the new millennium will tell of the more recent arrival in Tacoma of the Cambodians, Mexicans, Koreans, Polish, Vietnamese, Ukrainians, Filipinos, Moldavians, Salvadorians, Peruvians and people from every corner of the earth. The city's human tapestry is constantly being enriched by the contributions of a thousand new minds thinking thoughts that had never been imagined here before.

"In Tacoma," a city official once mourned, "you could be arrested for optimism." Today a new spirit pervades this corner of America. This may, perhaps, be the best of times. It is our destiny to become a great people and to build a great community on the foundation of those who have gone before us and about whom Dr. Gallacci writes so eloquently.

Enjoy the read. You are now a part of the history.

—Bill Evans
Tacoma City Council

Old Town Photo Studio

Washington State Historical Society, Photo by Charles E. Taylor

Introduction

Writing a history is an awesome task, especially for us living in Tacoma and Pierce County who have Murray Morgan's shoes to fill. He died while this work was in process and my one regret is that I was not able to share this manuscript with him. Murray was always a beacon for us stumbling through historical unknowns, and a person that any of us could call upon when our research led us to documentary dead ends. He was a true teacher — a one of a kind — who could so easily resurrect the past in ways beyond belief.

This history is designed to be a balance of both the old and new in terms of historical scholarship. As I looked at a broader time period than that covered by past historians, organizing the text proved a special challenge. My solution was to provide the reader with a chronological overview up to the eve of World War II, and then treat you to a more extended history of certain themes crucial to the understanding of the history of Tacoma and Pierce County.

The prologue introduces the reader to the landscape shaped and used by the Native Americans prior to the arrival of explorers, traders and settlers, and recounts the events leading up to the creation of Washington Territory in 1853. Following independent historical overviews of both Tacoma and Pierce County there are separate discussions of race and ethnicity, work, the creation of Tacoma's harbor and the construction of all that went into the physical infrastructure necessary to explain how and why we are what we are today. While the focus of the history is the first 100 years of Tacoma and Pierce County, this account also carries the story into the final decades of the 20th century. History always moves forward and so shall we.

Murray Morgan's work guided my writing, but so too did many other historians committed to explaining the characteristics of the region. The works of some are acknowledged in the bibliography or cited in the text. Others require a special show of appreciation. The Tacoma Historical Society sponsored this publication and without its support the history never would have been written. Conversations with Dr. Ronald Magden, Ron Karabaich — photo editor for this work — Cheryl Miller, and Joe Ursich have enabled me to put what is a very complex history into perspective. Thomas R. Stenger graciously made his private collection available to both the author and photo editor, providing in the process his own insights into Tacoma's history. And finally there is Gary Fuller Reese, who created the Tacoma Public Library's Northwest Room almost a quarter of a century ago. Without his endeavors historians truly would be lost.

One always fears, when sorting through the vast accumulation of historical data and opinion, that something significant is left out. I do apologize for all those omissions. Consider them as a motivation for all of you out there to continue the research, writing and publication of histories of Tacoma and Pierce County. History is, after all, a collective enterprise where the story is never complete as long as people retain their curiosity about the past.

—Caroline Gallacci

PROLOGUE

LAND OF THE NATIVE AMERICANS

The first Euro-American visitors to Pierce County encountered a landscape rich in variety, beauty and potential. In 1792 Captain George Vancouver called it an "enchantingly beautiful" landscape comparable to the "most elegantly finished pleasure grounds in Europe." For him there was "no reason to imagine that this country had ever been indebted for any of its decorations to the hand of man," and pondered what might happen once the land was "enriched by the industry of man with villages, mansions, cottages" and farms. Commerce too had a place in Vancouver's imagination as he observed the various waterways of Puget Sound. The natural inlets, when settled, could serve as the centers for an interior trade and as a safe haven "for such vessels as would necessarily be employed in those occupations."

The landscape described by Vancouver and his crew was limited to the shoreline in this maritime voyage of discovery. They observed steep bluffs and thick, forested interiors upon the peninsulas and islands that form western Pierce County. Seen too were open, or cleared, areas used as village sites by the Native Americans. Many were located near inlets and harbors fed by numerous streams and rivers.

The voyagers' observations of the rest of Pierce County were few but significant, especially Vancouver's description of Mount Rainier made in May of 1792:

"For having passed around the point, we found the inlet to terminate here in an extensive circular compact bay, whose waters washed the base of Mount Rainier. ... The forest trees and the several shades of verdure that covered the hills gradually decreased in point of beauty until they become invisible; when the perpetual clothing of snow commences, which seemed to form a horizontal line from north to south along this range of ragged mountains, from whose summit Mount Rainier rose conspicuously... the whole producing a most general and picturesque effect."

From the beginnings of the Euro-American presence in Pierce County, "The Mountain" was a geographical icon, one easily seen no matter where you happened to be.

For years historians considered this a portrait of George Vancouver. It has now lost its reputation as a likeness of the man and the painting has been removed from the National Portrait Gallery in London. Unfortunately, no image exists of this remarkable man. *MSCUA, University of Washington Libraries*

(Opening photo) Mount Rainier from Admiralty Inlet as sketched by John Sykes in 1792 *From A Voyage of Discovery to the North Pacific Ocean by George Vancouver. MSCUA, University of Washington Libraries, Native American Collection*

While Vancouver was able to portray the shorelines of Puget Sound in considerable detail, later English and American explorers helped to complete the geographical profile of an inland Pierce County bounded by the White River on the north, the Nisqually River on the south, and the Cascade mountain range to the east. Here the glacier-fed rivers of both the Carbon and Puyallup extended westward from the mountain's forested foothills to form natural valleys rich in agricultural potential. Farther west toward Puget Sound open prairies covered with indigenous grasses shared the landscape with thick, unpenetrable forests. Linking the two environments together was a system of lakes stretching southward from the future Tacoma townsite toward Eatonville in eastern Pierce County.

The land that the first Euro-American visitors saw, however, was not void of the "hands of man" as Vancouver assumed. For centuries local Native American tribes had been manipulating the environment in ways not seen by the new observers. Even as late as 1833, when William F. Tolmie contemplated the agricultural potential of the plains surrounding the new Hudson's Bay Company post at Fort Nisqually, he regretted "that a country which so easily could afford subsistence to man is yet uninhabited."

As a matter of fact, both the trails Tolmie walked along and the prairie he described were products of Native Americans living in Pierce County. They called the plains stretching from South Tacoma toward the Nisqually River Bau-kum an open place. Squa-szucks, a prominent point, identified the future Tacoma townsite. The Puyallup Valley eastward to the Cascades was Wheek, meaning both "a distant view," or "barely seeing it," referring perhaps to the visibility of Mount Rainier.

The prairies were not, however, really prairies but landscapes created by controlled burning. "Native fires were strategically set," explains historian William G. Robbins, "when seasonal and fuel conditions were conducive to low-intensity burns."

Ambrose J. Russell, one of Tacoma's early architects, created this painting of Mount Rainier in 1895. *Washington State Historical Society*

While this sketch drawn by Charles Wilkes in 1841 shows Native Americans fishing on the Chehalis River south of Pierce County, the Puyallup and Nisqually Indians used similar methods. *From Narrative of the United States Exploring Expedition by Charles Wilkes, MSCUA, University of Washington Libraries, Native American Collection*

Native Americans created the prairies by burning to enhance the growth of plants both to attract game for hunting and to develop food for harvesting. Opening the forested tracts also improved travel and provided a way to graze horses. It is an incontestable fact, claims Robbins, "that Indian cultural practices had profoundly influenced the character of the landscapes that Europeans reported." We don't know for sure how much of the Pierce County landscape was modified in this manner. What we do know is that once Euro-Americans stopped the Native Americans from burning, forests appeared where early explorers and settlers had only seen open prairie.

The Native Americans in Pierce County lived on sites near important fisheries and hunting grounds in a complex of summer and winter villages extending throughout the region. The cultural landscape also included sacred places and burial sites, as well as land set aside for horse racing and other sports. And while the Native Americans did not know it at the time, they had prepared the land for future foreign settlement. Their villages covered the county and became the places where Americans chose to create towns, cities and farms. The burned prairie

Native American fires created the prairies of Pierce County. The landscape was probably similar to this sketch of the grasslands surrounding Klamath Lake in southern Oregon. Trees appeared on the Nisqually Plains when the burning stopped. *From Reports of Explorations and Surveys to Ascertain the Most Practicable and Economic Route for a Railroad. Washington State Historical Society*

Native Americans spearing fish off Point Defiance around 1898
Washington State Historical Society

surrounding the Nisqually River and Steilacoom (Chambers) Creek proved uniquely useful to first the Hudson's Bay Company and then the earliest American settlers.

Puyallup native villages dominated the future Tacoma townsite. These centered on Hylebos Creek and Commencement Bay, including the Puyallup River upstream to Clarks Creek. According to Herbert Hunt, an early Tacoma historian, "the hub of their dominion was a large pool or inlet at what is now the foot of Fifteenth street." South of this location "there stood a large Indian cabin, with two or three smaller ones about it." Two miles west of this village site was a sheltered lagoon called Shu-bahl-lip. Between these two sites — located near a spring — was a "great rock, some seven or eight feet in height" which the Northern Pacific Railroad buried when the company began harbor development. It contained the image of a man on the surface, a feat credited to The Changer, a spirit able to turn humans into inanimate objects.

The Puyallup controlled the defenses around Commencement Bay and the Narrows. The bluff at South 9th and A streets in Tacoma was a signal station. In order to command the water routes into Puget Sound the tribe established villages at the head of Wollochet Bay, in Gig Harbor and at Quartermaster Harbor on Vashon Island. The defensive system did not go unnoticed by Americans later on when military planners recommended the creation of military reservations at Point Defiance, Gig Harbor and on Vashon.

Native Americans in south Pierce County were more closely tied to the Nisqually, a tribe whose economies and village life focused more on the rivers than on Puget Sound. There was one salt-water site, however, at Medicine Creek located within the Nisqually delta. Other major sites were on Sequalitchew and Muck creeks and on the Mashel River near Eatonville. In 1853, Territorial Governor Isaac I. Stevens selected the Medicine Creek village as the place for negotiating treaties with the South Sound Native Americans.

Between the areas of Puyallup and Nisqually influence were places of shared associations. The Steilacoom extended their influence toward Spanaway Lake. Native villagers at the confluence of the Stuck and Puyallup rivers had strong contacts with the Duwamish in King County. Those who lived on South Prairie were related to tribes on the Green River and moved to the Muckleshoot Reservation when required to leave their traditional home.

All these native associations produced a rich and complex cultural tapestry. In addition, Marian Smith, who studied the Puyallup and Nisqually in the 1940s, noted that the permanent or winter villages were "frequently an hour away by canoe or trail," suggesting an intricate system of transportation which earlier Euro-Americans used but did not completely document. Two trails are well known, however. One crested at Naches Pass in the Cascades and served as a northern route between the Yakamas and Pierce County tribes. The Brackenridge-Johnson party of the Charles Wilkes expedition used this route in 1841 during the first American exploration of the region. A decade later Theodore Winthrop immortalized the name Tacoma when traveling toward the land of the Yakamas. The

Naches Pass Trail became a route for pioneers, a military road during times of Indian troubles and a cattle and sheep trail when life became more settled.

A second road entered the region from the south and meandered northward to Commencement Bay. Settlers named it to honor Indian Henry, a Nisqually leader whose village was located near the trail on the Mashel River. This route also linked Puget Sound and eastern Washington Native Americans. Indians called the trail's end at Commencement Bay Swad-hum or Wad-hum-shum referring to the Plains natives who came westward to trade with the Puyallups.

By the time Captain George Vancouver sailed into Puget Sound, the Native Americans of the West had developed a sophisticated trading network that linked local Indian villages to the outside world. Key to the commerce were the Chinook, located along the Columbia River, the Nez Perce in eastern Washington, Oregon and Idaho, and the Plains Indians farther east. The Nisqually and Puyallup were connected to this larger trading network through their well-used trails and through their associations with tribes located along the waterways of Washington and British Columbia. Here coastal natives had been trading in sea otter furs with Europeans as early as 1778. On Puget Sound, beaver skins became the primary trade item.

The Puyallup and Nisqually were not isolated tribes when the whites first came. Puget Sound Indians were aware of the Europeans' interest in the sea otter and offered "the soft gold" in trade for goods the whites provided. The associations went beyond trade, however. Vancouver reported the countless depopulated and deserted villages, and the deathly effects of smallpox. The disease was "not only common, but it is greatly to be apprehended as very fatal amongst them, as its indelible marks are seen on many." Diseases of this nature were a clear sign of exposure to white culture even before Vancouver's arrival and partially explain why local Indian tribes were not able to resist Euro-American settlement. "The death of so many Indians," maintains historian John Findlay, "had essentially cleared the way for the flood of white settlement" into the Pacific Northwest.

By the time the English arrived in 1792, therefore, Euro-Americans were known to the Indians of Puget Sound through their exposure to both trade and disease. Vancouver was probably not aware of the native knowledge regarding the strangers. He had come for an entirely different reason.

Trade linked the Columbia River Chinook to the Puget Sound Native Americans. A.T. Agate captured the interior of a Chinook lodge during the 1841 Wilkes Expedition. *From Narrative of the United States Exploring Expedition by Charles Wilkes MSCUA, University of Washington Libraries, Native American Collection*

European Rivalry and Puget Sound

George Vancouver and his Lieutenant Peter Puget may have been the first to describe the interior waterways bordering Pierce County, but the two mariners were in reality among the last European explorers to venture to the north Pacific coastal region. Many had come before their celebrated voyage to claim the vast regions for their respective foreign crowns. The Spanish arrived first in 1707 although accounts suggest the Sir Francis Drake had declared the Pacific Northwest a possession of Queen Elizabeth I in the 1500s. The Russians appeared within a generation of the Spanish, putting into motion a round of European explorations and trading ventures which established Nootka Sound off Vancouver Island as a trading center.

All this means that the Pacific Northwest was not an isolated or unknown region when colonists on the Atlantic coast declared their independence from England and formed the United States. Indeed at the time the founding fathers were writing the Constitution Spain and England were threatening to go to war over an incident begun by the Spanish at Nootka. Hostilities were averted by means of a treaty allowing both countries to settle and trade in the region. The English sent George Vancouver to Nootka to make sure the terms of the agreement were carried out. It was while waiting for his Spanish counterpart to arrive from California that Vancouver launched his explorations leading to the exploration of Puget Sound.

He was not alone upon the waters. He encountered one Spanish explorer who shared his maps with Vancouver. Such generosity assured that some Spanish place names survived the English transformation of the landscape. Vancouver also met the American trader Robert Gray. He told Vancouver of his discovery of the Columbia River, prompting the English explorer to sail across the waterway's treacherous bar to assure ownership of the land for King George. It was Gray's second voyage to the region and while he didn't think much about it at the time, his discovery gave the United States a claim to the Pacific Northwest.

All early traders arrived in Puget Sound through the Strait of Juan de Fuca. T. Strothard captured its entrance during one of John Meares's voyages. *From Voyages Made in the Years 1778-1812 by John Meares* MSCUA, *University of Washington Libraries, Native American Collection*

Americans were also helped by events in Europe where the French Revolution and the rise of Napoleon allowed Boston traders to dominate the Pacific Northwest fur trade. President Thomas Jefferson's purchase of Louisiana Territory from Napoleon was an added blessing. By 1804 Meriwether Lewis and William Clark had begun their expedition through the new American acquisition toward the Columbia River, furthering United States interests in the Pacific Northwest. John Jacob

(Far left)
George Simpson, corporate manager of the Hudson's Bay Company, was determined to keep Puget Sound out of the hands of the Americans.
MSCUA, *University of Washington Libraries*

Fort Nisqually, established in 1833, was the first settlement in Pierce County. Within a decade of its founding Puget's Sound Agricultural Company sheep were grazing throughout the area.
Washington State Historical Society
Sketch by Alden

Astor solidified United States claims even further by establishing a fur trading post near the mouth of the Columbia at Astoria.

By 1819 American interests in the Pacific Northwest were enhanced by the Adams-Onis treaty whereby Spain surrendered all of its claims to the United States. One year prior to this agreement a treaty between the United States and Great Britain had promised joint occupation of the region by the two countries. Diplomatic assurances were no guarantee of a future American domination, however. Astor had been forced to surrender his outpost to the British during the War of 1812. Within a decade Oregon Country was under the sway of the Hudson's Bay Company (HBC). The firm was a monopoly blessed with all the power and authority the British parliament could bestow upon a private corporation.

The strategy of its governor, George Simpson, centered on one major assumption. The future boundary between the United States and Canada would follow the Columbia River, leaving Puget Sound to the British. To ensure this ultimate end Simpson in 1824 established Fort Vancouver on the north side of the river. He then ordered his trappers to completely destroy the beaver population on the south side, hoping that this would delay or remove the American presence. Finally he sent his trappers into Puget Sound in search of new locations for trading posts.

These HBC employees found Americans around the inland waterways. By one account Boston traders annually collected over 10,000 beaver pelts at prices way higher than what their British competitors were willing to offer. "In consequence of the American Coasters of late years frequently visiting the Strait of De Fuca," maintained John McLoughlin at Fort Vancouver, the company found it necessary "to keep a party constantly in Puget Sound." And so it came to be that in 1833 Simpson authorized the construction of Fort Nisqually in Pierce County near Sequalitchew Creek as a way to drive the Americans out.

For a while the British company was successful. Fur trading proved unprofitable, but the land surrounding the fort proved ideal for livestock production. In 1839, after Hudson's Bay officials decided to diversify their commerce through the creation of the Puget's Sound Agricultural Company, Fort Nisqually became headquarters for the new subsidiary. John Galbraith, a contemporary, also thought that the company farms, owing to their location, would serve as a "possible British counter in the Oregon dispute" that was beginning to preoccupy foreign diplomats in Washington, D.C. and London.

By 1846 some 8,000 sheep were grazing between the Puyallup and Nisqually rivers. Small, scattered farms and temporary shepherd stations were connected to each other and to Fort Nisqually by a system of trails. The company constructed wagon roads to Nisqually Landing located below the fort, and to Steilacoom (Chambers) Creek to the north. In most instances they improved upon the road

The Puget's Sound Agricultural Company established herder's stations for those tending the animals. One, the Sales Station, was located near Spanaway Lake. *Washington State Historical Society*

system created by the Native Americans, but adding farms to the landscape was a significant change.

Following the creation of the Puget's Sound Agricultural Company in 1839 the HBC tried to lure settlers from its Red River Colony in Canada to Fort Nisqually. Two years later 13 families arrived to farm the prairie between Sequalitchew and Steilacoom creeks. By 1845 all had left for the Willamette valley. Traditional farming was not profitable, especially when each family had to give a share of what they earned to the HBC. One settler, John Flett, did return later, however. When he came back he spent some time on South Prairie before moving to farm near Tacoma close to a creek that still bears his name.

Charles Wilkes was the first American to officially survey Puget Sound on behalf of the United States government. MSCUA, *University of Washington Libraries*

The company also tried to attract settlers from England and Scotland. Only one man, Joseph Heath, answered the call. He settled near Steilacoom Creek in 1844 on land first occupied by a Red River settler. Unlike the Canadians Heath stayed, planted wheat and built a farm complex Americans would find useful following his death in 1849 at the age of 44.

The motive behind British attempts to settle the region was obvious, at least to George Simpson. A United States-Canadian boundary at the Columbia River required a stronger English presence than what the HBC and its agricultural subsidiary could provide. The endeavor was doomed to fail. The company was, after all, a private monopoly concerned primarily with its own bottom line. Farmers were sharecroppers under the control of the company and not free subjects of Queen Victoria.

Furthermore, officers of the firm viewed themselves as owners of the land and were not willing to transfer that right to new settlers. There was a sense of bondage underlying HBC efforts to settle the territory, something that neither Englishmen nor Americans could really tolerate.

The American Ascendancy

The Hudson's Bay Company was never really able to keep the Americans away from Puget Sound. In 1839 the Methodist missionaries came. They hoped to both convert the Native Americans to Christianity and, in the words of Cecelia Svinth Carpenter, to "place a foothold in the land area north of the Columbia River for the United States." The church and school were located on the north side of Sequalitchew Creek near Fort Nisqually on land provided by the HBC. The missionaries, headed by Dr. John P. Richmond, abandoned their efforts three years later. Why is unclear, but the farming needed to subsist was poor, as were both Dr. Richmond's health and the relationship between the Nisqually Indians and the Methodists. In 1842 the group departed, leaving later Americans to claim the first foothold on Puget Sound.

The American naval officer Charles Wilkes was a far greater threat to the HBC than American missionaries. In 1838 he had embarked on the first major United States maritime expedition to the Pacific Northwest, one that led him to the Antarctic prior to his surveys of the Pacific Northwest. Wilkes had the opportunity to officially view Puget Sound through American eyes and what he saw and experienced changed the course of history. After his ship

Charles Wilkes named Commencement Bay and his reports convinced Congress that the region had to be part of the United States. This is a reproduction of one of his charts. *MSCUA, University of Washington Libraries*

went aground on the Columbia River bar and he had surveyed the waters to the north, he shattered all HBC hopes of a boundary settlement that would give Puget Sound to the British.

Wilkes arrived at Fort Nisqually in the spring of 1841 and established an observation post overlooking Puget Sound. Separate crews surveyed both local waterways and land to points extending towards Grays Harbor, the Columbia River and Idaho. Following his return to New York in 1842 Wilkes published the results of his expedition thereby focusing a spotlight on the northern reaches of Oregon Country.

The exploring expedition did two other things that collectively symbolized official American interest in the Puget Sound region. One occurred on July 5, 1841, when the crew, Methodist missionaries, Fort Nisqually employees and Native Americans celebrated Independence Day for the first time in the Pacific Northwest. Dr. Richmond's speech, as retold by Murray Morgan, must have really ruffled British feathers:

"We entertain the belief that the whole of this magnificent country, so rich in the bounties of nature, is destined to become a part of the American Republic.... The time will come when these hills and valleys will be peopled by our enterprising countrymen, and when they will contain cities and farms and manufacturing establishments, and when the benefits of home and civil life will be enjoyed by the people. ... The future years will witness wonderful things in the settlement, the growth and the development of the United States and especially of this coast."

To accent future domination by the United States, Wilkes covered Puget Sound with American place names. Granted some — Anderson, McNeill and Kittson — served to honor the generosity of his British hosts. He named most places, however, either after members of his crew, or as geographical references to the work of the exploring expedition. Commencement Bay was where the survey began, for example. Gig Harbor was a safe haven for small boats. Names honoring his crew members covered many of the islands, inlets, bays and harbors encompassing Pierce County.

Wilkes' place-naming was a significant and important piece of work. George Vancouver and Peter Puget certainly didn't make much of an effort to cover the terrain with English titles. Wilkes filled the void, and by placing American nomenclature upon the landscape he helped others to view the region as a possible United States possession.

Even before Wilkes published his account, "Oregon Fever" hit the nation. By 1845 almost 5,000 people had moved westward across the Oregon Trail. It is not known how many more came by ship. Most saw the Willamette valley as their final destination, but Michael T. Simmons and George Washington Bush looked northward to Puget Sound. In that year they became the region's first American, and African American, settlers. They were not Pierce County's first. Both settled south of the Nisqually River near Olympia. James McAllister, another member of the Simmons-Bush party, settled near the Medicine Creek Indian village on the Nisqually delta. Even so, their arrivals introduced a permanent American presence in the region.

One year later Congress recommended an end to the joint occupation agreement that had governed American and English relations in the Pacific Northwest since 1818. Turmoil preceded the decision. In 1844, just when the British government proved willing to give Puget Sound to the Americans, supporters of Presidential hopeful James K. Polk had launched a "54-40 or fight" campaign demanding a border along the Alaskan panhandle. By 1846, however, the main issue was free trade. After England opened its markets to wheat and cotton, Americans lost interest in any war against Great Britain and accepted a boundary along the 49th parallel. The United States and the English signed the Oregon Treaty on June 15, 1846.

The agreement did not mean the end of the Hudson's Bay Company or its agricultural subsidiary. By the terms of the treaty the Puget's Sound Agricultural Company owned its lands in Pierce County until the United States decided to buy them.

Years of negotiation followed and it was not until after the Civil War that English and American diplomats agreed to a sale price of $650,000. "The blight of foreign influence on our soil," to use Territorial Governor Isaac I. Stevens' words, did not keep settlers out of Pierce County but it did slow matters down a bit. Not until 1869 were the first residents able to get secure deeds for the land they had occupied sometimes for over a generation.

The United States Army came to Pierce County in 1849. Fort Steilacoom remained a center for settlers until its closure in 1868.
Washington State Historical Society

The treaty mandate was a difficult one for local settlers to accept. The ink was barely dry on the document when Americans began to find their way to Pierce County. The newcomers were trespassers in the eyes of the Hudson's Bay Company. Then too Congress was slow to provide expected government protection to the area. Native unrest and the deaths of missionaries Marcus and Narcissa Whitman near Walla Walla in 1847 finally forced Congress to act. In August of 1848 an area encompassing Oregon, Washington, Idaho and parts of Montana and Wyoming became Oregon Territory. From this time until 1853, when Congress created Washington Territory, a group of politicians located far away in Salem, Oregon, governed Pierce County residents.

Native unrest also brought the American Army to Pierce County in 1849, when the military selected Joseph Heath's farm as the ideal location for Fort Steilacoom. Dr. William F. Tolmie, representing the Puget's Sound Agricultural Company, accepted an offer of $50 per month for the property and by December of that year the men of Company M had moved in. The U.S. Army remained until 1868 providing both security and companionship to American settlers finding their way to Puget Sound.

It is not easy to determine exactly who the first arrivals were. Settlement in the late 1840s might be better explained as a quiet infiltration. The process was really an evolutionary one. Thomas M. Chambers, who established a claim on Steilacoom Creek in 1849, was certainly one of the earliest Americans. But the HBC still farmed its scattered sites between the Puyallup and Nisqually rivers. "Each farm or station was assigned to an individual employee," explains Cecelia Carpenter. "Francois Gravelle and John Ross each operated their own farms under contract with the Company. Walter Ross was sent out... to take charge of... the farm site near American Lake... and business continued as usual."

But not for long! Not all employees proved loyal to the Hudson's Bay Company. Some opted for American citizenship when Congress offered free land in the new territory. The lure prompted French Canadians and Englishmen to stay, especially those who had Native American wives. The promise of land also invited more Americans to venture to this isolated region of the country. Together they all formed a community and when that happened, Pierce County was truly born.

CHAPTER ONE

PIERCE COUNTY: A HISTORICAL OVERVIEW

Settlement in Pierce County began amid tremendous changes elsewhere in the country. As a result of the Mexican War between 1846 and 1848, the nation acquired the southwestern parts of the United States. Toward the war's end a workman discovered gold in John Sutter's millrace in the Sacramento Valley, and the California Gold Rush was on. Both of these events were to have an impact on how Pierce County grew and developed during its formative years. The war ultimately led to a new federal Indian policy which placed Native Americans on reservations. The Gold Rush brought the first economic boom to Puget Sound and ultimately led to the formation of Washington Territory in 1853, the same year Oregon legislators created Pierce County.

Events closer to home in the Willamette Valley also shaped the local future. Here what captured the attention of most people was land ownership. Many Americans had claimed and farmed property before the boundary settlement with Great Britain. To provide clear title for the farmers living in Oregon and to encourage future settlement, Congress passed the Oregon Donation Land Law in 1850. The act, which expired in 1855, allowed white husbands, wives and men over the age of 21 to claim 160 acres of land and to buy more if they wished at $1.25 per acre. When Washington was separated from Oregon, the law also applied to the new territory.

According to county historian William Pierce Bonney, 103 men or families filed Donation Land Claims in Pierce County by 1855. Of these, 84 eventually acquired title to their land. "The owners of these claims were all real pioneers," Bonney explained in his history. "It was natural for the first settlers to seek land near the water courses, springs and lakes of the county." The newcomers also selected areas that would be easiest to farm and were therefore drawn to

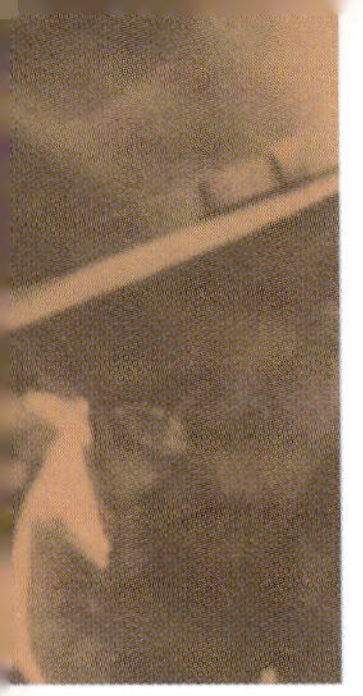

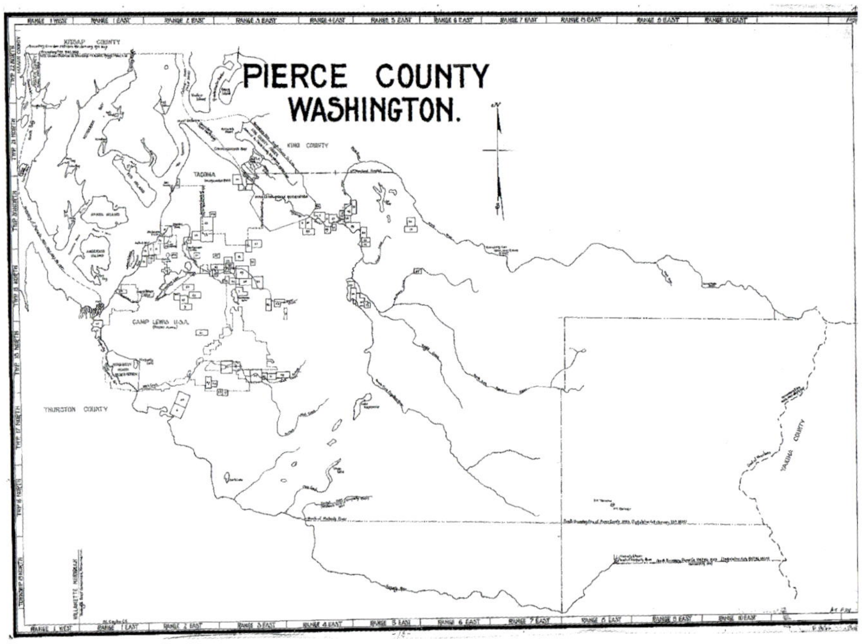

Donation Land Claims were the first evidence of American settlement in the region. William Pierce Bonney introduced this map of local claims in his 1927 *History of Pierce County*. *Washington State Historical Society*

the open prairies created by Native American burning and still grazed by Puget's Sound Agricultural Company sheep and cattle. The areas that proved most attractive during the county's formative years extended outward from Fort Steilacoom along Steilacoom (Chambers), Muck and Lacamas creeks and their nearby lakes. Later settlers chose sites in the rich agricultural lands bordering the Puyallup and Stuck rivers.

These first settlers were a varied lot. Some, such as Isaac Bastion and Francois Gravelle, were French Canadian former employees of the Hudson's Bay Company. At least one, Charles Wren, was the offspring of the union between a Native American and a British employee. Others like Martin Fahy and James Minson were discharged soldiers from Fort Steilacoom. Many came from Midwestern or border states, seeking to escape both economic depression and the dividing tendencies of slavery. They traveled alone by ship, sometimes stopping at the California gold fields along the way. Or the newcomers joined the 33,000 people using the Oregon Trail between 1850 and 1855. Finding little land in the Willamette Valley, the migrants moved north. The largest number to arrive at one time, however, came in 1853 after crossing the Cascade Mountains through Naches Pass.

Upon their arrival the new settlers began the business of farming, raising families and creating the community life familiar to them back home. One observes a record of marriages among these first migrants between the children as well as the widows and widowers of those losing their spouses along the way. The men became officeholders, jurors and road builders while the women organized schools, churches and social functions needed to tie the various settlements together. Communication with the outside world was secured in 1852 when the federal government approved the creation of a post office at the freshly platted town of Steilacoom. Security was provided by the men of Company M stationed at Fort Steilacoom.

There were problems, however. For one, the Puget's Sound Agricultural Company still claimed ownership of the lands now occupied by donation land claimants. For another, the center of territorial government at Salem was too distant to aid the residents of "Northern Oregon." The Oregon Territorial Legislature, in response to local concerns, reorganized the northern counties, first by forming Thurston County — one that included both Pierce and King — and then by dividing the three into separate entities. In January of 1853, the Legislature designated Steilacoom the county seat of Pierce County and appointed Thomas Chambers, William P. Dougherty and Alexander Smith the first county commissioners. A governing body of three commissioners was to serve Pierce County until 1981.

At the same time that Northern Oregonians were seeking county status, they were petitioning Congress for a government closer to home. In March of 1853 their demands were met when Washington became a territory and Isaac I. Stevens became its appointed governor. Stevens had more to do than simple administration, however. On his way west he was to survey the landscape for a railroad

(Opening photo) In 1937 forest ranger Ed Gross discovered a wheel from one of the wagons lost on the Naches Pass in 1853. *MSCUA, University of Washington Libraries, Photo by R.N. Cullough* route across the northern United States. Upon his arrival in Washington he was to assume his role as Superintendent of Indian Affairs.

Reservations and War

By 1854 the Puyallup and Nisqually Indians found most of their village sites claimed by Americans. Part of Isaac I. Stevens' responsibility, therefore, was to negotiate treaties with the Native Americans so that each tribe would relinquish its rights to the land. In exchange, the federal government was to reserve specific areas upon which the Indians would live and be taught the ways of American civilization. Stevens selected a site at Medicine Creek on the Nisqually River delta to settle matters with the Pierce County tribes. Discussions began on December 24, 1854.

Stevens dominated the proceedings, treating those present as children in need of his fatherly care. Furthermore, the treaty document was not a negotiated matter but one already used elsewhere in the country. With no apparent discussion with local tribes, the governor established the sites for the reservations and forced those locations on the chiefs and subchiefs attending the meetings. Translators read the treaty to the assembly in Chinook, a trade language not easily applied to the complexities of the treaty. Therefore, most of the Indians who signed the agreement on December 26, 1854, were provided little opportunity to fully understand — or to debate — what their conformance meant.

The Medicine Creek Treaty, which Congress ratified on April 10, 1855, established two reservations for Pierce County Indians. The Nisqually were to settle on forested land east of the river delta in Thurston County. The Puyallup reservation was to be located along the south shore of Commencement Bay. As Stevens traveled eastward to complete his negotiations with other tribes, local Indians began to realize the full impact of the agreement. The Nisqually, explains Cecelia Carpenter, "had not fully anticipated the poor choice of reservation land... They had wanted river frontage for fishing and prairie grassland for their horses." The same held true for the Puyallup, whose reservation was also in the forests and away from traditional villages. Stevens returned to Puget Sound in January of 1856 to fight an Indian war that had begun three months earlier on Connells Prairie in northeastern Pierce County.

Many historical themes are encompassed in the Puget Sound Indian War of 1855 and 1856. Before Stevens returned, acting territorial governor Charles H. Mason ordered that all Pierce County Indians be interned on Fox Island (other Puget Sound tribes received similar treatment). Stevens' first act upon his arrival was to order the extermination of all hostile Native Americans, thereby encouraging members of the territorial citizen militia under the command of H.J.G. Maxon to kill all Indians, including women and children, at a Mashel River village. In addition, Stevens declared martial law in Pierce and Thurston counties and jailed and

While many Pierce County settlers fled to Fort Steilacoom during the Indian Wars of 1855-56, others built blockhouses to protect themselves. *Washington State Historical Society*

attempted to court-martial settlers — especially those with Indian wives — who refused to participate in the hostilities.

Additionally, his behavior led to continuous discord with U.S. Army officers at Fort Steilacoom. Stevens had resigned his military commission to accept his political appointments and his relationship with the local army was at best uneasy. Those stationed at Fort Steilacoom were convinced that Stevens, who considered himself commander of the citizen militia, was acting outside the law in his treatment of both American citizens and native warriors.

The most controversial episode was Stevens' insistence that Chief Leschi be tried and hanged for the killing of volunteer Colonel A.B. Moses during the course of the war. Following Leschi's arrest in November of 1856, two trials were necessary to prove the defendant guilty. Army officers at Fort Steilacoom who aided in the arrest of Sheriff George Williams thwarted the first scheduled hanging. When Leschi's supporters failed to obtain a pardon, he was again scheduled to hang on February 19, 1858. Officers in charge at Fort Steilacoom refused the use of Army land for this purpose. Instead the gallows were constructed about a mile east of the fort — there is a shopping center there now — and on the appointed day Leschi was hanged.

The war had ended a few months prior to Leschi's arrest. Even though the Indians were militarily defeated, their initial aim — better reservations — was achieved when Stevens met the Native Americans on Fox Island on August 5, 1856. At the council the governor agreed that his initial choice of reservations was wrong and moved the two locations to better sites. The Nisqually now found themselves skirting both sides of the river on lands encompassing traditional village sites, including one on Muck Creek in Pierce County. The Puyallups' reservation included all their river delta eastward toward the shore and the surrounding hills of Commencement Bay, and southward into the river valley. An Executive Order signed by President Franklin Pierce on January 19, 1857, solidified the agreements Stevens made at the Fox Island Council.

The resolution of the conflict did not end the story of American-Indian relations, for they continue to the present. Both reservations became coveted real estate toward the end of the 19th century, albeit

In July of 1895, tribal members reburied Chief Leschi on the Nisqually Indian Reservation. In this view Bill Quiemuth is on the far left and George Leschi stands with hat in hand. Yelm Jim holds the rope. *Washington State Historical Society*

Charles Grainger, His Executioner, on Leschi

"I felt that I was executing an innocent man. I had charge of Leschi two weeks before he was taken to Steilacoom. He was cool as could be — just like he was going to dinner. On the scaffold he thanked me for my kindness to him. He said that he was not guilty; that Rabbeson had lied when he said he saw him in the swamp, and that he would meet him before his God and that he would tell him there he lied. He said he was miles away when Moses was killed.

"Leschi was a square-built man, and I should judge would weigh about one hundred and seventy pounds. He was about five feet six inches tall. He had a very strong, square jaw and very piercing, dark brown eyes. He would look almost through you, a firm but not a savage look. His lower jaw and eyes denoted firmness of character. He had an aquiline nose, and different kind of features than those flathead Indians — more like the Klickitats. His head was not flattened much, if any at all. He had a very high forehead for an Indian.

"I saw Leschi in 1853 at McAllister's on the Nisqually. McAllister told me he was a good, faithful Indian. George McAllister and Joe Bunton both told me that Leschi met them on the way and helped them.

"He did not seem the least bit excited at all — nothing of the kind, and that is more than I could say for myself. In fact Leschi seemed to be the coolest of any on the scaffold. He was in good flesh and had a firm step and mounted the scaffold without assistance, and as well as I did myself. I felt then I was hanging an innocent man, and I believe it yet."

— *History of Pierce County, Washington* by W.P. Bonney

Chief Leschi
Washington State Historical Society Watercolor by Raphael Coombs

for different reasons. Until then, however, federal Indian agents made conscientious attempts to keep Americans from settling on reservation lands and tried to create a new life for the displaced Native Americans. By the end of the Civil War the Puyallup Indian Agency headquarters had become a stopover and supply station for Americans seeking both farmland and townsites in Pierce County.

In 1862 Congress passed the Homestead Act, luring more settlers westward. Two years later Stevens' role as railroad surveyor bore fruit with the incorporation of the Northern Pacific Railroad charged with the construction of a line between Lake Superior and Puget Sound. Both events, along with the federal purchase of Hudson's Bay Company lands in 1869, energized the county as more people came, acquired land and began to speculate on where the railroad terminus might be. The Puyallup and Nisqually Indians were never far removed from these events fueling the county's history.

The Making of Pierce County

To talk about the history of Pierce County after the Civil War is not simply to tell the story of a single place. There are different regions of the county, each with its own distinct story to tell. Some settlements were born long before Tacoma arose as the terminus of the Northern Pacific Railroad transcontinental line in 1873. Other communities emerged because of the railroad. While all eventually became part of Tacoma's hinterland, each also was a settlement in its own right.

There are common threads in this tapestry. Community life usually centered on a post office, a school, churches and a general store. Modes of transportation were identified by wagon roads or train depots, or wharves for those facing Puget Sound. The settlements were family-oriented and designed

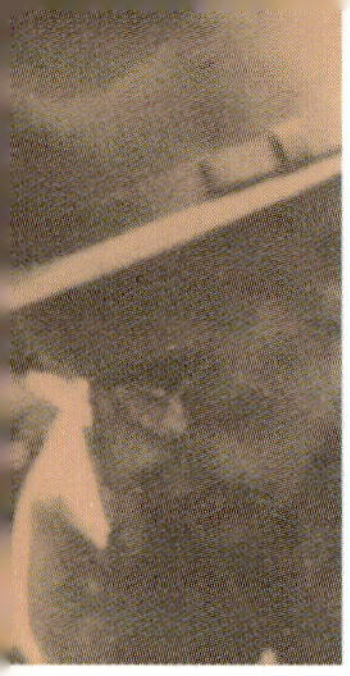

Rose Emma Atkinson completed this painting of Frank Spinning's Puyallup River cabin in 1888, long after the Northern Pacific Railroad had begun to reshape the idyllic portrait of a Pierce County homestead.
Washington State Historical Society

Portable sawmills roamed Pierce County during the early years, allowing settlers the luxury of a wood frame house rather than a log cabin.
Washington State Historical Society

around the largess of nature — trees, coal or fish — or the productivity of the soil. When the land proved unaccommodating, dairy production, chicken farms and cattle grazing provided adequate substitutes.

The resulting environment was not really unique. The first Pierce County settlers, after all, brought their culture with them and they were never far from influences back home. Newspapers and letters kept folks abreast of the latest political or cultural trends. With time, mail order catalogs enabled Pierce County settlers to get all the necessities of life, from houses to tombstones. In other words, Pierce County was never completely isolated from the rest of the world, but sometimes the snail's pace of communication made the earliest settlers feel very much alone and highly dependent on each other.

Association and governance were the essence of community life. Most often the first institutions formed by settlers were school districts. These dotted the landscape and served as the focus of the various settlements until district consolidations began in the 1940s. Voting precincts also defined the early communities, as did the road districts created by the Pierce County commissioners. When the population grew and more government was needed, residents agreed to the incorporation of cities and towns. Pierce County now has 21 such entities dating from Steilacoom in 1854 to Edgewood and Lakewood in 1996. All of these organizations emphasized the importance of participatory democracy as the foundation of community development.

Settlements arose first within the Nisqually plains where the new arrivals remodeled the Puget's Sound Agricultural Company farming stations into American creations. Communities then spread eastward into the agricultural valleys and westward onto the islands and peninsulas of Puget Sound. When Northern Pacific officials discovered coal in northeastern Pierce County in the 1870s, settlement took a different form. In that region, company towns emerged as industrial suburbs of Tacoma. To the south, the railroad line of the Tacoma Eastern spread development to the present boundary of Mount Rainier National Park. Other unique enclaves in and around Tacoma, such as Ruston and Salmon Beach, have also added to the rich variety of community life defining Pierce County.

It is not possible to provide the histories of all the settlements, for there were literally hundreds of them. What follows is a sampling of regional highlights and events that best characterize some communities dating from the beginnings of Pierce County to the eve of World War II.

The Greenwater River marks the far northeastern boundary of Pierce County. C.B. Talbot photographed the Allen settlement in 1895. *Washington State Historical Society*

British Occupation Transformed: The Nisqually Plains

When Pierce County first began, all roads led to Steilacoom. Lafayette Balch and John Chapman were the town's two founders when one platted Port Steilacoom and the other Steilacoom City on their adjacent Donation Land Claims facing Puget Sound. The town incorporated in 1854, shortly after the Oregon Territorial Legislature declared it the county seat. For almost 30 years Steilacoom was the center of urban life, losing out to the railroad and Tacoma in 1880. At that time local voters decided to move Pierce County government offices to the new City of Destiny.

Initially the region surrounding Steilacoom — an area bounded roughly by Chambers Creek, Spanaway Lake and the Nisqually River — was agricultural and it remained so for many years. But early on, the land began to acquire an incredible mixture of things. The first noticeable diversion from farming occurred following the abandonment of Fort Steilacoom in 1868 when Congress approved the use of the land as an "asylum for the insane," or what is known today as Western State Hospital.

The rural nature of the Nisqually plains was transformed further following the arrival of railroads and streetcars after 1873. The first Northern Pacific line entered Pierce County near the junction of Lacamas and Muck creeks, and there in 1884 James M. McNaught platted the town of Roy. Four years later, north of this new town, Lake Park was platted on the east shore of Spanaway Lake as one of the first suburbs linked to Tacoma by streetcar. William Wilson and Frank D. Nash platted Parkland and Brookdale just north of Spanaway in 1890.

Henry Holt painted this view of Day Island in 1904. The Puget Sound island was a summer retreat for local residents, including the owners of the Holt Art Store located in Tacoma. *Washington State Historical Society*

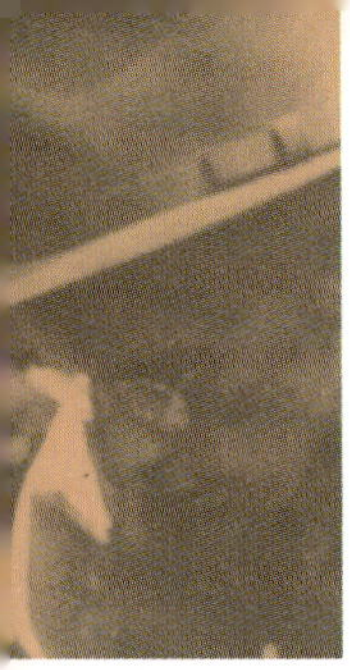

The lakes south of Tacoma attracted the Hudson's Bay Company and many of the first settlers long before the waters became recreational havens for city residents. MSCUA, *University of Washington Libraries*

DuPont, located on the original site of Fort Nisqually, became the second company town. Edward Huggins, who had acquired much of the property after the British left, sold it to the E.I. DuPont de Nemours Company in 1906. The firm constructed the Village of DuPont between 1909 and 1916 to house the families of those working in the plant. Most of the land, however, was reserved for the production of mining explosives. The enterprise continued until 1976 when the Weyerhaeuser Real Estate Company purchased the property and began planning the development of Northwest Landing as a new town surrounding the original village.

By the 1890s the region had also proved attractive to Methodist and Lutheran educators seeking sites for institutions of higher learning. University Place was to be the location of the University of Puget Sound. In 1895, landscape architect E.O. Schwagerel proposed a plat of lots bordering winding boulevards, circles and malls whose sale would fund the college. The project never materialized after officials decided to hang onto their Tacoma roots. In 1894, near the same time that the Puget Sound school was considering a site north of Steilacoom, other educators established Pacific Lutheran University at Parkland, thus providing a major cornerstone for the fledgling community.

The early years of the 20th century saw additional changes brought on by both industrialization and urbanization. The result in two instances was the creation of company towns. In 1908 the McKenna Lumber Company selected a site on the Nisqually River south of Roy for its mill and developed a town for its workers. The firm also attempted to develop a rural community as an adjunct to the town by irrigating Yelm prairie in Thurston County and giving jobs to the workers who bought the irrigated land. Observers at the time termed the venture a semicooperative experiment in farming and industry.

Urbanization yielded a different kind of change to the Nisqually plains. By the 1880s, Tacoma's businessmen began to view the lakes region as an ideal spot for recreational homes. From this interest grew residential suburbs designed to attract those families who wanted to live outside Tacoma but worked downtown. By 1910, Lakewood lots were a hot item on the real estate market. "While Lakewood is to be a suburb of Tacoma," explained one news reporter, "it is planned to give the residents there every convenience of a separate community, and it is intended to make the locality the business center of the larger region." Norton Clapp enhanced this early vision in 1937 by constructing Lakewood Center, one of the first planned suburban shopping centers in the region.

By the eve of World War I the area still remained somewhat agricultural, explaining perhaps why the land extending south from American Lake toward Roy attracted the attention of those wanting a military reservation in Pierce County. The idea wasn't new at this time. Tacoma's businessmen had been talking about the possibility since 1895. The Army, however, was not willing to pay for the land. The matter was resolved on January 16, 1917, when Pierce County voters approved a bond issue to establish Camp (later Fort) Lewis.

Both negative and positive results emerged from the decision to create the base. On the one hand, condemnation suits removed all residents from some 109 square miles of settled farm and forest land. In addition, the action necessitated the loss of that part of the Nisqually reservation and cemetery located in Pierce County. On the other hand, the presence of Fort Lewis improved economic conditions for the entire region. It also served as a settlement magnet for military retirees who liked what they saw in Pierce County and decided to stay.

The Puyallup Valley

Somewhere on Elhi Hill near Bonney Lake is a culturally modified rock named Skystone by today's archaeologists. The Puyallup Indian observatory overlooks the Puyallup Valley near the Naches Pass trail not far from Connells Prairie, the site of native hostilities in 1855 and 1856. It is not known whether the first settlers were aware of this significant cultural artifact, but it helps to explain why many of the battles during the Puget Sound war were fought near this sacred site. The report of its rediscovery in 2000 helps to remind people that Native Americans treasured the valley beyond the stone long before the first settlers arrived.

The Naches Pass trail brought many of the first families to the Puyallup Valley in the 1850s, but it was the arrival of the Northern Pacific Railroad 20 years later that ensured the survival of the farmers. Perhaps it is better to say that it was the discovery of coal beyond the confines of the Puyallup and Stuck rivers that spurred community development. In order to get to the mines, the railroad had to construct a line through the valley. That meant necessary stops along the way, chances to build towns and opportunities for land speculation. Farmers had another reason for welcoming the railroad. Hops were king in the Puyallup and Stuck valleys in the 1880s and growers needed a quick way to get the produce to market.

Post offices sprouted along the line from Tacoma through Puyallup and southward toward Orting. An additional spur, one which would eventually

Charles Graham provided an illustration for the October 20, 1888, issue of *Harpers Magazine* showing the importance of Native Americans in harvesting Puyallup Valley hops. MSCUA, *University of Washington Libraries, Native American Collection*

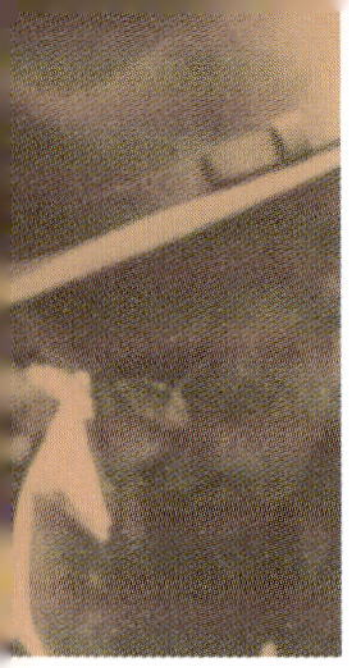

link Tacoma to Seattle, ran through Sumner and followed the Stuck River northward into King County. Town plats accompanied the railroad. Ezra Meeker filed one for Puyallup in 1877 after the railroad created a siding on the J.P. Stewart land claim. A similar pattern ensued at Orting where the siding first inspired a post office and then a town plat filed by F.E. Eldridge on Daniel Varner's claim in 1887. George H. Ryan platted Sumner in 1883. By 1891, all three towns had incorporated.

Also in 1891, a hop lice began to invade the Puyallup Valley fields, destroying that industry. A worldwide economic depression followed in 1893, reducing farm prices to a significant low. Both happenings meant that local farmers never again would rely on a single crop for their livelihood. Instead William H. Paulhamus introduced "three-story farming" as a way to combine berry cultivation, poultry and fruit orchards. By the 1920s, fields were diversified further when growers began to plant King Alfred daffodils imported from Holland, a change that inspired the first Daffodil Festival in 1926.

Not all viewed the Puyallup Valley as a place for farming. In 1890 John S. McMillin platted Lime Kiln to exploit a mineral vein he discovered along the railroad line between Alderton and Orting. Within a couple of years all the lime had been mined, but McMillin, as the town came to be, remained as a focal point for local farmers. At Elhi the Tacoma Oil Company platted a town around its one well site. The project was abandoned when no oil was discovered. Milton, which incorporated in 1907, was originally the site of several lumber and shingle mills. Dieringer began as a farming community in the 1880s but was more closely tied to the Pacific Power and Light Company (now Puget Sound Energy) hydroelectric power plant completed in 1912.

The McCarty Place in the Stuck River Valley *Washington State Historical Society*

The Western Washington Fair first began in 1900, thanks to the generous donation of $82 from local businessmen and farmers. MSCUA, *University of Washington Libraries*

On the whole, the changing nature of diversified agriculture defined the history of the valley. The Western Washington Experimental Station, founded in 1891, was (and is) one symbol of this dominance. The role of the facility was best explained by Superintendent Dr. J.W. Kalkins in 1929. "We have no interest in scientific problems which involve purely scientific aspects," he said in a newspaper interview. "In our researches we are striving to devise agricultural methods, proven by scientific tests, that will aid the farmers in every possible way. And then having devised these methods, to acquaint the farmer with them and assist him in putting them into practice."

A second symbol remains the Western Washington Fair, founded by L.A. Chamberlain,

W.H. Paulhamus, J.P. Nevins and George D. Spurr in 1900. The first event, held in downtown Puyallup, was made possible through the $82 donation of Puyallup Valley merchants. Except during World War II, when the grounds became Camp Harmony to assemble Japanese-American internees, the fair has been held at its present site since 1901.

The city of Puyallup became the center of this farming region. Besides being the place where farmers came to shop, Puyallup also became the marketing center for their produce. Local growers formed the Puyallup and Sumner Fruit Growers Association in 1902 and constructed their first cannery on Main Street in 1905. Other packing companies followed. News stories reported the intricacies of agricultural production along with reports of a local economic boom during these years.

Puyallup's growth caused local boosters to compete for Tacoma's suburban dwellers, especially following the completion of the Puyallup-Tacoma Electric Short Line in 1908. Newspaper editor Robert Montgomery expected "that large numbers of persons... will move their homes to Puyallup, where they can enjoy all the comforts and conveniences of an ideal suburban life without losing any of the advantages of the city life." By the eve of World War II his vision had yet to materialize, but by then Puyallup had become the second-largest city in Pierce County.

With the arrival of the Puyallup-Tacoma Electric Short Line in 1908, the intersection of Meridian and Stewart became Puyallup's city center. *Washington State Historical Society*

The Lands of the Mosquito Fleet

The marine geography of Puget Sound united the history of Pierce County's islands and peninsulas. The region displayed common characteristics first described by George Vancouver in 1792. Bays and inlets led to open clearings used by Native Americans as fishing villages during the annual runs of salmon. The interiors contained dense forests that the first Americans had to clear before getting down to the business of farming. The settlers found the work a

Until the second Tacoma Narrows Bridge opened in 1950, automobile and passenger ferries transported people to and from Pierce County's islands and peninsulas. Here people posed for a ferry ride to Gig Harbor. MSCUA, *University of Washington Libraries*

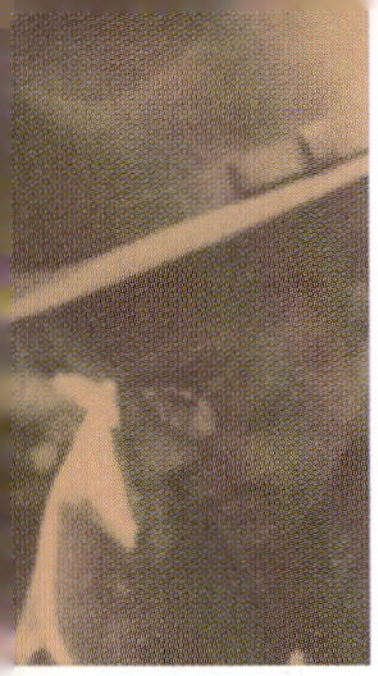

lucrative endeavor, for the cord wood they produced was needed to fuel the steamers of the Puget Sound Mosquito Fleet, their sole link to the outside world until replaced by automobile ferries and the Tacoma Narrows Bridge.

F.A. McCarty filed the only Donation Land Claim on McNeil Island in 1855. Little did he know that his property would become the site of Washington's territorial prison and one of the first federal penitentiaries on the West Coast. Ownership of the land passed on to Jay Emmons Smith and John Swan, who in 1870 offered the site facing Puget Sound across from Steilacoom for the prison. This use, however, did not keep farmers from settling the remainder of the island. By 1900 two post offices served island residents, one located on Still Harbor, where various members of the Julin family handled the mail, and another at Bee, located on prison grounds.

The first cell block on McNeil Island was small but attractive. Prisoners and local farmers easily mingled in this open environment until the 1930s, when the federal government purchased the entire island. MSCUA, *University of Washington Libraries*

In part, the informal mingling and easy interaction between residents and criminals at Bee ultimately led to the removal of all settlers from McNeil. The Department of Justice began buying the rest of the island in 1925 and completed the purchases in 1936. Then the federal prison began to house some of the nation's more infamous criminals, at least until its transfer to Washington state ownership in 1981.

Artondale, located on the head of Wollochet Bay, became the Gig Harbor peninsula's first post office. Miles B. Hunt established his claim at this location in 1876. He began delivering mail two years later, also constructing the boats needed to haul the mail, freight and passengers. A similar pattern arose on the Longbranch peninsula where in 1871 William Creviston had become the first settler at Lakebay. A post office and shipyard followed in 1882 and 1884. By the end of the 1880s, settlements in all the major bays — Minter, Gig Harbor, Rosedale, Purdy and Vaughn — were communities of farmers, lumbermen, loggers and ranchers. Most of the remaining smaller inlets were under development by the end of the 1890s.

The region was remote but not isolated from the rest of Pierce County. By the turn of the 20th century, ferry and streetcar connections from both Steilacoom and Higgins Beach provided easy access to downtown Tacoma for those not wanting to take Mosquito steamers directly to the Municipal Dock. Tacomans in turn were being lured to the region. By 1912 the Chamber of Commerce was promoting "Bay Island Country" as a place to invest. There still were lands to be logged, suggested a brochure printed in that year. And once cleared there was prime real estate for resort colonies. Arletta, Vaughn, Delano Beach, Longbranch, Lakebay, Fox and Anderson islands were some of the desirable locations selected for the Tacoma investor's attention.

Noticeably missing from the Chamber's list of desirable locations was Home. In 1897 George Allen, O.A. Verity and L.F. O'Dell had located the Mutual Home Association on Von Geldern Cove just north of Lakebay as one of Puget Sound's several utopian colonies. Philosophically, residents could think and do as they pleased, provided they respected

O.A. Verity, one of the founders of the utopian colony at Home, joined other members of his family for this group portrait. MSCUA, *University of Washington Libraries*

the rights of others to behave in a similar manner. Through the community's newspaper, Home attracted the attention of the nation's anarchists, socialists and other free-thinkers who came to either settle or visit. The colony survived until 1919. By then, residents had come under attack by "self-appointed guardians of the status quo," to use Murray Morgan's description of Tacoma's reaction to the anarchists in their midst. Internal dissent over such issues as nude bathing didn't help either. The association was dissolved and residents became private landowners of one of Puget Sound's first planned communities.

Even though the town did not incorporate until 1946, Gig Harbor emerged early as the major settlement within this region of peninsulas and islands. Originally the head of the harbor was an Indian village, and its long house served as the first school. James A. Tyrer initiated mail service in 1885 to accommodate the farmers who began arriving shortly after the Civil War. On April 28, 1888, Alfred M. Burnham filed the town plat. Early development was dependent upon lumber mills, the establishment of a major Puget Sound boat yard and the salmon fishing fleet headquartered in the harbor. Community growth was also aided by its location. Gig Harbor was the nearest settlement to Tacoma and was outside the immediate confines of the hazardous Narrows. The ease of communication enabled the town to quickly become the service center for the broader region.

Improving surface transportation throughout the region remained a constant problem far into the 1920s and 1930s. The symbol of this endeavor was, of course, the Narrows Bridge. Tacoma's neighborhood organizations and Chamber of Commerce were promoting the construction of this bridge long before its dedication in the summer of 1940. The collapse of the bridge on November 7, 1940 — four months following its opening — was more than just an engineering embarrassment. The loss of "Galloping Gertie" severed a new and important transportation link just as World War II was approaching. Any further changes to a community life centered on farming, fishing and recreation would have to wait until the end of hostilities in Europe and Asia.

Coal Country

Northern Pacific Railroad officials knew of the coal in the Cascade foothills as early as 1875. Within two years the company had constructed a line to its mines near Wilkeson, ultimately extending the route southward along the Carbon River toward Mount Rainier. Other corporate entities joined the Northern Pacific to create an industrial landscape far different from the farming communities located elsewhere in the county. Laborers and their families encompassed this environment of mines, coke ovens and logging camps. Granted, there were farms surrounding this region of coal, but the true symbols were the mines and company towns.

Carbonado was one such place. In 1879 the Carbon Hill Coal Company sent Robert Wingate to Pierce County to locate coal deposits. The result was the development of mines and coking facilities all along the Carbon River. Charles Crocker, Leland Stanford and Collis P. Huntington acquired the mining interests of Carbon Hill in 1882 for the Southern and Central Pacific railroads in California. Carbonado, with David P. Davies as superintendent, became the company town for this operation and remained so until 1937.

Burnett became another coal country community when Charles H. Burnett opened the South Prairie Coal Company in 1881. Two towns emerged from this development, one immediately around the mine and another along South Prairie Creek, an area now known as Lower Burnett. Coal from this mine was good for steam production and was used by the Mosquito Fleet once cordwood ceased to be in abundant supply.

The Carbon River area farther south and east of Carbonado developed into remote communities of miners, loggers and homesteaders all tied together by a Northern Pacific spur line. Fairfax was the first to receive a post office when, in 1896, Theron B. Corey became its postmaster. Other company towns followed at Melmont, Montezuma and Manley-Moore. Settlement in this far corner of Pierce County had only just begun, however, when Congress in 1899 created Mount Rainier National Park. Presidential executive orders set aside additional land surrounding the park as national forests, thereby limiting future industrial development along the river.

Carbonado was one of several coal mining company towns located in the isolated foothills of Mount Rainier. MSCUA, *University of Washington Libraries*

The mine for the Carbonado workers was located on the Carbon River just below the town. It provided fuel for the Southern and Central Pacific railroads in California until 1937. MSCUA, *University of Washington Libraries*

In the annals of Western history, company towns were not uncommon but were something of a mixed blessing. Workers were rarely able to own their own homes, for example, and were at the mercy of the company store. On the other hand, the various mining firms provided schools, churches, recreational centers and sports fields for the workers and their families. Additionally in Pierce County, towns not company-owned were just a short train ride away.

Wilkeson was the only town in the coal region not owned by the coal companies. It survived the closing of the mines to become a gateway to Mount Rainier National Park. *Washington State Historical Society*

Wilkeson was located adjacent to the Northern Pacific mines and near the quarry whose sandstone is still found in buildings throughout Washington state. Platted in 1889 and incorporated in 1909, Wilkeson became the major town in the coal region and, during World War I, the center for the only coke-producing area in the United States west of Utah.

Other towns in the coal region were the product of railroad construction but also dependent upon the miners for their survival. Francis Bisson platted South Prairie in 1888 after the location became the major junction for the Northern Pacific's transcontinental line across the Cascades. Alexander Wickersham platted Buckley the same year. This community's hinterland was more diverse, however. During the early years of settlement, logging activity dominated the landscape while small portable mills cleared the land for farming. With agriculture established, Buckley became a service center for both farmers and miners.

Significant changes came in the 1920s and 1930s. Coal became too expensive to mine because of the area's convoluted geology. Then, after oil replaced coal as a major power source, one by one the mines closed. In addition, the Northern Pacific moved its major Cascade junction from South Prairie north into King County. While farming and logging continued in the region, a gradual shift occurred from an industrial landscape to one centered on recreation. Easing the transformation was highway construction into the area and the completion of the Carbon River bridge in 1921. Tourists were then welcomed and Wilkeson became a new automobile "Gateway to Mount Rainier."

The Tacoma Eastern Area

Many combined themes are necessary to explain the historical development of the southeastern region of Pierce County. As elsewhere, the story begins with farming homesteaders. Robert Fiander, who filed his claim in 1874 in the Ohop Valley, may have been the first to settle in the area. He, as well as those who followed, was partly dependent upon local Native Americans for help in supplying the first seeds for planting. Indian Henry, whose village above the Mashel River survived the removal of the Nisquallies to their reservation, was particularly helpful. Not much is known about this generous man. According to local lore, however, either his real name was Sotolick and he was a Cowlitz native, or he was from Eastern Washington and was forced to leave his village after killing a native doctor who did not cure his father. Regardless of his origins, the first settlers honored him because he contributed to their survival at a crucial time.

By the 1880s and 1890s, farming settlements extended from Leber and Tanwax to Alder, Elbe and

Ashford. Town building soon followed. Thomas C. Van Eaton founded Eatonville in 1890, followed by Henry Lutkins in 1902 at Elbe, and Walter Ashford in 1904 for the town that bears his name. By this time, however, the economic landscape was changing in this region of Pierce County. Ashford platted his town in that year because it had become the terminus of the Tacoma Eastern Railroad.

The Kernahan home near Ashford was a stopping place for tourists traveling to Mount Rainier by train. *Washington State Historical Society*

Tacoma businessmen had long dreamed of a railroad extending into the timber-rich areas of southeastern Pierce County. The dream became a reality through the endeavors of John Bagley. Construction of the line, one ultimately acquired by the Chicago, Milwaukee and St. Paul railway, began in 1900 and extended south from Tacoma through such places as Frederickson, Graham and Kapowsin on its way to the terminus at Ashford.

Logging, lumber mills and new communities appeared as the tracks moved southward. The Kapowsin Lumber Company established a sawmill at that location in 1901. By 1905, the Pacific National Lumber Company had created a company town near Ashford called National. All along the route, small logging and sawmill concerns helped clear the land for fruit, dairy and poultry farmers. Then, too, some communities evolved simply because they were necessary stops along the way. Thrift, located east of Graham, was one such place. It was a passenger stop located at the farm of Charles and Minnie Thrift. Because the train stopped there, a small farming community grew up around this residential station.

The railroad, however, was not the only community attraction. The development of hydroelectric power also placed a unique stamp upon the landscape. Electron, a Puget Sound Power and Light Company project under way by 1903 on the Puyallup River, was the first. Tacoma's hydroelectric power dam on the Nisqually at La Grande followed soon thereafter. Completed in 1912, the project gave birth to a post office and general store in 1910. During World War II Tacoma expanded the complex along the Nisqually toward Alder, a farming and logging community Martin Hotes had platted in 1905. City officials began moving Alder residents in 1943 before flooding the older settlement to create Alder Lake behind a new dam. The present-day Alder was the result of that move and the completion of the dam in 1947.

Beyond the farming, logging, railroads and river dams that have historically tied this area together, the people living in the region have always had one thing not possessed by other county residents. They lived along the various "Highways to Paradise" which linked the outside world to the main entrance into Mount Rainier National Park. The Mountain Highway began as a Native American trail — the Indian Henry Trail perhaps — and was gradually widened and improved to accept wagons then automobiles. It has been a part of the Pierce County landscape for more than the 100 years marking the park's creation.

Beginning in the 1830s, when William F. Tolmie first tried to climb The Mountain, Mount Rainier has attracted tourists. Here a few of them prepare to camp at Longmire Springs. *MSCUA, University of Washington Libraries*

Other routes joined the main highway, one by road from Puyallup through Eatonville and another by train on the Tacoma Eastern. Therefore, when park development began in earnest just before America's entry into World War I, transportation was in place to ensure a direct route to Rainier. Other economic incentives might have come and gone from this part of the county, but residents along the way were ready to provide the proper accommodations for those ready and willing to experience The Mountain.

At the beginning of Pierce County's history, all roads led to Steilacoom. Long before the eve of World War II, however, the center of transportation and commerce had shifted to Tacoma. Indeed, by the turn of the 20th century, Pierce County had become "Greater Tacoma" to the businessmen boosting the city's economic development. Those living in the various settlements could maintain singular identities based on location or economic endeavor, but they became highly dependent upon the City of Destiny for a wide array of services and support. This reality made all the regional communities a part of Tacoma's hinterland. Therefore, it is now time to take a look at Tacoma to see how the city came to be one of the major cities in Washington state.

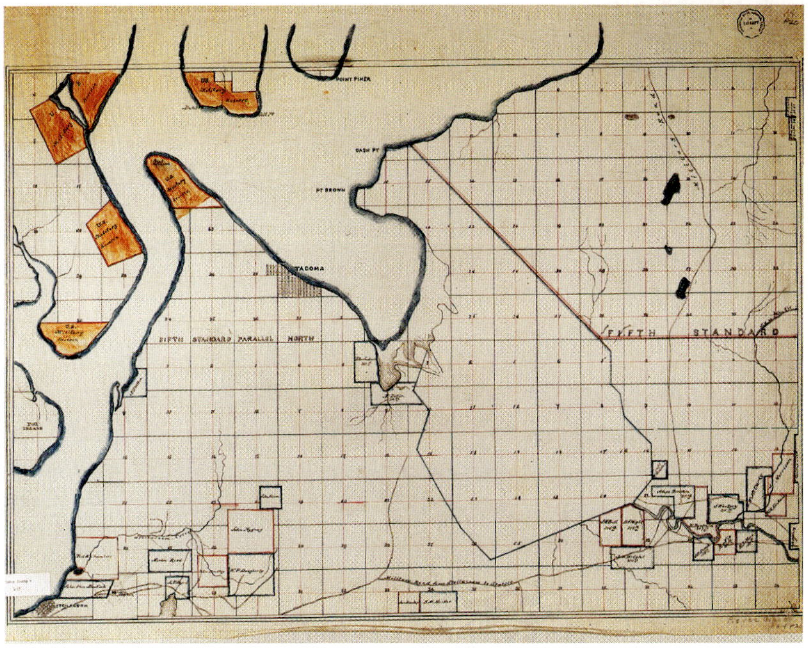

Colored portions of this undated map show the proposed military reserves designed to protect Puget Sound from foreign foes. Also visible are the boundaries of the Puyallup Indian Reservation and the very first Tacoma City plat. *Washington State Historical Society*

CHAPTER TWO

TACOMA: THE CITY OF DESTINY

The history of Tacoma began with the impenetrable forest that once dominated the landscape. This environment did not really invite town building. The first Americans saw the tangled web of trees and undergrowth as a detriment to settlement and chose instead the prairie land located along the future city's southern boundary. The shoreline and waters of Commencement Bay provided additional barriers. At the head of the bay, constant silting within the Puyallup River delta did not lure commerce. Neither did the south shore where steep bluffs and deep water meant few possible locations for the wharves so necessary for urban development in the 1850s. The earliest settlers therefore ignored the area and looked toward Steilacoom as the metropolis of the future.

The trees that drove most settlers away, however, were magnets for others. The California Gold Rush had produced a market demand for lumber in San Francisco and inspired the creation of sawmills throughout the Puget Sound region at such places as Tumwater, Seattle, Port Gamble and Port Blakely. In 1852 Nicholas Delin added another to the list when he filed a Donation Land Claim at the head of Commencement Bay. By the end of the year his mill was in operation with local settlers providing the logs.

The development attracted others. In 1853 Peter Judson filed a Donation Land Claim north of Delin's on land encompassing both the Puyallup Indians' main winter village and signal station. He and his sons began logging their homestead to feed the sawmill and gradually moved their activity northward along the bay. They stored the timber in the sheltered lagoon at Shu-bahl-lip before towing it by rowboat to Delin's operation. William Sales came to work

in the mill and settled on the Puyallup River. North of the Judson claim, Chauncey Baird began manufacturing barrels for the area's first commercial fishermen, John Swan and Peter Reilly.

All went well until 1855. "With logging, farming, barrel-making, seining, and fish-packing underway," notes Murray Morgan, "the little community seemed ready to coalesce into a town. Instead there was war, and all was lost." This settlement was located on Indian land before Isaac I. Stevens had established treaties with the Puyallup tribe. War forced the settlers to flee. The Judsons resettled in south Pierce County. Nicholas Delin stayed at this mill until 1861 but then sold it to James L. Perkins, who in turn sold it to Milas Galliher. By then, however, overproduction and poor quality had put a strain on the Puget Sound lumber market. In addition, silting in the Puyallup delta continued to make access to the mill almost impossible.

(Opening photo) St. Peter's church on North Starr Street was built in 1873. The cedar tree used as the bell tower made it the oldest one in the world. *MSCUA, University of Washington Libraries, Washington State File (Tacoma) Photo by Hannah Maynard*

Thomas Hood purchased his own Homestead claim in 1868. His cabin was located west of the future New Tacoma townsite. *Washington State Historical Society Watercolor by James A. Anderson*

To protect his claim on Commencement Bay, Job Carr built his cabin during the winter months of 1864 and 1865. *Ron Karabaich Collection Oil painting by Ted Grunden*

The Indian war also led others to the future Tacoma townsite. In 1859 U.S. Army officials proposed the abandonment of Fort Steilacoom and the creation of a new installation at Point Defiance. According to Herbert Hunt, General W.S. Harney thought that "Fort Steilacoom was badly located... He was of the opinion that the impenetrable forests forever would preclude railroad transportation and that the Sound would have to be depended upon." On September 22, 1866, President Andrew Johnson approved the location of a new military reservation on this site, along with others on the eastern shore of Gig Harbor and the southern tip of Vashon Island in King County. Batteries of guns, Army planners concluded, "would close the head of the Sound to the largest fleet."

As America entered the Civil War, there was little hint that what Delin, Judson and the other settlers began would be anything more than an abandoned ghost town. History would prove different, however. Delin had located his mill near the head of today's Thea Foss Waterway. Judson's farm would become the heart of Tacoma's downtown business district and the lagoon where he stored the timber for Delin would become the log pond for a future mill. Point Defiance eventually became one of the city's first urban parks.

Equally significant, logging cleared the forest along the south shore of Commencement Bay sufficiently to attract the first townsite speculators. For them to come, however, literally required an act of Congress.

Tacoma City

Tacomans have a hard time settling on a date for the founding of the city. There were originally two towns platted at different times, Tacoma City in 1869 and New Tacoma in 1874. There were also two separate city governments incorporated in 1874 and 1880. It also has become increasingly difficult to credit all who were responsible for the city's creation, development and survival during the formative years. Speculation fueled Tacoma's birth, just as the collective desire for land ownership propelled families westward to settle the region. Even though local lore has acknowledged a privileged few — Job Carr, M.M. McCarver, Charles B. Wright and John W. Sprague — the hundreds of others who became urban midwives must also be remembered.

The road leading to Tacoma's creation began in Washington, D.C., on July 2, 1864, when Congress incorporated the Northern Pacific Railroad Company. The firm was to build a transcontinental railroad and telegraph line from Lake Superior to Puget Sound using Isaac I. Stevens' 1854 survey as a guide. It took corporate officials six years to develop the financing and begin construction, during which time land speculators converged on Puget Sound, each one certain that his development would become the railroad terminus.

Job Carr was one of the many who came. He had just been discharged from the Union Army when he heard of the Congressional action "and immediately resolved to go to Puget Sound and locate at the western terminus of said road." Later in life Carr wrote an account of what followed from his initial decision:

"I arrived in Olympia on the 13th day of Nov. of that year, never having heard of any other place on the Sound before my arrival and supposed of course that would be the terminus. On seeing the place (then in a very dilapidated condition) I was convinced that no sane company would ever locate the terminus of a Trans-Continental R.R. there if there was any other place to go. On making inquiry I learned the extent of Puget Sound and examining maps and charts at the land office, I concluded I would explore the country a little. After traveling round, about a week, I reached the Puyallup Indian Reservation, keeping my own counsel as to my ultimate designs, but telling those whom I met that I wanted a place near the water for a fruit farm... On Christmas Day of 1864 in company with others, I went over to Gig Harbor fishing. Mr. Billings telling me there were several nice places along the shore of the Bay, as we went along in our canoe, when we came opposite to where Tacoma now stands I raised on my feet and exclaimed Eureka Eureka, and told my companions there was my claim."

Job Carr, Tacoma's first permanent settler
Mel Carr Collection

He then filed a pre-emption claim, lured his sons and daughter westward, and began constructing a cabin north of Shu-bahl-lip.

Nothing outstanding happened for four years while land speculators throughout Puget Sound waited for Northern Pacific officials to begin work on the railroad. The company's biggest problem was financing. While Congress had granted 40 million acres of the public domain as payment for the line, officials could only sell specific parcels when the trains were running. The Northern Pacific therefore turned to Jay Cooke, who had successfully financed the Civil War through his private investment schemes, to help the project along.

Something else happened during these years. Congress approved a change in the route through Washington territory. Initially legislators envisioned a line directly through the Cascades to the Sound. By the end of the 1860s, railroad engineers were

He Forgot
(An Ode to the City Beautiful)

He wanted a city beautiful.
A city that should be fair.
A city where smoke should never roll
In billows upon the air.
He wanted a city where art should be,
A city of splendid halls,
Where culture's touch should appear upon
The battlements and walls.

He called for a city beautiful;
He shouted it day by day;
He wanted a city where noise was not,
Where the spirit of art should sway;
He wanted a city that should be fair,
Where filth might never be seen,
And forgot, in spite of the zeal he had
To keep his back yard clean.

— *Tacoma Daily News,* April 6, 1907

WIELDING A BIG STICK

The North End Improvement Club launched a war against billboards as one way to make the city beautiful. The August 8, 1907, *Tacoma Daily News* lent its editorial support to this neighborhood endeavor.
Poem, 4/6/1907
Cartoon, 8/8/1907

requesting another one taking the line southward along the Columbia River and then northward from Vancouver along a well-worn transportation corridor. Congressional approval came with one condition — a rail line had to reach Puget Sound no later than December 31, 1873.

The change was a boon to Portland, Oregon, businessmen who now saw a direct advantage to investing in terminus sites. They began sending land agents northward to secure townsite locations. James Law was one such individual. He held a blanket power of attorney "to be used in securing locations for a number of Portland people." Morton Matthew McCarver was another. Behind him were bankers Lewis M. Starr and James Steel. In 1868, McCarver came upon Job Carr's claim, purchased a portion of it and platted Tacoma City, naming four of the streets in honor of the two Portland bankers behind the project, Job Carr and himself. To provide a sense of permanency to the whole endeavor, residents acquired a post office in March of 1869 with Job Carr as the community's first postmaster.

There is something very traditional about Tacoma City's beginnings. The area bounded by North Starr, Steel streets and Commencement Bay held all the firsts — school, church, hotel and hospital — that cities hold dear. McCarver was also able in 1869 to get Charles Hanson and John Ackerson to build a mill around the Shu-bahl-lip lagoon. The first photographic views of Tacoma City show a frontier town whose only difference from many in the American West were the thick forests surrounding the small community.

Even so, Tacoma City was supposed to be different. McCarver boosted the town to the point where local observers found it easy to deride his pretensions. Here is Clark P. Crandall's opinion of the Commencement Bay community in 1871.

"The founder found it two or three years ago, lying around loose, and as it was the only place not then appointed and ordained for terminus purposes, he went for it, bought it, and had it regularly platted and set down as the place where the job of building the world was commenced... and where the job of building the Northern Pacific Railroad... is to be finished. Nothing has, however, happened to prevent the possible extensions of the town site. There is room yet for Tacoma to spread as much as she likes."

Today, however, people admire McCarver's foresight. His energetic style did draw the Northern Pacific's attention to Tacoma. And he unquestionably played a role in the company's decision in July of 1873 to locate the railroad terminus two miles south of Tacoma City.

Tacoma City looked like this in 1875 when Job Carr became the town's first mayor.
Old Town Photo Studio

Unfortunately for McCarver, the terminus was to have a new city located south of his townsite. Thomas Prosch, McCarver's biographer, maintained that the town's founder was devastated upon learning that Tacoma City was not to benefit from the decision. "It did not occur to him that the railroad men... would use the means he had given them to inflict upon him their hardest blows, that they would endeavor to destroy his town by building a rival town two miles away, by robbing it of its name, by leading its people to their own town, and by these and similar methods ruin him and those with him in the town he had projected and fathered."

This account, while overblown, reflected the opinion of many at the time. Much speculative energy had gone into the making of Tacoma City, and along with it the expectation that the terminus would increase land values to unheard of levels. This was not to be. Instead, the town became a temporary camp for newcomers who came in droves to await the arrival of the first train to the new terminus.

New Tacoma

It is hard to imagine the sense of urgency felt by Northern Pacific officials as construction began westward from Duluth, Minnesota, in 1870. Remember, Congress said that trains had to reach a Puget Sound terminus by the end of 1873. To meet the deadline the railroad company decided to concentrate on the two farthest ends of the line. So, in 1871, while construction progressed toward Bismarck, North Dakota, from the east, the Northern Pacific appointed Civil War general and engineer John W. Sprague to manage the construction northward from the Columbia River to an unknown terminus. If the whole transcontinental line could not be done in time, the company was going to make sure that at least one train arrived on Puget Sound before the deadline.

Sprague selected a site some 15 miles north of Vancouver, Washington, for the start of the line and platted a town called Kalama. From there, construction moved northward while officials pondered the terminus location. In 1872 the corporate directors paid a site visit and listened to the various town boosters pandering their options like vendors at a trade convention. It is not known for sure why the railroad chose Tacoma over the likes of Olympia, Seattle, Everett or Port Townsend in July of 1873. But the Judson and Delin abandoned claims south of Tacoma City were one major selling point for the townsite developers. Railroad engineers liked the Commencement Bay shoreline where they envisioned terminal wharves on tidelands bordering the deep water.

On the other hand, one cannot dismiss the possibility that Tacoma became the terminus because by the summer of 1873 the Northern Pacific had run out of money. The techniques Jay Cooke used to finance the Civil War didn't work for this transcontinental railroad. Within two months of

the terminus selection, Cooke's bank had failed and there was a real danger that the route would not be completed by the end of the year. In November workers decided to strike for back wages. John C. Ainsworth, then managing director of the railroad on the West Coast, paid the workers out of his own pocket and guaranteed their credit at the Hanson, Ackerson mill store in Tacoma. With assurances and back pay in hand, the railroad made its way to Tacoma just in time.

Charles B. Wright became president of the Tacoma Land Company in 1873 and platted New Tacoma the following year. *From Tacoma: Its History and Its Builders by Herbert Hunt*

There were several things going on during this hectic time and each was important to Tacoma's growth and economic development. In 1873 in Tacoma City the construction of two docks was under way at the feet of Starr and McCarver streets. Adjacent to the town, the Hanson, Ackerson mill was in full operation. It too had a wharf for timber exports along with a company store and boarding house. Until railroad workers completed the terminal wharf late in 1873, these facilities were the new city's major link to the outside world. By the end of the year the Northern Pacific wharf was operational, complete with a new hotel run by William and Alice Blackwell.

All this activity along the south shore of Commencement Bay produced three separate residential settlements. One was at Tacoma City, where housing quickly sprouted to accommodate the new arrivals waiting for the completion of the terminus. A second community formed behind the mill. There Hanson, Ackerson officials allowed workers to construct their homes in what became Mill Town, Tacoma's first of many working class neighborhoods. In 1873, however, all eyes were focused on the third settlement on the hill above the Northern Pacific Railroad terminus. Those converging on Tacoma City after July had come to purchase lots in New Tacoma. Even so, months would pass before the Tacoma Land Company — the railroad subsidiary formed to market the town — was ready to satisfy the land-hungry speculators.

Charles B. Wright, then president of the land company, was primarily responsible for the delay. He dreamed of a planned city for the new terminus and in September of 1873 hired Frederick Law Olmsted to produce a fitting design. Olmsted was a good choice. He was well known for his park designs, especially Central Park in New York City, and for residential suburban plans of curvilinear streets.

Olmsted's proposal for New Tacoma came as a real shock to local residents. According to Thomas Prosch, then editor of Tacoma City's *Tacoma Pacific Tribune*, the map was "the most fantastic and astonishing plat of a town that ever was seen."

"It covered a thousand acres, two miles along the front of the hill top. Everything was curvilinear. There wasn't a straight street, a right angle, or a corner lot. The blocks were shaped like melons, pears, and sweet potatoes. Some were short and others were long. One block, shaped like a banana, was 3,000 feet in length, and had 250 lots. The lots were 25 feet wide, but were all sorts of lengths, averaging 180 feet. It was a pretty fair park plan."

Charles Wright dismissed Olmsted and hired a railroad engineer named William Isaac Smith to create the New Tacoma plat among more traditional lines. By April of 1874 the Tacoma Land Company finally began to sell lots in New Tacoma.

For the next 10 years Tacoma's history was a painful process of survival. When Jay Cooke's financial empire collapsed, Henry Villard obtained control of the Northern Pacific. The results were devastating for the Puget Sound terminus. Villard's economic interests resided in Portland and along the Columbia River where his navigation companies monopolized commerce. Therefore, when under his leadership the railroad transcontinental line was finally completed in 1883, Portland — not Tacoma — was the primary beneficiary. Corporate headquarters remained in Oregon while trains were ferried across the Columbia to Kalama and Puget Sound. But at least one of the train ferries was given the name *Tacoma*.

New Tacoma's Pacific Avenue in 1875
Washington State Historical Society
Drawing by Clinton P. Ferry

New Tacoma was not completely ignored during these years. Railroad officials continued work on the terminal wharves and began filling in the bay for the Half Moon Yard. The discovery of coal in eastern Pierce County in the mid-1870s brought more construction along the shoreline in the form of coal bunkers that dominated the waterfront for decades. All the work required a sawmill — the Hatch Mill — to locate on the Northern Pacific wharf. As the 1880s approached, the railroad proceeded to dredge southward into the head of the bay, beginning an engineering endeavor that would ultimately create the Thea Foss Waterway.

Gradually the elements of a city took form. The Tacoma Land Company was a cautious landowner when selling townsite lots, usually requiring improvements before deeds were transferred. Charles Wright was also generous, reserving land for churches, schools and parks — notably Wright Park. In 1877 the land company gave $10,000 to the Northern Pacific to move its construction and repair shops from Kalama to a site near South 17th Street and Pacific Avenue. And as the transcontinental line neared completion, the firm hired architect Stanford White of New York's McKim, Mead and White to design a hotel to lure investors to the City of Destiny. This activity was not fast-paced. Tacoma's population was only 1,098 in 1880 when voters approved a move of the county seat from Steilacoom. Enough had occurred, however, to allow the city to take root and to grow at the proper time.

Conditions began to change shortly after the completion of the transcontinental line in 1883. Like Cooke before him, Villard's economic empire collapsed, leaving a void that Charles Wright willingly filled. With him now heading both the Northern Pacific and Tacoma Land Companies, corporate policies changed. Tacomans now felt they had a future and agreed late in 1883 to combine the separate and competing Tacoma City and New

Annie Wright Seminary, located on the corner of Tacoma Avenue North and Division, opened as a school for girls in 1884.
MSCUA, *University of Washington Libraries, Washington State Files (Tacoma)*
Photo by Hannah Maynard

Early Tacoma was surrounded by trees that had to be logged before the city could expand. *Thomas R. Stenger Collection* *Photo by French*

Tacoma governments. When the city of Tacoma began operations the next year, municipal officials also had authority over a larger area. The vote to merge also included an agreement to expand urban boundaries westward toward Point Defiance and eastward to the Puyallup Indian Reservation.

One specific hope fueled Tacoma's optimism, that the Northern Pacific officials would complete the railroad line through the Cascade Mountains. Construction of this direct line to Puget Sound had been slow during the Villard years and Tacomans were elated when early in 1885 the board of directors agreed to finish the work. The decision was a significant one, for local businessmen had also learned that Chinese and Japanese merchants wanted to initiate trade with the city. The completion of the Cascade Line and commerce with Asian countries was expected to pull Tacoma out of the economic recession that had plagued the nation throughout the mid-1880s.

It is within this context that one must understand why Tacomans, by November of 1885, had expelled all the Chinese who had resided in the city since the arrival of the railroad. While this tragic episode is discussed later on, it is necessary to explain here the economic motivations which led to the unanimous opinion that the "Chinese must go." Workers feared that the Northern Pacific would continue its practice of hiring Asians to build the railroad across the Cascades. Businessmen felt that a Chinatown in downtown Tacoma would keep new investors away just when an economic boom was in sight. So even though improved conditions were to be based on trade with Asian

The last spike of the Northern Pacific Cascade Division was driven here in 1887. Tacomans spent the 4th of July celebrating the first train to arrive from eastern Washington. *MSCUA, University of Washington Libraries,* *Photo by Davidson*

countries, the Chinese were forced out of their homes and placed on a train headed to Portland.

Tacoma was not very big when residents forced the Chinese to leave. In 1885 there might have been around 5,000 people living in Old Town — the former Tacoma City — in Mill Town and in Tacoma proper. The latter settlement was a walking city or at best one traversed by horse and buggy. It was a frontier town where vice, gambling, prostitution, and law and order were constant concerns. But it was also a mixture of other things. Commerce dominated the shoreline north of the Tacoma Land Company townsite. Industry, specifically the Northern Pacific railroad shops, marked the town's southern boundary. In between were houses, schools, churches, meeting halls and businesses along with families and proprietors all waiting the arrival of the first train across Stampede Pass. When that happened in July of 1887 Tacoma was truly transformed.

"Jacks" Epitaph

Oh, bear the bear unto the bier,
His days are past — the end is here.

Eight years of happy life he led,
On hotel dainties he has fed;
And never yet has it been said
He's hurt a hair of human head.
A righteous life, alone he led,
His actions have been told and read.
Subdue the voice, bow down the head,
Approach the pit with softened tread —
For all is o'er, and "Jack" is dead.

From life in woods where he was free
To fettered chains within a pen;
A stroll through town — a shot — and then
He had through death gained liberty.

— *Every Sunday*, March 19, 1892

Jack the Bear was a constant attraction in downtown Tacoma. A policeman who caught him roaming the city streets at night cut his celebrity status short in 1892. *Thomas R. Stenger Collection*

Boom and Bust

The rail line across and through Stampede Pass revolutionized Tacoma. By the time the first trains arrived, the Northern Pacific had moved its headquarters from Portland to a new building at the northern end of Pacific Avenue. Across the street Tacomans built their city hall. Southward from these two visual anchors, owners constructed brick business blocks to replace the earlier generation of wood structures. This expansion forced many residents from their downtown homes. But by the early 1890s the city's residential areas were already moving outward along railroad and streetcar lines. Tacoma's growth was really amazing at this time. Census takers found 36,006 people living here in 1890, an increase of 34,908 since their 1880 enumeration. Most of the newcomers arrived after 1885.

From 1888 until 1892 Tacoma was, maintained British journalist Rudyard Kipling, "literally staggering under a boom of the boomiest." Land speculation fueled the frenzy as over 500 individuals and firms platted and marketed the hundreds of additions defining Tacoma today. This rush for land, however, should not be confused with actual development. When the real estate boom collapsed in 1892, it left a legacy of unsold and undeveloped lots, some located far from the city's downtown. Most selling

Thomas Rutter photographed Tacoma from the roof of the Northern Pacific headquarters building in 1888. Within months the city's first land boom transformed the downtown.
Old Town Photo Studio

To promote his North End real estate development, Allen C. Mason constructed his own mansion on North Stevens Street in 1892. He lost it during the 1893 depression. Whitworth College used the building from 1899 to 1912.
Old Town Photo Studio

the lots were not really interested in urban growth and rarely moved beyond a legally required survey. They did not clear the land or even construct the streets needed to attract residents. Indeed, some of the additions platted at this time were still undeveloped on the eve of World War II a half century later. Even so, the activity prompted the incorporation of 20 square miles of territory to the municipality in 1891, the largest in Tacoma's history.

Not all land speculators were ambivalent towards Tacoma's growth. Allen C. Mason, when planning one of the city's first residential suburbs in the North End, demonstrated a real interest in the future city. He envisioned an upper-class clientele for his neighborhood and engineered an environment suitable for their tastes, an idea that also included the creation of parks and boulevards fronting the homes. Mason hired R.B. Mullen to log, clear and grade streets, and built a few houses to illustrate the type of residence he expected in his development. He then topped off his project by constructing both a public library and his own house on a prominent bluff overlooking Commencement Bay. Edward Fuller's *Every Sunday* lauded Mason's achievement in 1892 as ideal:

"Here is a purely residence district, dotted with well-built and well-kept homes, with comfortable and luxurious surroundings, graded streets and planked sidewalks, street railway transportation, public light and water supply systems, churches, schoolhouses, and all other conveniences of first class suburban residence districts.... If a stranger were dropped from a balloon into its midst it would be difficult for him to account for the existence of such a perfect, well improved and regularly laid out townsite, far removed from the bustle of business."

Allen C. Mason proved unable to survive the depression that shook the world in 1893, but his vision of a fashionable residential district remained and took root when the city came upon better times after 1900.

While some developers centered on residential areas for the upper class, others catered to workers. One of the earliest opportunities came in 1890, when the Northern Pacific Railroad decided to move its construction and repair shops from South 17th Street and Pacific Avenue to a vacant prairie located about three miles from the city center. Land developers then began to promote property near the shops as ideal for the "thrifty skilled mechanic." Villa Park, platted by Chauncey Griggs and P.D. Norton of the St. Paul and Tacoma Lumber Company, was to be "a new Arcadia of grove and gardenland, where the weary workman from the shops can rest in an Eden of his own," or so an advertisement claimed in 1891. South Tacoma grew from these beginnings as workers settled in the area, bought property and built their homes close to their place of work.

In 1890 the Northern Pacific moved its railroad repair shops to South Tacoma, creating a new residential neighborhood in the process.
Old Town Photo Studio

Other neighborhoods began to take shape as streetcar lines moved outward from Tacoma's downtown, creating a new kind of city in the process. When Tacoma began, everything was confined and mixed together. Now with space to grow, people began to live in residential neighborhoods and commuted to work in other parts of the city. Neighborhood commercial areas sprouted up along the streetcar lines where transfer points invited trade.

All the routes converged in downtown Tacoma, creating a central business district of businesses, hotels, department stores, theaters, banks, specialty stores and grocers. The result of all this activity was the city seen today — a central business district connected to residential and commercial areas stretching outward to embrace McKinley Hill, Roosevelt Heights, Portland Avenue, Oakland, Larchmont, Manitou, Sixth Avenue, Proctor Street, Fern Hill and many other neighborhoods. Not all was in place in the 1890s, but the movement of families into the developing districts had begun and would continue long into the 20th century.

Fern Hill began as a separate pioneer settlement outside Tacoma's boundaries and was linked to the city by streetcar. The area was annexed to Tacoma in 1909.
Old Town Photo Studio

People came to create these neighborhoods because there was work. There was great promise that the completion of the Cascade line would enhance the local business, commercial and industrial environment. Expectations bore fruit when Tacoma became a commercial center. By 1901 two miles of warehouses and grain terminals lined the shoreline northward along the Thea Foss Waterway and Commencement Bay. Imports from around the world were traded for such things as timber, coal and wheat. Tacoma quickly became the wholesaler for a wide array of products shipped eastward along the line of the Northern Pacific.

Manufacturing and industry came as well. In 1888, Dennis Ryan located the Tacoma Smelter near Point Defiance. Two years later William R. Rust organized the Tacoma Smelting and Refining Company. At the same time, the St. Paul and Tacoma Lumber Company formed under the corporate leadership of Chauncey Griggs, Henry

Hewitt Jr., A.G. Foster and George Browne. They purchased some 90,000 acres of timber from the Northern Pacific, much of it located in eastern Pierce County, and proceeded to build a mill on land on the Puyallup River delta. Other mills followed, including the Willam C. Wheeler and George R. Osgood company also located on the tideflats. By the early years of the 20th century, Tacoma called itself the "Lumber Capital of the World" because of the many mills lining the shoreline and because the economic well-being of the city depended so much upon timber exports.

Lumber was not, however, Tacoma's only industry even if it employed the most workers in 1890. There were also blacksmiths and bakers and manufacturers of clothing, shoes, wagons and beds. Carpenters, painters and plumbers were numerous enough to catch the attention of census takers. So too were brick-makers, tinsmiths and jewelers, along with foundries, photographers and boat builders. Doctors and other medical practitioners led the list of professionals along with lawyers and those selling real estate. Dominant too were nurses, hat makers, seamstresses, grocers and proprietors of boarding houses — the work done by women when not taking care of their families. City directories show people of many races and ethnicities contributing to Tacoma's economic development at this time, documenting the point that diversity was always a significant part of the urban landscape.

George Francis Train coined Tacoma the "City of Destiny" and in 1890 launched a 67-day tour around the world to promote the city. He introduced a poem titled, "Seattle! Seattle! Death Rattle, Death Rattle; Tacoma! Tacoma! Aroma, Aroma" to show that the northern city was in no position to outdistance the railroad terminus. And up until 1893 there was some truth to the allegation that Tacoma would be the major city on Puget Sound. It was, after all, home to the region's only transcontinental railroad.

Tacoma in 1873 and 1874
As Told by Alice Blackwell

"Just before we came the town site had been cleared of trees, the small ones with trimmings, piled in three huge bonfires and burned, the ground as well burned over, leaving only ashes and blackened stumps where the future great city was to be. There were a few tents on the ground where the workmen had been living.

"All business was at the wharf — the railroad and express offices, telegraph, two small stores — afterward a printing office; also three families lived there. A few people were on the hill in rough shanties or boarded-up tents.

"My first visit to Pacific Avenue was in March following our coming. The only way of getting to the town site from the wharf was a single footpath down hard in the mud. In front of where the Odd Fellows Temple now stands, was a deep mud puddle, which has had enough rubber in it to start a good business — overshoes sucked off the feet of pedestrians. That summer a plank walk was laid up the hill, consisting of two boards laid lengthwise."

— Tacoma: Its History and Its Builders by Herbert Hunt

New Tacoma in 1878 — five years after the Northern Pacific arrived in Tacoma the city was still quite small. To the left of the drawing is an idealized version of the terminal wharves. To the right the unfilled inlet marks the location of a Puyallup Indian village. *New York Public Library Drawing by E.S. Glover*

Tacoma lost its momentum during bad economic times. Residents found the city embroiled in lawsuits and political acrimony when Edward Orr and Angelo Fawcett both claimed to be mayor at the same time. The city was at odds with the Northern Pacific for the company's refusal to provide space for a municipal dock, and with Charles Wright over the costs of purchasing the Tacoma Light and Water Company. These were contentious times indeed, but they were also signs of a city adapting to changes that came with rapid growth. It was just as well that the city grew only some 1,700 people during the depression years. There was time to catch one's breath and prepare for the next round.

Between 1888 and 1984 Ruston's "Tacoma Smelter" was an industrial icon along the south shore of Commencement Bay.
Old Town Photo Studio

"Watch Tacoma Grow"

By 1920 Tacoma's population had more than doubled its 1900 count to reach 96,965. The increase was so obvious during the first decade of the 20th century that the Tacoma Boosters created a new slogan to reflect what was clearly a major demographic happening. Industrial development, new railroads and an expanding port all helped to explain what turned out to be the largest influx of people in the city's history.

Lumber and timber products dominated the local economy at this time. January 3, 1900, saw the creation of the Weyerhaeuser Timber Company when Frederick Weyerhaeuser and Northern Pacific's William H. Phibbs agreed to the purchase of 900,000 acres of the railroad's land grant. The firm established its headquarters in Tacoma and proceeded to consolidate its logging empire. Weyerhaeuser never built a mill in the city, but the company didn't really need to to aid the local economy. By 1910 there were over 30 other companies manufacturing timber with many dependent on Weyerhaeuser's logs.

The first decade of the century also saw significant changes to Tacoma's smelter. In 1902 William R. Rust converted the facility to an electrolytic copper refinery, "the first on the Pacific Coast," according to Murray Morgan. Within three years the private

Many mayors guided Tacoma's development along, but Angelo V. Fawcett was best known at the turn of the 20th century. His son C. Val Fawcett, pondering here at his father's portrait, was mayor from 1943 until 1950.
Tacoma Public Library

company had attracted the attention of the Guggenheim brothers and their newly incorporated American Smelting and Refining Company. After prolonged negotiations, including the intervention of Wall Street wizard Bernard Baruch, Rust sold the plant in 1905. A community of workers lived nearby in a town platted by the Tacoma Smelter and Refining Company in 1891 and 1901. Ruston, named to honor William R. Rust, incorporated in 1906 and remains a separate town surrounded by Tacoma and Commencement Bay.

Railroads also were changing the face of Tacoma. Up until 1904 the Northern Pacific had been able to maintain a tight monopoly over other railroad lines entering Tacoma. Two factors changed this scenario after that year. For one, the U.S. Supreme Court in the Northern Securities Case outlawed the railroad's actions. At the same time, Congress allowed Puyallup Indians to sell their land allotments on the reservation east of the river. It is important to remember that after this time, Tacoma's business community began planning for a new port area separate from the wharves constructed by the Northern Pacific. The move was in some ways a declaration of independence, one producing a land boom on the Puyallup River delta.

The Supreme Court decision and the new port area were open invitations to railroad companies other than the Northern Pacific. Besides the Great Northern, the Union Pacific and the Chicago, Milwaukee, and St. Paul companies decided to come to Tacoma. The Milwaukee Road became the third transcontinental carrier in Washington state and in 1911 the second to establish its terminus in the City of Destiny. The Union Pacific arrived from the south. When the company threatened to build a parallel and competing line adjacent to the Northern Pacific, the two firms agreed to share the existing infrastructure. The symbol of this concord is the Union Depot, a passenger station completed by 1912 to accommodate the needs of both companies.

Also at this time, the Northern Pacific restructured its main route into Tacoma. Prior to 1912, when the work began, trains passed through South Tacoma and crossed Pacific Avenue near South 17th Street at grade level. As the downtown area grew, the crossing became

One of the Old Town officers with residents
Old Town Photo Studio

The completion of the Union Station in 1911 symbolized a joint-use agreement between the Union Pacific and Northern Pacific Railroad companies.
Old Town Photo Studio

Workers constructing the Point Defiance tunnel between 1912 and 1914 established a residential community below the western portal. It evolved into Salmon Beach, one of Tacoma's several waterfront neighborhoods. *From Tacoma: Its History and Its Builders by Herbert Hunt*

increasingly dangerous. To solve the problem, railroad engineers designed a new route — the one still used today — that entered Tacoma from the south along Puget Sound after passing through a 4,400-foot tunnel underneath Point Defiance. Nelson Bennett, the contractor for the Stampede Tunnel in 1888, supervised the work. The tunnel's opening in 1914 ended major railroad construction in Tacoma, at least for the time being.

With economic growth came people, the expansion of residential areas, and more annexations. In 1907 the council agreed to incorporate east Tacoma into the city. Two years later government officials extended the boundary south to include Fern Hill. Other annexations — the port area east of the Puyallup River and northeast Tacoma — were to follow later in the century, but by 1910 most of the city's present-day boundaries were firmly established.

Streetcars took new residents to a wide array of economically and culturally diverse neighborhoods. As more families came to settle there was increasing concern about the future growth and development of the various communities, and city officials devised new techniques to make sure that residential areas remained residential. By 1895 Tacomans had already begun to establish zones where certain uses — specifically saloons — were allowed or prohibited. Now local property owners could reject the location of other businesses within the residential parts of the city. By 1918 Tacoma had a zoning code, one dividing the city into industrial and residential areas. The city's first planning commission followed two years later.

Planning arose because of another phenomenon of the times. The creation of distinct residential areas led to the formation of neighborhood improvement clubs. It is not known who was first, but by the 1920s there were close to 20 active organizations blanketing Tacoma. In 1907 the members of the various groups even formed a citywide federation in order to provide a stronger voice when petitioning the city council for major improvements. There was not always complete unanimity, of course, but the collective activities of the clubs contributed significantly to how the city evolved.

Improving Tacoma's appearance dominated the minds of both neighborhood residents and downtown businessmen. These years saw the dedication of the Carnegie Library (1903), the conversion of the burned-out Tourist Hotel into Stadium High School (1906) and the construction of Stadium Bowl (1910). Downtown Tacoma acquired mature

Residential developments surrounded the city's downtown by the late 1880s. Hawthorne, now the site of the Tacoma Dome, grew into a working-class neighborhood and home to many Italian immigrants.
Thomas R. Stenger Collection
Photo by Thomas Rutter

urban characteristics as businessmen embraced both new architectural styles and the technologies which allowed the city to grow upward. But new construction placed the remnants of Tacoma's past into bold relief and local businessmen decided that something had to be done.

Their solution was a "Make Tacoma Clean" campaign launched by the Tacoma Boosters in 1907. The educational program was designed to embarrass owners into eliminating the "Things That Mar Tacoma." Charles F. Cutter produced a lantern slide show illustrating the city's worst eyesores — including what tourists first saw when entering Tacoma by rail, boat and even automobile — and published the photographs in the *Tacoma Daily News*. Boosters also initiated a campaign against residential owners who had yet to landscape their yards. Their attack on weeds got major press coverage then, and even though it might sound silly today, Tacomans viewed unkempt yards as a health hazard as well as something that might keep others from settling here.

Park development was also a way to make Tacoma beautiful. The creation of city parks had begun in 1883 when Clinton P. Ferry set one aside in a platted addition. He was the first in a long line of landowners, including the Tacoma Land Company, who deeded parks to the city. Not only did the latter firm grant substantial parcels of land, it mandated municipal participation in their development and maintenance, beginning in 1886 when it deeded Wright Park to the city. What captured the imagination of city dwellers, however, was Point Defiance. Since federal authorities had not developed the site as a military reservation, and since timber thieves were denuding the site of trees, local citizens in 1888 successfully petitioned Congress to grant "the use of certain lands in Pierce County...to the City of Tacoma for the purposes of a public park."

Within four years of the Wright Park grant, the city had acquired almost 700 acres of land reserved for park purposes. On June 9, 1890, the city council created a Board of Park Commissioners to "take charge and exercise control over all parks belonging to the city," including the acquisition of new properties for park purposes. As Tacoma's neighborhoods took form, new parks were added, including McKinley Park in 1901. In addition, the city itself did not hesitate to reserve its own surplus property for park purposes. In 1905, for example, the council authorized the creation of a "park and parkway" along Tacoma's abandoned water flume right-of-way

Name of the Mountain

"To the Editor: Judging from legislative action — whether in joke or earnest — it would seem that the old question of changing the name of Mount Rainier has for the second time circled its quarter century and is with us once again.

"When American explorers came to the Pacific Northwest more than a century ago, the names of most of the geographical features had been given by previous British and Spanish navigators and discoverers. Practically the entire Puget Sound and Cascade nomenclature is based on these records....

"Beautiful and appropriate as is the custom of applying where possible names suggesting the original Indian designations, there is no more reason for a change of name of Mount Rainier than of Mount Baker or Mount Hood. All have equal authority, recognition and usage for more than a century. Fortunately the early American explorers found two of the great snow peaks of the Cascades which had escaped the eyes of the navigators.... Thus Mount Adams and Mount Jefferson honored the names of the two greatest Americans, after Washington.... If Hood, St. Helens, Rainier and Baker had not then received names already recognized, it is probable than names like Franklin, Madison, Hamilton and Marshall might have completed a processing of American statesmen along the Cascade range.

"If after a century and a quarter of recognition the spirit of change demands that Rainier must go, why should we delve in the mysteries of Indian lore, or awaken memories of a controversy best forgotten, by attaching the name of the fine city of Tacoma to the great mountain?

"Surely we have not been unmindful of aboriginal names in this vicinity. A slavish attempt to perpetuate Indian names of localities would compel us to change the name of the city of Tacoma to something like Chebaulip. While this might establish a euphonious kinship with Puyallup and be a rival for pronunciation exercises with Steilacoom and Kapowsin... we ought to be grateful that the beautiful city on Commencement Bay has spared us the name of Chebaulip.

Mount Rainier is located in Pierce County and dominates the City of Destiny skyline. For years local residents tried to change its name to Mount Tacoma.
Old Town Photo Studio

"This is a day of dedication to the truest patriotism and noblest Americanism. Is not the time opportune to rededicate this greatest of our mountain peaks to the name which must ever stand closest to Washington in our great Hall of Fame — Lincoln?

"If we must change Rainier, let us take the opportunity this Lincoln's birthday to make a real change, one that is truly worth while. Forgetting controversy, let us honor ourselves by dedicating 'the mountain that was God' by giving it the new name Mount Lincoln."

— George Cotterill, Olympia, *Seattle Post Intelligencer*, February 5, 1917

"The East Side is growing rapidly and the residents are entitled to a public pleasure ground," claimed a news editor in 1901. McKinley Park was the result, one of many donated to the city by the Tacoma Land Company.
Tacoma Public Library

running northward from Spanaway Lake into the city's downtown, and created South Park near the Northern Pacific Railroad shops in South Tacoma.

By 1907, commissioners were having difficulty funding park development and maintenance. The solution devised by one of its members, Stuart Rice, was a new state law allowing cities to form metropolitan park districts. These were to be separate taxing entities governed by elected commissioners empowered to develop parks and parkways. A month after state legislators approved the law, Tacoma's voters approved the creation of the Metropolitan Park District of Tacoma by electing J.E. Jones, R.P. Shaw, W.C. Beardsley, A.M. Craig and Stuart Rice as commissioners.

One of the board's first projects was a plan to construct a series of wide boulevards linking together all of Tacoma's major parks. These roads were to radiate outward from the central business district, stretching north and south from Point Defiance Park to South Tacoma and east and west from McKinley Park to Puget Sound. It was a magnificent piece of work conceived by Stuart Rice and Allen C. Mason. Unfortunately, the grand plan was never implemented because in April of 1909 voters rejected the necessary bond issue. Even so, some work was done

Classes began at Tacoma High in 1906. The stadium bowl built next to it four years later gave a new name to the school.
Old Town Photo Studio

The Northern Pacific Railroad had begun the construction of a tourist hotel in North Tacoma before the 1893 depression halted the development. In 1902, Tacoma architect Ambrose J. Russell provided an idealized view of a building that soon became Stadium High School.
Washington State Historical Society Watercolor by Ambrose Russell

Commercial development along Sixth Avenue formed the nucleus of what was originally called Tacoma's "West End" neighborhood.
Old Town Photo Studio

on the system and can be seen along Union Avenue in Tacoma's north end.

Most of what happened in Tacoma during the early years of the 20th century defined urban development for years to come. The neighborhoods of today, complete with schools, churches, parks and commercial centers, are primarily the product of this era. The commission form of government approved by voters in 1909 was to rule the city into the 1950s, as would an industrial environment centered on timber. But the second spurt of growth began to wind down as World War I approached. When hostilities ended in 1918, Tacomans awoke to an entirely different world.

From War to War

Just before America entered World War I, the local Chamber of Commerce began to talk about a "Greater Tacoma," a phrase with two distinct meanings. On the one hand, the city's business leaders began a massive advertising campaign to sell Tacoma as a great place to live. On the other, the Chamber began to define the city as one whose well-being was highly dependent upon what was taking place elsewhere in the world. The notion of economic development grew from these two ideas and molded Tacoma's history for decades to come.

The nation was truly transformed because of World War I. Changes had actually begun locally before the declaration of hostilities in April of 1917. The opening of the Panama Canal in 1914, the year war broke out in Europe, held great economic promise for Puget Sound residents by easing commerce between eastern and western ports. The engineering wonder also caused Americans to look more closely on the political behavior of neighbors to the south. Therefore, when Pancho Villa launched raids across the Mexican border in 1916, National Guard troops joined General J.J. Pershing on a punitive expedition to capture the revolutionary. Soldiers were just returning from this adventure when President Woodrow Wilson asked Congress to declare war against Germany. Troops from Washington state participated in this Mexican campaign. They were trained at and departed from a location near American Lake, now the state National Guard headquarters at Camp Murray.

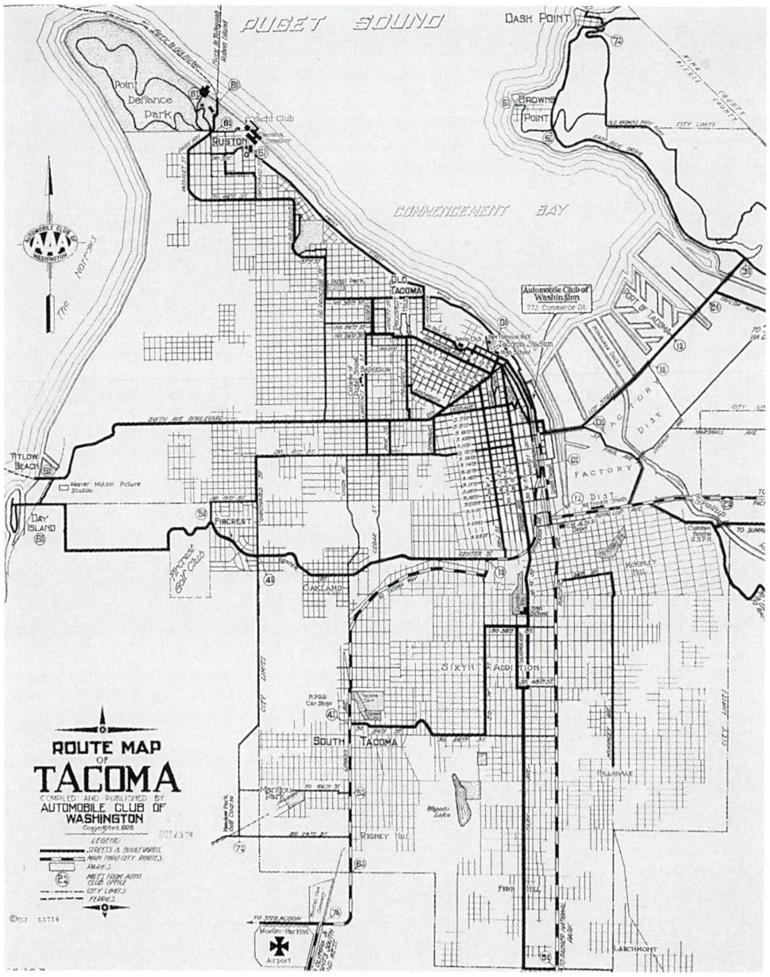

The Automobile Club of Washington produced this route map of Tacoma in 1928. MSCUA, *University of Washington Libraries*

the Puyallup River, an area still outside the city's municipal boundaries. Here property owners along Hylebos Creek formed a commercial waterway district and were dredging southward into the tideflats by 1914. Of equal significance, voters approved the creation of the Port of Tacoma in November of 1918 with Charles Orton, Edward Kloss and Chester Thorne the first commissioners. Therefore, both private owners and the port district built the commercial wharves and industrial sites needed for economic expansion after the war with development underway by 1927 port ownership petitioned for municipal incorporation successfully. Tacoma's boundaries expanded to include the port and parts of Northeast Tacoma. This annexation would be the last one for Tacoma until 1948.

The campaign to add an Army base to the National Guard encampment began while local troops were still stationed along the Mexican border. According to *Tacoma News Tribune* historian Paul Harvey, the agreement to create the fort was brokered by the newspaper's publisher Frank S. Baker, along with Stephen Abbleby and Jesse O. Thomas, a local banker and realtor. Baker was a personal friend of Secretary of War Newton D. Baker, "and this intimate association proved of much advantage to Tacoma." Indeed it did! In January of 1917 voters approved a proposal to acquire 70,000 acres of land on the Nisqually plains, which was then given to the Army. The construction of Camp Lewis and the influx of soldiers after the beginning of hostilities in Europe was of tremendous economic significance to Tacoma.

Creating Fort Lewis was the first manifestation of the Chamber's "Greater Tacoma" concept. Other efforts centered on the developing port area east of

Not all attempts to market the Tacoma name were successful. Between 1917 and 1925 Seattle and Tacoma businessmen locked horns over the name of Mount Rainier. The city's efforts centered on the restoration of the correct name of the mountain after the National Board on Geographic Names had officially deemed it Mount Rainier in 1890. Tacoma obtained a 1917 memorial from the Washington state Legislature requesting the board to reconsider its original decision. When this maneuver failed, Tacomans approached Congress. The Dill-Johnson bill passed the Senate in 1924 but never made it out of the House Public Lands Committee.

The bickering between the two cities got a little heated as each accused the other of "converting the house of God into a market place," or so the *Tacoma Times* reported in 1921. The *Tacoma Daily Ledger's* editor insisted that the mountain was named Rainier "to protect the trademark of a brand of beer." Tacoma was the gateway to the mountain, claimed another writer. "Anything that belongs to a person... as closely... as the mountain belongs to Tacoma should have the ownership acknowledged by the outside world."

By the end of the hearings it became clear that both cities saw the mountain primarily as a major economic asset. For residents in the City of Destiny, changing the name to Tacoma would be one way of inviting potential visitors "seeking a new location for a mill or industrial plant" to stay and invest in the city. Seattleites saw the Mount Rainier name as a registered trademark owned by that city. Indeed, J.J. Underwood, representing its Chamber of Commerce, made the point quite clear at the final Congressional hearing. After itemizing a list of projects totaling over $10 million all "made under the assumption that the name could not be changed," he contended "that if the name of this mountain is changed it would be the same as changing the name of Ivory Soap, or anything else which had a nationally known name."

And so the arguments and acrimony continued into the 1920s. By 1929 the issue centered on Tacoma's request to have the aircraft carrier *USS Lexington* provide power to the city. The circumstances leading to the request were unique at the time, for cities were dependent upon rain to fuel their hydroelectric power plants. This particular year the region encountered a drought, one that found Tacoma unable to provide electricity from its 3-year-old plant on Lake Cushman and the older La Grande dam on the Nisqually River. With water levels dangerously low, governmental officials and local businessmen petitioned the U.S. Navy for assistance.

Both the city of Seattle and the privately owned Puget Power and Light Company lobbied against the Navy's approval. Why is not clear in the newspaper accounts reporting the event. The two entities argued that the drought did not affect their facilities and therefore Tacoma's problem was the result of poor management. Their allegations failed, however, and in late December 1929 Tacomans welcomed the arrival of the Lexington to Baker Dock where the ship supplied electricity until the rains returned and Lake Cushman could provide power once again. The irony of this story is that Seattle soon found itself requesting the same service from the *Lexington*, a request the Navy denied.

An airport finally brought the two cities together. The Tacoma City Council's involvement in this new form of travel had begun following a 1919 letter from the Service Aviation Training and Transportation Company requesting a landing field for commercial airplanes. Government officials decided "to take up [the] matter with [the] Speedway Association for purposes of making arrangements for use of [the] speedway grounds for such a landing place." Before the city could act, however, R.A. Mueller and L.W. Harkins acquired the raceway located on Steilacoom Boulevard — now a part of Clover Park Technical College — and developed a private airfield. Until the late 1920s the Mueller-Harkins field was also the Tacoma Municipal Airport.

In November of 1928, Pierce County voters approved a $300,000 bond issue to develop another municipal field. The next year, county commissioners selected a part of John Rigney's pioneer farm adjacent to the government dirigible mooring mast, north of Fort Lewis, for the new Tacoma Municipal Airport. The facility had a short life, however. By 1933 the U.S. Army began to show an interest in the field because of its possibilities for military defense. McChord Field — now McChord Air Force Base — was dedicated in July of 1940 just as mobilization for a new war had begun.

Tacoma's 1938 gift to the Army left the city without an airport. At this very same time Seattle approached local governmental officials for financial help in the construction of an international airport 10 miles south of the Emerald City near Bow Lake. Tacoma Mayor Harry P. Cain agreed to the proposition provided Tacoma's name was indelibly attached to the new facility. Sea-Tac was the result of the negotiations, and while Tacomans continued to search for an airport closer to home, the effort proved fruitless until 1963, when the city established one of its own on the Gig Harbor Peninsula.

Tacoma in 1889

Rudyard Kipling

"We passed down ungraded streets that ended abruptly in a fifteen foot drop and a nest of brambles; along pavements that beginning in a pine-plank ended in the living tree; by hotels with Turkish mosque trinketry on their shameless tops and the pine stumps at their very doors; by a female seminary, tall, gaunt and red, which a native of the town bade us marvel at, and we marveled; by houses built in imitation of the ones on Nob Hill, San Francisco, after the Dutch fashion; by other houses plenteously befouled with jig-saw work, and others flaring with the castlemented, battlemented bosh of the wooden Gothic school.

"The hotel walls bore a flaming panorama of Tacoma in which by the eye of faith I saw a faint resemblance to the real town. The hotel stationery advertised that Tacoma bore on its face all the advantages of the highest civilization, and the newspapers sang the same tune in a louder key. The real estate agents were selling house-lots on unmade streets miles away for thousands of dollars. On the streets — the rude, crude streets, where the unshaded electric light was fighting with the gentle northern twilight — men were babbling of money, town-lots and again money.... I think it was the raw, new smell of fresh sawdust everywhere pervading the air that threw upon me a desolating homesickness."

— Reprinted in *Puget's Sound: A Narrative of Early Tacoma and the Southern Sound* by Murray Morgan

The Tacoma Hotel located on South A Street opened for business in 1884. *Thomas R. Stenger Collection* *Photo by Thomas Rutter*

Juaquin Miller

"This is a red town... with her endless avenues of red brick and her continuous trees, which serve to emphasize the red with the contrasting green. The city is built of red brick, with limestone rock in the rough for the first story, as a rule. But beside the red brick, the roofs of the houses are painted red; and as the city is on a hill, with the blue waters of the inland sea below her, and a crescent of dense green forest crowding close around and closing in to right and left, why, you see, Tacoma is a tower and battlement of red, brilliant by contrast with sky and sea and somber wilderness.

"And for fear I have given the broad impression that this is a sort of mining camp, so far as comfort is concerned, I must write it down now... I have secured quarters in a hotel so elegant that I am filled with astonishment at its perfection. You would mistake this airy red hostelry for a palace of the Middle Ages. Now, this is saying very much for a city so new that it continually smells of paint whichever way you pass as you walk the streets; but I know what I am about. The edifice is a copy of the Ancono, I should say. At least, I am certain I have seen its airy and red counterpart — its high light gables, its tile imitations, its countless curves and turns of roof and wall and corner — by the banks of the Adriatic sea, or somewhere along there, in and about Ancono and Ravena.

"These hotels are not so crowded thus by those who are building that city. Strangers on the balconies that look out into the inland sea from this island of red are, as a rule, merely the better class of seaside loungers. I should say that the greater portion of those who fill the first class houses here at this season of the year are the wealthier and healthier of the Newport or Long Branch people, who, with a bit of an eye to business in the way of land speculation, are merely taking a longer "run" down to the seaside. Certain it is that I see the same quiet manners here, the same absence of care and business concern that marks the well-bred American in your famous great resorts on the other side of the Republic."

— *The Journal*, August 31, 1889

Cable cars ran up and down South 11th and 13th streets until 1938.
Old Town Photo Studio

All these events occurred during a time of war and depression. Hard times did not come to the Pacific Northwest as a part of the Stock Market crash in 1929. It came with the end of World War I. Industries that had grown during hostilities, shipbuilding is one example, slumped when government orders were canceled. The price of timber fell, putting a particular strain on Tacoma's mill workers. Poor agricultural prices received by Puyallup Valley and eastern Washington growers alike affected local commerce. There was some stability by the mid-1920s, but gone were the booms of the past. From this time forward, Tacoma's population experienced a slow but steady growth from 96,965 to 109,408 in 1940.

In the words of historian John Findlay, "the Depression took an already troubled economy and destroyed it even further." This circumstance probably explains why disproportionately high levels of federal dollars flowed into the region during the New Deal. Tacoma, as well as other Pierce County communities, received their fair share for projects both large and small. Public Works Administration monies paid for the construction

In 1938, the same year construction began on the first Narrows Bridge, Tacomans celebrated the end of the streetcars and the beginnings of bus transportation.
Old Town Photo Studio

of the first Narrows Bridge, while separate Congressional appropriations allowed for the expansion of Fort Lewis, the construction of McChord Field and new dredging in the port-industrial area. The Works Projects Administration funded schoolhouses and park facilities throughout the county. Bonneville and Grand Coulee dams on the Columbia River promised more public power to aid new chemical and aluminum industries.

The New Deal also brought federal planning to the region in the form of the National Resources Planning Board. In 1940 the federal agency selected Tacoma — along with Salt Lake City, Utah and Corpus Christi, Texas — to create new planning procedures for the "post-defense deployment of men and materials in city rebuilding." As explained by Philip J. Funigiello, the board "hoped to attain a new level of sophistication in urban planning by treating the city not simply as an artifact but integrating social, economic, and cultural factors into the planning process."

Tacoma Mayor Harry P. Cain got the whole city involved. He sent letters to all the neighborhood and commercial organizations asking for their ideas on ways to improve the city. Their collective responses were incorporated into the municipality's first published planning document entitled *Tacoma, the City We Build.* While the whole endeavor received mixed reviews at the time, the city's involvement in this federal experiment ultimately led to the creation of a city planning department following charter revisions in 1952.

Tacoma's economy began to improve when President Franklin D. Roosevelt ordered a general mobilization for war in 1940. Hostilities after Pearl Harbor brought more soldiers and airmen to Fort Lewis along with new industrial workers, many of them women who did everything from pump gas and drive buses to build ships and airplanes. To meet a housing shortage, the federal government built new residential neighborhoods, including Salishan and Lincoln Heights in Tacoma and American Lake Gardens east of Lakewood. The city also attracted soldiers on leave. Downtown Tacoma became a place to have fun during these years, so much so that businessmen were always worried that the Army would place the City of Destiny off-limits to the servicemen if proper decorum was not maintained.

Tacoma Mayor Harry P. Cain was probably the only local governmental official to protest the internment of American citizens following President Roosevelt's February 19, 1942 Executive Order #9066. This decree led to the removal of all Japanese living along the West Coast of the United States and their placement in concentration camps located in Idaho and eastern California. The fairground in Puyallup — renamed Camp Harmony — became the embarkation point for the Puget Sound Japanese. In Tacoma they had embraced a commercial and residential area situated westward from the downtown along South 15th Street. Photographs taken at the time show the Japanese Americans boarding guarded trains at the Union Station. Others show Camp Harmony as a place less satisfying than the barracks at Fort Lewis.

Ultimately the Japanese were allowed to return to Tacoma, but the city had changed while they were away. The population had grown by 34,265 to reach 143,673 by 1950. Houses were beginning to fill the areas left vacant since 1893, and by 1948, construction had begun on a new Narrows Bridge promising even more expansion outward from the central business district. Downtown businessmen were concerned again about the general problems of vice, prostitution and urban decay. They discovered upon approaching the city for help that municipal government was also a part of the problem. The commissioner form of government proved unable to keep pace with a city altered by war. Therefore, in 1952 Tacoma's voters approved a change, one that replaced city commissioners with a council designed to determine urban policy and a manager to administer the daily affairs of the city.

A century before this particular election, Nicholas Delin had established his sawmill where a major industrial waterway stood in 1952. He would not have recognized the place after 100 years of development. Neither would have Job Carr, Charles B. Wright or the hundreds of other early settlers, promoters and boosters who came to Puget Sound. So much had happened to create the city of their dreams. But this story is not yet finished. Having described the events that shaped the City of Destiny and the county that gave it economic sustenance, now it is time to consider the people who made it all happen.

The Tacoma Narrows Bridge just after its dedication in July of 1940 — four months later "Galloping Gertie" collapsed into Puget Sound.
Old Town Photo Studio

CHAPTER THREE

STREAMS OF MIGRATION

Those who came to Pierce County to live and work were part of a highly complex movement involving people from all over the world. Ordinarily this migration is thought of as a westward one where folks left the eastern part of the United States for a better life in the Pacific Northwest. This portrait is certainly true for the many who used first the Oregon Trail and then the various railroad lines. Others came by ship, traveling around Cape Horn or across the Isthmus of Panama. Pierce County residents following these routes came primarily from New England, the mid-Atlantic states or the Midwest.

Not all came this way, however. People traveled from all directions to settle Pierce County. European or Asian immigrants oftentimes arrived directly from their foreign homes, especially when family members or countrymen had already paved the way. Ethnic or racial enclaves were the result, communities where foreign traditions were preserved through schools, benevolent associations or churches. French and British Canadians migrated from the north, while Hispanics — along with others from Oregon and California — came from the south. Asians and Pacific Islanders, beginning with Hawaiians who arrived during the earliest years of the fur trading, came from the west.

They came for a variety of reasons. Poor economic conditions back home motivated the majority. Land hunger inspired others. Immigrants from Europe were also escaping political instability and totalitarianism, religious persecution and wars requiring permanent standing armies and mandatory military service. To lure newcomers westward toward Pierce County, the Northern Pacific Railroad circulated immigrant guides advertising all the economic

(Opening photo) The Puyallup Indian Tribe never abandoned Tacoma. They continued to congregate, joined by African Americans, on the shoreline near their traditional village sites. *Old Town Photo Studio*

advantages to be found along their route leading to the City of Destiny.

By the turn of the 19th century, Pierce County was a rich cultural tapestry. Over half of the residents were of foreign stock, with the English from Canada, Swedes, Germans, Italians and Croatians dominating the list of those migrating from outside the United States. Almost 900 African Americans lived in Pierce County by 1910, along with some 2,000 Japanese. The Puyallup and Nisqually Indians were also a part of this diverse human landscape.

When heavy snowfall buried tracks on the Stampede Pass switchback, railroad officials employed Chinese workers to clear it by hand. This view was taken in 1886 while the route was still under construction and one year after Tacomans expelled the Chinese from the city. *MSCUA, University of Washington Libraries*

Dealing with such a human mixture was bound to be difficult, especially for whites not able to tolerate racial, religious or ethnic differences. When problems arose, the native-born Americans expected Congress to protect them against the foreigners. Such was the case in 1882 and 1885, when the House and Senate passed first the Exclusion Act prohibiting Chinese laborers from the United States, and then forbade the importation of all contract foreign labor. Tacomans viewed both measures as ways to remove the Chinese from their midst. When they realized that the new legislation did not apply to workers already living in the city, local residents decided to take matters into their own hands.

"The Chinese Must Go"

Tacomans today acknowledge that the vigilante methods used to forcibly expel the Chinese from the city in November of 1885 was a terrible mistake, but that was not the case at the time. Then, almost every resident supported the endeavor, and for years afterward elections were won or lost based on the position a candidate took concerning this rather delicate matter. Herbert Hunt tells that even women were a part of the melee as they looted dishes and furnishings from the vacant Chinese shops. Tacoma was not the only place along the Pacific Coast whose citizens viewed the Chinese as a menace to be rid of, and in many ways their discriminatory treatment and violent behavior paralleled events elsewhere. But an International District — or Chinatown — never emerged in the City of Destiny. What happened in 1885 explains why.

It is not known for sure how many Chinese lived in the area in 1885. The majority, however, were contract workers hired by the Northern Pacific. The earliest settlements were located near present-day Tacoma at the Hanson, Ackerson mill, on the railroad wharf and above the Half Moon yard. Chinese dwellings and businesses were scattered throughout the downtown area. The population had grown from approximately 250 in 1873 to over 500. An additional 200 lived near Pierce County's hop fields and mines. Not all the Asians were workers. They were also merchants, laundry owners and other businessmen. Sing Lee was one of the few who owned land. Most leased property from whites.

Real estate speculators were the first to voice displeasure over the Chinese in Tacoma, calling them "one of the perils of buying" land in the city. According to Herbert Hunt, "the possibility of having a Chinese for a neighbor" caused at least one Sinophobe to pay one to move off an adjacent lot so as not to impair the value of his own property. Between 1881 and 1884, the city tried even more direct measures. Tacoma City ordered the removal of a Chinese cemetery. New Tacoma outlawed laundries in the downtown area, forbade contractors from hiring Chinese workers on public projects and banned "the using of any yoke, pole or balance pole" when conveying "slop, swill, offal [or] garbage... upon or along any sidewalk or street crossing in the city."

Pacific Avenue looked like this at the time Tacomans forcibly expelled the Chinese living there. MSCUA, *University of Washington Libraries*

Ordinances of this nature were introduced to force the Chinese to peacefully leave the city. Tacoma's businessmen especially wanted them out of the downtown area where they feared that the scattered settlements would meld into a Chinatown encompassing the entire townsite. When the new laws did not achieve their desired effect, members of the Chamber of Commerce considered the possibility of providing land for a Chinese district — an Asian ghetto — far removed from white businesses. The project failed for lack of support and because no landowners came forward to offer property for the purpose.

Businessmen were not alone in their efforts. During the time city council members were legislating against the Chinese, Tacoma's workers had organized at least six labor unions, including the Knights of Labor. On May 5, 1884, one of its members, J.R. Weisbach, replaced Northern Pacific's John W. Sprague as mayor. Labor radicalism came with the Knights, along with men like William Christie, who had helped to forcibly expel the Chinese from Eureka, California, early in 1885. The tone of the local debate now became more heated as laborers joined the municipal government and Tacoma's business elite in what one newspaper called a movement to reform the city.

The final round of agitation began in May of 1885 when Tacoma councilman William Pierce Bonney introduced a new health code that prohibited public laundries not connected to sewers and the public display of freshly slaughtered animals. The law also mandated "500 cubic feet of air space to each occupant" in a sleeping area. Newspapers published Mayor Weisbach's inspections of Chinese houses and businesses, reports which inevitably proved violations of the city code. It is not known if anyone else in Tacoma broke the new law because city officials seldom if ever looked beyond the living conditions of the Chinese.

Inspection raids continued into the summer months, encouraged by the Tacoma Anti-Chinese League formed in June. The focus now changed from the health code to opium use and wine smuggling, culminating in a joint federal customs and city police raid on the Northern Pacific wharf in July. During the course of the raids, newspapers reported mass meetings and demonstrations, all designed to portray Tacoma as laboring under an extreme danger because of the presence of some 500 Chinese.

All matters came to a head in October when the Anti-Chinese League appointed an expulsion committee composed of some of Tacoma's most distinguished businessmen — the Committee of Fifteen — to inform the Asians that they had to be out of the city by November 1. Murray Morgan explained the initial results of the demand:

"Many Chinese left quietly. More than a hundred were reported to have caught the train to Portland

or the boat to Victoria. Others had no funds to buy tickets anywhere. And some, especially those who had been in town for years, who had jobs, or businesses, who felt they had friends, stayed on, unable to believe force would be used against them. They were encouraged by men like former Mayor Sprague, who assured the Chinese who consulted him that this was the United States, they were in Tacoma legally, their rights would be protected."

Those who hesitated to leave became victims of the "Tacoma Method," a vigilante effort led by the Knights of Labor Committee of Nine on November 5, 1885. Street by street and block by block, armed men methodically and forcibly cleared the city of Chinese. The same men marched them to Lakeview, a Northern Pacific station located some six miles south of Tacoma's downtown. Once there the Chinese were expected to pay their own way to Portland on the next passenger train. Those with no money were put on freight cars.

Fires deliberately set near the Hanson, Ackerson mill and around the Northern Pacific wharf followed the Chinese expulsion. Herbert Hunt maintained that were it not for the efforts of the Reverend Peter Francis Hylebos, the entire city might have been destroyed. The Roman Catholic priest reminded the potential arsonists that if they set the fires they "might burn the entire city and forever ruin its reputation... while if the shacks, which had been built by the Chinese on leased land, were allowed to remain they would revert to white owners of the land and the community would benefit by it." Father Hylebos' argument prevailed downtown, but no one stopped those who slashed the fire hoses spreading water on the torched homes and businesses of Tacoma's Chinese.

George R. Epperson, editor of the *Tacoma Weekly News*, was one who called the forcible expulsion of the Chinese a reform. For him, "the majority of the citizens have surely accomplished a great victory... in demonstrating to the world the fact that an earnest, intelligent and peaceable community is capable, without violence or disorder, of accomplishing a great reform." Not all agreed. United States Attorney William H. White attempted to convict those responsible for a violation of federal conspiracy laws. A jury indicted 27 community leaders and public officials, but none were found guilty of any crime.

The federal government indicted 27 men for their role in expelling the Chinese from Tacoma in 1885. None were brought to trial. All, along with their wives and children, were locally honored as heroes. *From Tacoma: Its History and Its Builders by Herbert Hunt*

The story of Tacoma's Chinese did not end in 1885. The symbol of their continuing presence was the arrival of the *Phra Nang* in June of 1892. At that time the Chinese government informed local businessmen that steamship trade with Asia required Chinese merchants in the city. Therefore, while labor groups protested, the firm of Wong Chung and Kong, representing the Oriental Trading Company, established its business in the Bostwick block at South 9th Street and Broadway. Even so, anti-Chinese sentiment lingered far into the 20th century, along with the persistent rumors that tunnels used for smuggling Chinese and their wares honeycombed the ground underneath Tacoma.

The Chinese were not the only minority population of local interest at this time, however. While Tacomans were forcibly expelling Asians, Northern Pacific officials announced their own efforts to remove Puyallup Indians from the Commencement Bay shoreline. The company was not alone in seeing the Puyallup Indian Reservation as a problem to be solved — as a barrier to urban growth. Unlike the Chinese, though, the Puyallup natives had treaty rights and could not be forcibly expelled. Again, Congress came to the rescue, this time through the Dawes Act of 1887.

Undoing the Puyallup Reservation

The Dawes Act was not specifically designed to help only Tacoma, but it proved exceedingly useful for those who saw the Puyallup River delta as an ideal location for a new harbor. The measure was really designed to make American citizens out of all the Western tribes by allowing each to own land on their respective reservations. Once the Native Americans received their personal allotments, the surplus land was to be sold to the highest bidder, a legal provision guaranteed to transfer ownership to whites.

The legislation as amended over the years established a time after which individual tribal members could lease or sell their lands. For the Puyallup Indians, Congress allowed sales after 1903. By then, however, most of the original Puyallup Indian Reservation was in the hands of a small group of Tacoma real estate speculators. How this came to be was, like the story of the Chinese, a terrible mistake acknowledged today. But at the time Tacomans viewed the alienation of the Puyallup Indians Reservation as absolutely vital to the future of the city.

Old-time Tacomans are convinced that Chinese tunnels lie underneath the county. The entrance to this one, really an engineering test for the Union Pacific Railroad, was located in Fircrest.
Tacoma Public Library, Boland Collection

Puyallup Indian Reservation allotments, 1886
Washington State Historical Society

Children sent to Indian schools in the United States were expected to become "American" in dress and habits. This included abandoning Indian music and playing in a brass band.
Tacoma Public Library

Opposition to the Puyallup Indian Reservation was regular fare in Tacoma's first newspapers. In 1883, for example, R.F. Radebaugh, founding editor of the *Tacoma Daily Ledger*, considered "Indian policy and reservations" as "relics of the past... Indians themselves prefer to accept the true status of manhood, instead of being confined upon reservations as an inferior and dependent race." Radebaugh, however, was not the first to criticize the existence of the Puyallups living close to the Tacoma townsite. Between 1872 and 1873, Northern Pacific Railroad President Frederick Billings and Western Manager John W. Sprague had unsuccessfully explored the possibility of moving the Puyallup Tribe to the Tulalip Reservation north of Everett.

By the mid-1880s, the Indians lived on individual allotments initially assigned to them in 1874. According to Puyallup Indian Agent Edwin Eells, there were 167 allotments in 1890, the year a Puyallup Indian Commission set out to determine if any of the land could be sold to outsiders. The commissioners decided that close to 13,000 acres, or 73 percent of the reservation, could be taken from the Indians and auctioned off. Just under 5,000 acres was to remain in Puyallup ownership. And with Congressional approval, a commission of three began the process of selling the land to Tacoma developers.

Between 1892 and 1893, therefore, the Native Americans began to see the beginning of the end of their reservation. By that time local concerns centered on who was to benefit from the economic windfall. One Tacoma newspaper editor, while acknowledging his wish to see surplus land sold, also thought that "Congress should protect the interests of 'poor lo' against the wiles and schemes of unconscionable real estate sharks anxiously waiting to make fortunes out of these lands through their special seductive methods... largely to the exclusion of the general public." His unheeded advice was directed at a land syndicate, headed by Frank C. Ross, which in 1889 had begun to enter into lease-purchase agreements with the Puyallup Indians.

Through written contracts, the Native Americans "granted, bargained, and sold" their individual allotments to the land syndicate. This process clearly began before Congress had authorized the sale of reservation land and before its members established 1903 as the year Puyallups could sell their own parcels. Even so, by the time of a Puyallup Indian Commission investigation in 1892, 40 percent of the reservation land had been pre-sold in this fashion.

The Commissioners were able to identify 26 contractors, some of whom — like Jerry Meeker — were Indians. Of the total, Hugh C. Wallace and Frank C. Ross controlled almost 75 percent of the acreage under contract. Ross also lobbied Congress to appoint Puyallup Indians working with the land speculators as the commissioners who appraised and sold the unalloted lands. While this effort failed, in 1897 Congress replaced the original three commissioners with a single individual, and the syndicate managed to get one of their own, Clinton A. Snowden, appointed to the position. Two attorneys were also a part of the scheme. James Wickersham, one of the Committee of Fifteen which supervised the expulsion of the Chinese, was one. The other was James M. Ashton, whose name is most closely tied to the project.

The final undoing of the Puyallup Reservation centered on a jurisdictional dispute over the ownership of the tidelands fronting the reservation, land that the Ross syndicate had purchased from the state of Washington. A territorial survey done in 1864 placed this valuable property outside the reservation. However, a survey conducted by Isaac I. Stevens in 1856 had included them. The Puyallups, therefore, claimed ownership and in 1906 sued the land syndicate for the recovery of their tidelands. The case was decided in Federal District Judge Cornelius Hanford's court three years later.

Upholding Puyallup Indian ownership of the tidelands required Hanford to accept the possibility that the Native Americans had legally acquired them as a part of their original land patents. This he refused to do. He maintained instead that Congress had removed all Indian rights to their land through the Oregon Donation Land Act of 1850 and the Medicine Creek Treaty of 1854. The tidelands, in other words, really belonged to the state, not the Indians.

With one swoop of the pen, Judge Hanford granted more than half the Commencement Bay tidelands to the Tacoma land syndicate. The undoing of the Puyallup Reservation was complete. In 1970 the American Friends Service Committee reported that "no more than thirty-five acres of the Puyallup reservation remain in trust status." Some 200 to 300 acres were still owned by Indian allottees.

Tacomans had hoped that the end of the reservation would lead to the assimilation of the Indians into American culture. Such was not to be the case. The Puyallups never lost their identity as a people. They retained their cultural institutions and traditions. The same was also true for many others who migrated to Tacoma and Pierce County over the years.

In 1928 the Woman's Club of Tacoma considered it appropriate to dedicate a marker that commemorated, among other things, the award of U.S. citizenship to Puyallup Indians in 1903. *Tacoma Public Library, Boland Collection*

The Cushman Hospital provided services to Indians throughout the Pacific Northwest until its closure in 1959. The Puyallup Indians reclaimed the property in the 1970s and it now houses tribal headquarters. *Tacoma Public Library*

Pierce County Ethnicity

Discussing ethnic diversity in Pierce County is full of hazards simply because it is not possible to include everyone. Like the communities formed through the various streams of migration, many people were responsible for making the county what it is today. And like the communities they created, one can only provide a sampling, a small taste, of a rich human smorgasbord.

According to the 1900 federal census, Germans led the list of the foreign born, and while they settled throughout Pierce County, Elbe served as a magnet for many. Their community symbol was the Evangelical Lutheran Kirche built in 1906. Services were conducted in German and therefore attracted parishioners living throughout southeastern Pierce County. Scandinavians were close to the Germans in numbers, especially the Swedes. Many established farms on the peninsulas and islands of Puget Sound. In addition, the Netherlands American Manufacturing Company acquired property on the west side of Anderson Island, inspiring a community called New Amsterdam.

Many students spoke German when they first attended the Rosedale School located on the Mountain Highway between Eatonville and Elbe. A.W. Stuhrman was the teacher when classes first began in 1892.
Washington State Historical Society

The Saints Peter and Paul Polish Catholic Church on Portland Avenue is one of many religious landmarks marking where immigrants settled in Tacoma.
Tacoma Public Library

Some immigrant enclaves centered on religious belief, such as Tacoma's Jewish population. There were two distinct phases to their settlement throughout Puget Sound, maintains historian William Toll, both based on a close association with the Jews of Portland. From that Oregon city "the wandering young Jewish men were following to the logical geographical limits the desire to stake out traditional trading services. They moved back and forth between Portland, the Oregon and Washington hinterlands, San Francisco and New York to complete transactions. Only at a later stage in their lifestyle would they settle permanently in one city or another." By means of this process, Jews began to settle in Tacoma at least by the early 1880s, and many were instrumental in shaping the city's early growth and development.

The Temple and Jewish cemeteries — Chevra Kadisha and Home of Peace — are symbols of their local history. The First Hebrew Benevolent Society platted the Home of Peace cemetery on December 14, 1891. Isaac Pincus was president of the organization at that time and Louis Wallerstein was secretary. Members of the local Jewish community organized the Temple Beth Israel the following year. A second temple also formed early in the 20th century, but in 1960 the two Jewish congregations united to form the present-day Temple Beth El.

Churches and cemeteries located elsewhere in the county also help to identify the centers of other ethnic populations. In the town of Wilkeson, for example, one finds the Russian Orthodox Holy

Ethnic celebrations included weddings where old country relatives and friends would be photographed with the bride and groom.
Old Town Photo Studio

Croatian immigrants in Old Tacoma created their fraternal and benevolent organization in 1901.
Old Town Photo Studio

Trinity Church. Constructed near the turn of the 19th century, it joined Our Lady of Lourdes Roman Catholic church built in 1894. Their existence pointed to the large number of Russians, Slovene, Croatian, Polish and Italian miners who congregated in Pierce County's coal region. Lutheran churches, schools and cemeteries surrounding Parkland and Spanaway document the role played by Scandinavians in settling these particular communities.

In Tacoma, foreign immigrants were initially drawn to certain neighborhoods. Here the formation of benevolent societies and meeting halls marked their presence. These organizations were a place of refuge for the new arrivals. The societies provided financial aid in times of trouble and assured a decent funeral for their members. The meeting halls were places where immigrants could celebrate their own cultural traditions while also learning how to adapt to a new life in the United States through classes in English and American citizenship.

Maintaining a cultural identity while still becoming American underscored activity of this nature. Many Croatians, for example, were attracted to Puget Sound because it reminded them of the Adriatic Sea fronting their native villages, and they formed settlements in both Gig Harbor and Old Tacoma. From their attempt to adapt traditional fishing methods to new waters came some of Tacoma's first major boatbuilding concerns and a fishing industry centered on the purse seine. At the same time, Croatians formed a benevolent association in Old Tacoma and persisted in retaining their cultural traditions.

So did many others in Tacoma. Italians, many settling in the Hawthorne district at the foot of McKinley Hill, had the Sons of Italy to provide help to the new immigrants. West of downtown both Germans and Norwegians constructed meeting halls for their respective organizations. But the insistence that cultural traditions be preserved was not just limited to immigrants from Europe. Migrants from Japan and African Americans from other parts of the United States were also here seeking a better life.

The African Americans in Tacoma

African Americans made their mark in Tacoma even before the arrival of the railroad, when in 1869 the Workingmen's Joint Stock Association of Portland, Oregon, platted the Alliance addition to the city. By 1910 there were 778 blacks living in the city, and this area west of the downtown business district had become the northern anchor of an African American neighborhood stretching south along the city's Hilltop. "These nineteenth-century urbanites were," maintains historian Quintard Taylor, "influential far beyond their numbers as the organizations and institutions they created... the

African Americans were part of the early railroad crews. James McFaddon (foreground left) worked with a team surveying the Northern Pacific Cascade Division route along the Green River. *MSCUA, University of Washington Libraries*

goals they sought through politics and civil rights influenced successive generations well into the twentieth century."

Throughout the cities of the West, African Americans shared a common pattern of life. "Both men and women were personal servants for wealthy households, while black males worked as hotel waiters, railroad porters, messengers, cooks, and janitors. Some entrepreneurial blacks operated barbershops, restaurants, and boarding houses. By the 1890s most western black communities had a few doctors and lawyers and newspaper editors, who, along with ministers and schoolteachers, comprised the 'elite'." Tacoma was no exception.

Ralph Hayes, in his centennial portrait of African American pioneers, introduces some of Tacoma's earliest businessmen and public servants. John Conna, for example, was sergeant-at-arms for the first session of the Washington State Senate. Lawrence Sledge, in 1909, became the first African American attorney in Tacoma. Horace Prince Lawhorn drove a patrol wagon for the Tacoma Police Department in 1899. Edward Hollowell graduated from the London Royal School of Architecture and designed the Colored Women's Clubhouse at South 23rd Street and Yakima Avenue. In addition, the wives of the city's earliest African Americans were music teachers and nurses. The masthead of the *Forum*, the city's first black newspaper, lists Ellen Ryan, along with her husband, J.H., as editor.

Tacoma's African American community revolved around such organizations as the Sierra Leone Club, Odd Fellows and Masonic Lodges, the Black Republican and Colored Women's Republican Clubs, the Colored Women's Club, the Allen AME Church and the National Association for the Advancement of Colored People. Reverend A.M. Taylor, John Mason and William Moore were trustees of the church when it first organized in 1889. It became the cornerstone of Tacoma's black community. "Perhaps the strongest feature of Reverend Taylor's mission," concludes Dr. Ella Taylor in her centennial history of the congregation, "is the fact that he understood the spiritual value of a church congregation months before the territory became a state. His accomplishments brought spiritual peace and harmony to African Americans in an unsettled territory."

Nettie Asberry, whose husband, H.J., owned the barbershop in the Tacoma Hotel, established the city's branch of the NAACP in 1912. One finds the organization protesting against D.W. Griffith's film *The Birth of a Nation*. In 1916 the city council minutes report that "a delegation of citizens appeared before the Council asking for an amendment to Sec. 1, Ordinance 6179, relating to moving picture films portraying race hatred," a request city officials ignored.

Nettie Asberry established Tacoma's branch of the National Association for the Advancement of Colored People in 1912. She went on to help form additional chapters in Seattle, Spokane and Portland, Oregon. *Tacoma Public Library, Richards Collection*

The NAACP, however, remained an active voice and joined others in Tacoma seeking racial and ethnic equality. When in 1913 the Washington State Legislature considered a bill prohibiting interracial marriages between whites and Asians, Nettie Asberry successfully lobbied against the measure. Gustav B. Aldrich, a later secretary of Tacoma's NAACP, continued the African American support of local Asians following World War I. The partnership between other ethnic and racial groups also continued after World War II. In 1956, for example, today's Federal District Judge Jack Tanner, then an attorney for and president of Tacoma's NAACP, spoke at the Temple Beth Israel on "Brotherhood in Tacoma."

World War II revolutionized the urban African American landscape. From 650 living in Tacoma in 1940, the black population grew to 3,205, a 393 percent increase. Employment in war industries motivated many to come to Puget Sound, but so too did the military, especially the 5,000 soldiers and sailors stationed at Fort Lewis, Seattle's Fort Lawton and the Puget Sound Naval Shipyard at Bremerton. Again, to quote Quintard Taylor, "black military personnel frequently ended their enlistment at western bases, sent for family members, and settled permanently." And so it was in Tacoma.

The African Americans who arrived during the war to work in Tacoma's industries encountered a housing shortage compounded by the city's overall population growth and discrimination that confined black families to the segregated core along the Hilltop. Adjacent to this neighborhood, however, were the residences left vacant by Tacoma's Japanese following their internment in concentration camps. As in cities elsewhere along the Pacific Coast, blacks moved into the houses of the Asian Americans. The racial accord established between blacks and Asians prior to the war was shattered under the pressure and "gave way to migrant-dominated communities that, without

Following the assassination of Martin Luther King in 1968, the NAACP and the Tacoma Ministerial Alliance sponsored a memorial march. More than 1,000 people walked from St. John's Baptist Church to the County-City Building. *Tacoma Public Library*

the benefit of prior contact, often refused to acknowledge Asian grievances."

The discord was an unfortunate result of the war, but it also points to a major fact surrounding the history of race relations in Tacoma. The African Americans were never the only people of color living in the city. They joined Native Americans as well as the Chinese and Japanese in an urban environment where whites were at best ambiguous but usually hostile toward their collective presence. Within this scenario Tacomans treated Asian populations with the least regard. This was seen first with the Chinese in 1885. It is now time to consider the Japanese.

The Japanese in Tacoma and Pierce County

The event that brought Chinese merchants back to Tacoma — the arrival of the *Phra Nang* in 1892 — also introduced local residents to the Japanese in their midst. There were not many in Pierce County at this time, for the federal census lists only 56 in Tacoma in 1890. But the population grew to some 700 by 1900, most living in the City of Destiny where they formed a business community along Broadway (then C) Street.

Another decade saw Tacoma's Japanese population grow to just over 1,000. By this time, not all arrivals were proprietors of the barbershops, laundries, hotels and other businesses located downtown. Federal legislation prohibiting the immigration of Chinese laborers did not keep Tacoma and Pierce County lumber companies from hiring the Japanese. "Nikkei foremen... actually did the hiring," explains historian Dr. Ronald Magden. "The straw bosses earned four dollars a day to recruit and supervise lumber handlers. Each laborer made three dollars for working the night shift moving boards from the saw to the drying shed or sorting lumber on tables. The Japanese lived in separate bunkhouses and ate their meals apart from the whites."

The early decades of the 20th century saw an increase in the number of Japanese living in Pierce

Japanese women serving tea at a Tacoma Parent-Teacher Association meeting
Tacoma Public Library, Richards Collection

In 1942 President Franklin D. Roosevelt ordered the placement of all Japanese on the West Coast into internment camps. Most were American citizens. *Tacoma Public Library*

County outside Tacoma. While some were laborers — the Eatonville Lumber Company was a major employer — others were able to lease Puyallup Indian Reservation land in the vicinity of Fife. Such ventures were possible because of the emergence of the Tacoma City Market, first established in 1893 and moved to 11th and Market streets in 1909. When it became apparent that white grocers could not meet the urban demand for fresh vegetables and fruit, the Japanese filled the void. By 1920 the county's Asian population was almost equally split between urban and rural dwellers.

The Puyallup fairgrounds became Camp Harmony for the Pierce County Japanese. After their arrival here, families were transported to camps in Idaho and California. *Tacoma Public Library*

These decades were, says Dr. Magden, "the happiest years in the history of the Tacoma Japanese." Like their African American compatriots, community life revolved around social and sports events all reported in local Japanese newspapers. There were language schools in Fife and Tacoma, a Baptist Mission, Japanese Methodist and Buddhist churches along with a wide array of other organizations all designed to preserve cultural identity for Japanese immigrants and their American-born children. In addition, "the friendliness displayed

by whites toward the Japanese during the Peace Jubilee" ending World War I "gave the appearance of lasting harmony between the races" in Tacoma.

Perhaps so, but within three years of the armistice ending the Great War, Tacoma's Japanese faced public demands for their expulsion from Puget Sound. The arguments were not new to the 1920s. Tacoma's Congressman Albert Johnson, then chair of the House Immigration and Naturalization Committee, wanted to investigate "the growing menace of Japanese intrusion into the agricultural and commercial lines of business in the state," an explanation not too far different from the motivations underlining Chinese exclusion in the 1880s. This time, however, opponents of Asian immigrants used American citizenship and land ownership as the rallying cry in all the Pacific Coast states. If immigrants born in Japan could not be citizens and noncitizens were prohibited from owning land, so the argument went, then the Asians would be forced from their land and would go home.

In the spring months of 1921 the Washington State Legislature approved a measure that would prohibit immigrants not able to achieve American citizenship from acquiring land. Pierce County representatives, to their credit, did not unanimously vote for the law, and there are strong indications that Pierce County's Prosecuting Attorney James W. Selden did not aggressively enforce the Alien Land Act. But within a year of its passage, the U.S. Supreme Court decided two cases — one involving Takuji Yamashita of Pierce County — that foreign-born Japanese could not be American citizens even if naturalized in the past. Then, in 1924 Congress forbade the immigration of anyone ineligible for citizenship.

Measures such as these did not destroy the Tacoma and Pierce County Japanese communities, however. Farmland ownership was simply transferred to Nisei children, who as American citizens could legally own it. Business thrived in Tacoma's downtown up to the eve of World War II. Ironically, the

"Little Harlem Rondivoo," a celebration of jazz at 2503 Broadway on September 6, 1935 *Tacoma Public Library, Associated Photographic Services*

1940 war mobilization proved especially beneficial as white shipyard workers and servicemen frequented local Japanese cafes, hotels and laundries. Even as relations began to sour between the United States and Japan, Tacomans saw no reason to boycott local merchants or exclude the Japanese from community life.

All things changed when the Japanese attacked Pearl Harbor on December 7, 1941. War hysteria led to President Franklin D. Roosevelt's Executive Order No. 9066 authorizing the U.S. Army to exclude "enemy aliens" from the entire Pacific Coast region. On May 10, 1942, General J.L. DeWitt ordered all Pierce County Japanese to report to Camp Harmony, a makeshift collection center carved out of the Puyallup fairground. From there, families were transported inland to concentration camps. Neither the executive order nor Army personnel made a distinction between the Japanese born in their homeland or those born in the United States. Therefore, the executive order led to the mass incarceration of American citizens without due process of law — a constitutional right — simply because they were of Japanese ancestry.

Officials in Pierce and King counties objected to the evacuation because, explains Dr. Magden, the removal "would create havoc in harvesting the vegetable and fruit crops." Tacoma's Harry P. Cain was probably the "only mayor of a large West Coast city to oppose evacuation." In explaining his reasons for supporting racial minorities he replied, "If I don't fight to protect the other fellow's freedom, my own loss of freedom hangs by a very thin thread." Very few agreed with Cain or the other local officials, however.

With the war's end, Tacoma's Japanese returned to a changed downtown. Some shopkeepers sought to restore their businesses but lacked the funds to begin anew. Those who wanted to remain close to their prewar settlement found themselves competing with the African Americans who had arrived during the war. Of the 872 Japanese who were evacuated in 1942, only 174 returned to Tacoma. The others migrated elsewhere or lived in parts of the city removed from the central business district. And with time, city officials demolished many of the business blocks directly associated with the Japanese community as a part of Tacoma's first venture into urban renewal.

Reconciliation

In 1986 historian Richard White wrote that "minority peoples should be at the heart of historical claims for Western distinctiveness." If people don't consider how the various races and ethnic populations interacted with whites and with each other, the West "might as well be New Jersey with mountains and deserts." Accommodation was never a neat and tidy affair, and in spite of all the attempts to exclude some groups and discriminate against others, Dr. White's comments hold true for Tacoma and Pierce County where relations between Native Americans, the Chinese and Japanese, as well as Northern and Southern Europeans were significant components of local history.

Past racial relations in Tacoma and Pierce County are not a pretty story, but local whites were not unique in wanting to define an American as someone who was not Asian, African American or Indian. What is important to acknowledge is that with time, attempts were made to apologize for past wrongs. An economic settlement with the Puyallup Tribe of Indians in the 1980s compensated them for the loss of reservation lands. In 2000, plans were under way to construct a "Reconciliation Park" near the site of the Chinatown once located near Old Tacoma.

Of equal significance in terms of the history of the city and county is that people stayed (or refused to go) even when the odds were against them. James Weldon Johnson, NAACP national secretary in 1925, explained why this was the case for African Americans: "Your West is giving the Negro a better deal than any other section of the country. I cannot attempt to analyze the reasons for this, but the fact remains that there is more opportunity for my race, and less prejudice against it in this section of the country than anywhere else in the United States." Others clearly agreed. Opportunity — work — drew everyone to Tacoma and Pierce County.

CHAPTER FOUR

WORK

Work is the fuel that powers society. Most histories are therefore an account of the tasks people performed to shape events in one way or another. Some people opt for politics and the overwhelming challenges of creating a well-run government. Others become businessmen or capitalists who make sure the gears of commerce and industry remain oiled. Teachers, ministers, doctors and nurses make sure people are educated, spiritually inspired and physically healthy as they live their daily lives. One needs only to look at the pages of the classified section of any telephone book to see how much labor goes into the making of the communities where people live. Given the complexity of the working environment within cities, historians face a challenge when trying to identify those individuals who deserve the most attention.

The role played by businessmen in fostering growth and development in Tacoma is a good place to start. Merchants, entrepreneurs, the owners or managers of manufacturing or industrial firms, wholesale concerns, as well as other business owners, formed a nucleus of leaders commonly called the "movers and shakers." As with many things in Tacoma, however, there were so many individuals contributing to the city's well-being that it is practically impossible to credit them all. The corporate biographies that conclude this history volume give a sampling of a few.

One characteristic applied to all realms of work. Men and women organized themselves into associations to further their collective economic or social goals. A library association incorporated in Steilacoom in 1858 was probably the county's first. By the end of the 19th century in Tacoma, organizations catered to the needs of both businessmen and wage earners. Farmers in Pierce County had established Granges and had begun to experiment with producer

(Opening photo) Sandstone taken from a quarry near Wilkeson was used to construct countless buildings in Washington, including the State Capital campus in Olympia. MSCUA, *University of Washington Libraries*

cooperatives. Men and women had also created local branches of national professional associations linking residents to the outside world of work.

Members of these groups saw government as a necessary tool to ensure the growth and development of Tacoma and Pierce County. Therefore, people from all walks of life were involved in local politics. Members of the business elite, professional classes and wage earners all served on various elected bodies in the city. And while early campaign rhetoric accused political bosses of running the city, the voting patterns of the electorate fail to show that any one party could easily dominate the workings of government for very long. On the whole the business of Tacoma's government was business, and all the necessary work needed to see the City of Destiny grow.

Government worked differently then than it does today. In the 21st century the city council is expected to initiate a whole array of matters related to economic development. That was not the case in the 1880s. Nor was it always the case on the eve of World War II. During these years the initiative came by means of citizen petitions that council members themselves would research before making a decision. Early council minutes are full of all kinds of requests ranging from the NAACP petition to ban the movie *Birth of a Nation* to a municipal airport. Streets were built in this fashion. The council also permitted business licenses by owner petition, or rejected them if neighborhood residents objected too loudly.

When it came to matters of economic development, Tacoma's business organizations were the ones who came before the council. Of these, the Chamber of Commerce was clearly the most important. By the turn of the 19th century, this body was almost an administrative arm of city government. Its view of what was best for the city was incorporated into ordinances and planning documents that guided urban development. Chamber members in 1891, for example, wrote an ordinance providing funds to plant trees along city streets so as to attract newcomers to Tacoma. Beginning in 1903 and continuing far into the 1930s, the organization developed various plans

By 1890, professional firefighters had replaced volunteer hose companies in Tacoma. Station No. 6, located at South 9th and A streets, served as the department's headquarters. *Old Town Photo Studio*

first for the Army Corps of Engineers and then for the Port of Tacoma to develop the harbor area upon former Puyallup Indian Reservation lands. There was a clear working partnership between the city and the Chamber, one that both entities accepted as a normal way of doing business.

The Chamber's contribution to Tacoma's history was only one facet of the world of work and how labor related to the economic health of the county. When its members first began their endeavors in the 1880s, agriculture and the timber industry had already created the base upon which newer enterprises would build. Labor also had created an independent voice, one not always heeded by business representatives in defining what was best for the region. Women were a part of the workplace as well. Indeed, Old Tacoma's first entrepreneur was Janet Steele. Her hotel was the first in the city, and when DeWitt Clinton Davisson, the local sheriff, traded Janet's pearl-handed revolver for city lots, she became a real estate speculator as well.

Farming in Pierce County

Agriculture — as noted in the prior chapters of this history — was crucial to the settlement of Pierce County. The Puget's Sound Agricultural Company first introduced cattle and sheep grazing in the 1840s. Americans picked up where the British left off, and dairying still remains one component of the local economy. Poultry, along with fruit and vegetable cultivation, sustained other farmers, especially as Tacoma grew into a major city. Locally grown fresh produce was always in demand in any urban area before the days of refrigeration, rapid transportation and supermarkets. Farm settlements specifically on the peninsulas and islands and around Fife on the northern reaches of the Puyallup Valley were well suited to meet the demands of city dwellers.

Other farms grew out of a different kind of need. In the past, public institutions were expected to pay their own way by providing their own food, or by marketing produce as an export commodity. Therefore, Western State Hospital had its own farm.

Fannie Paddock

Mrs. Paddock was a woman of much executive ability and broad sympathies, and all through her married life she was a leader in benevolent efforts. She organized, and for years was the president of, the Sheltering Arms Nursery in Brooklyn and was associated with many other similar enterprises, and her first question, after her husband was made bishop was, "What do they need out there?" She was told that a hospital was the one crying need, and at once she began a campaign among her Brooklyn friends. "I'm going to build a hospital," she said. "Won't you give me a brick?" She brought West with her about five hundred "bricks."

When the news of her death [on April 29, 1881] reached Brooklyn, friends determined that a hospital should be her monument, and at once they began sending gifts to the Bishop. On the first anniversary of her death the Fannie C. Paddock Memorial Hospital, a frame building on Starr Street, Old Tacoma, was dedicated by Bishop Paddock, and it proved a Godsend to the community. Hundreds of men from mills and logging camps and railroads were cared for, and many a person, far from home and friends, found there kindly care, health and happiness.

— *Tacoma: Its History and Its Builders* by Herbert Hunt

Many historic views of Tacoma and Pierce County were taken by C.B. Talbot and printed using this blue print apparatus atop the Northern Pacific Railroad headquarters building at 7th and Pacific Avenue. *Old Town Photo Studio*

When disease destroyed hop production in the Puyallup Valley, farmers turned to other crops. The Koehler farm located near Orting turned to the cultivation of daffodil bulbs. MSCUA, *University of Washington Libraries*

The Puyallup and Sumner Fruit Growers Association Cannery around 1908 *Washington State Historical Society*

So did the federal penitentiary on McNeil Island. The Pierce County poor farm located south of Sumner on the Puyallup River provided a place for the homeless to both live and work. State legislators established the Washington Soldiers' Home and Colony outside Orting in 1891 because of the farmland located nearby.

John V. Meeker was one of the first to encourage agriculture as a large-scale business in the Puyallup Valley. In 1865 he planted hops on his land near Sumner. By the mid-1880s, hops were the mainstay of valley farmers, who were linked to world markets by the Northern Pacific Railroad's transcontinental line and by shipping docks at Tacoma. The profits and excitement brought by this one crop were incredible at the time. Local newspapers reproduced foreign commodity prices in hops much as Stock Market trading is reported today. Farmers were certain that, like wheat in eastern Washington, the monoculture would sustain local growers far into the future.

Plant lice destroyed the notion. So too did a worldwide depression that began in 1893. Both events reminded Puyallup Valley farmers how unstable their lives could be. By the end of the 19th century, they had diversified their crops, swearing never again to put all their eggs in one basket. Economic hard times told local farmers that they were part of a world market economy that they could not always control.

The shift from hop monoculture to commercial diversified farming in Pierce County in the 1890s occurred at the same time that Populism emerged as a national political movement. Farmers throughout the United States were enraged over the corporate power of the railroads, banks and shipping companies whose fees left the growers constantly in debt. Helping to voice the protest and to seek remedial reform from both state and federal governments was the Patrons of Husbandry, or the Grange. Washington farmers began to organize in 1889, just as Washington became a state.

The organization was not new in that year. Oliver Hudson Kelley had established the Patrons of Husbandry nationally in 1867. By 1874, one of his deputies, N.W. Garrettson, began creating Granges in the West. Pierce County claimed two in that year at Puyallup and Steilacoom with W.C. Kincaid and William Lyle the respective masters. Mary F. Meeker and M.F. Hawk were secretaries, and John S. Bozarth was the Pierce County deputy to the territorial Grange. It took 15 years, however, and a fear that corporate interests would dominate the politics of the new state, to see the Grange really come into its own.

"The civil-intellectual awakening of the farming population... had begun to bear fruit in an increasing political awareness," explained an early historian of the Washington Grange. Awareness "saw no hope for the nation except through such leadership and reform as might be generated within the ranks of farmers themselves." This insistence on grass-roots democracy, and the farmers' successful lobbying before the Washington state Legislature, led along the way to such things as the initiative, referendum, women's suffrage and Prohibition. From the Longbranch Peninsula to Ohop, Pierce County was blanketed with local Granges. In them all women participated on equal terms with men in an organization where "its members were bound together by fraternal vows and a ritual of agricultural symbolism."

There was more than just friendship and politics, however. Farmers were (and are) primarily businessmen and one of their major challenges at the turn of the 19th century was to increase profits. Creating cooperatives was one solution. To tell the story of Puyallup Valley's William H. Paulhamus and the creation of the Puyallup and Sumner Fruit Growers Association is one way to demonstrate how the ability of local growers to pool and collectively sell their resources proved highly beneficial to the county.

William H. Paulhamus pioneered the three-story diversification scheme of berries, poultry and orchards in the Puyallup Valley, organized the fruit growers association, and went into politics to make sure that the local farmers' interests were protected in the Washington State Legislature. He arrived in Sumner in 1890 and seven years later acquired E.C. Meade's 60-acre farm called "Maplelawn." Paulhamus tested all kinds of agricultural produce on this farm, especially the Cuthbert red raspberry and wild Evergreen blackberry, which he introduced to other farmers.

When berries became a major crop in the Puyallup Valley in the 1890s, growers were faced with the problem of marketing their produce. At that time each of them would individually sell their produce to commission men for whatever they could get, a process more beneficial to the middlemen than to the growers. To remedy this situation, Sumner farmers around 1901 formed the Sumner Fruit Growers Union. William Paulhamus encouraged that organization to combine with other valley farmers to form the Puyallup and Sumner Fruit Growers Association in 1902. Members of the association ranged from large-scale farmers to women growing berries in their backyard gardens.

The success of the association led to overproduction and a glutted market by 1905. Association members in turn constructed a cannery initially leased to Andrew Weber. Three years later, the growers decided to run the cannery themselves, with Paulhamus as president. By World War I, the facility was shipping frozen and canned berries,

William H. Paulhamus pioneered agricultural diversification in the Puyallup Valley and went into politics to make sure the interests of local farmers were protected in the Washington state Legislature.
Washington State Historical Society
Painting by Irene Muir McHugh

along with a wide array of other Puyallup Valley produce, to locations throughout the United States and Europe.

Problems related to shipping produce via the Northern Pacific Railroad led Paulhamus into politics. In 1909 local voters elected him to the Washington state Senate where he served until his death in 1925. While there, he became president of the Senate and was an advocate for good roads and flood control measures on the Stuck and Puyallup rivers. In addition, he ran for governor twice, in 1912 and 1924. With Paulhamus in a position of power, the railroad modified its freight rates, facilitating the shipment of both fresh and canned produce into eastern markets.

Farmers' associations went beyond the mere cultivation of the soil, however. "From the early days of statehood there were conditions peculiar to the region," explained one Grange historian, "which made for a close association and understanding between Washington farmers and organized labor." This circumstance was especially true in the timber industry, where farmers worked in the woods to get the cold, hard cash sometimes needed for taxes. Indeed, farming and logging were always closely intertwined during the early years.

The Timber Industry

When one looks at the history of Pierce County's many communities, one always finds a lumber mill nearby. The reason why is quite simple. In order to create the farms, towns and cities, local residents had to clear hundreds of acres of forests. While historians and economists alike tend to look at the forest industry within the context of timber exports, one must remember that initially much logging was a homegrown affair and a necessary component of settlement. Indeed, up until the 20th century when firms began to reforest the timberlands, lumber owners assumed that their function was to clear and sell the land to potential farmers.

The axe, saw, horses and oxen logged the Pierce County forests for the first settlers. Waterside mills also provided cord wood for the steam boilers of the "Mosquito Fleet." Timber was cut for the construction of the ships themselves, in addition to the docks they were tied to. Local forests made cabins and houses and some of the first roads, schools and churches. Portable mills moved throughout the county helping farmers clear the land.

Technology was to change all this, and logging the settlements evolved into a full-blown industry.

Building the highway from North Puyallup to Sumner in 1913 Cornell Brothers, Savage and Scofield were the contractors. MSCUA, *University of Washington Libraries, Washington State files*

Every Pierce County community had a lumber mill at some time in its past. These men worked at a shingle mill in South Prairie.
Washington State Historical Society

The introduction of the "steam donkey" into the forest in the 1880s was one symbol of the change. No longer would ox teams be needed to haul the fallen logs. Railroads were equally significant. Prior to their arrival, commercial logging was kept close to the water. Trees were collected behind a splash dam that tenders periodically opened to send the logs downstream to the closest mill. Railroads could extend far into the forest and haul the trees directly to mills on Puget Sound.

Production skyrocketed as a result of these changes. Statewide lumber production grew from 77 million board feet in 1859 to 1 billion in 1889. By 1905 Washington was the leading lumber producer in the nation and Tacoma was the "Lumber Capital of the World." Mills stretched along the south shore of Commencement Bay and extended into the Thea Foss Waterway. Some milled timber for export. Others specialized in such things as doors, window frames and the decorative "gingerbread" that went into the making of most houses at the time. The lumber industry was a real magnet for economic growth by providing a source of employment for thousands of people ranging from

Before Pierce County settlers could farm or build towns and cities, they first had to clear the vast forests from the landscape.
Old Town Photo Studio

By 1905 Tacoma was the "Lumber Capital of the World." Of all the mills, the St. Paul and Tacoma Lumber Company, organized in 1888, was the largest.
Old Town Photo Studio

the timber barons themselves, loggers and mill workers, to all those involved in the local real estate and construction industry and those who housed and fed the workers.

Of all the mills, the St. Paul and Tacoma Lumber Company was the largest. Its origins grew out of a proposal the Northern Pacific had first made to Frederick Weyerhaeuser in 1887, one where the railroad offered an extensive stand of its timbered land grant provided the lumberman constructed a mill in Tacoma. Weyerhaeuser refused the proposal, but Chauncey Griggs and other Great Lakes investors agreed to the deal and organized as the St. Paul and Tacoma Lumber Company in 1888. The firm, historian Robert Ficken reports, "agreed to purchase 80,000 acres of timber, to construct a railroad from this timber to Commencement Bay, and to build a large mill." Most of the forest was situated in eastern Pierce County. The mill, constructed on Tacoma's tideflats, began operations in 1889.

Part of the company's longevity rested on the realization that a mill's success was dependent upon owning the timber. Frederick Weyerhaeuser took this assumption one step further, making his company's role in Tacoma's economy slightly different. Believing that success in the lumber industry rested more in the ownership of timber than in mills, he concentrated — at first anyway — on purchasing forests. Therefore when he bought some 900,000 acres of the Northern Pacific land grant and incorporated the Weyerhaeuser Timber Company in 1900, Frederick had no mill in Tacoma in mind. But he established corporate headquarters in the City of Destiny and created employment for an increasing number of white-collar office workers.

The timber industry was the major indicator of economic growth in Tacoma during the early years of the 20th century and therefore a measure of hard times as well. Depression came early to forest production. Following World War I, the price of Douglas fir was cut in half. Logging companies were forced to lay off some 15,000 workers in Washington state, a decision that affected local mill workers as well. The Tacoma Mill Company, organized as the Hanson, Ackerson Mill in 1869, was one of the first to be affected when it closed in the early 1920s.

The Dickman Lumber Company closed its mill in 1977. It was the last to operate along the south shore of Commencement Bay. Its headsaw will be preserved in a new park located on the same site.
Ron Karabaich Collection
Watercolor by Vera Erickson

During these years the Washington state Legislature promoted a "back to the land" movement to lure unemployed workers onto the logged-off lands. The program was designed to make farmers out of the urban dwellers while giving the timberland owners a market for what they saw as overtaxed, worthless land. High taxes, forestry officials argued, kept them from replanting the logged acreage with trees.

The problem plagued the industry into World War II. By then, according to Ficken, "increased prices and decreased supplies of privately owned timber meant that there was a considerable financial incentive for reforestation." Millions of acres, some located in eastern Pierce County, were consolidated into private tree farms. The lumbermen also established a cooperative nursery near Nisqually where 6 million seedlings were under cultivation by the end of the war.

After World War I, pulp and paper manufacturing began to replace milled timber as a local industry. The Cascade Paper Company had established this mill on Chambers Creek by 1924. *Washington State Historical Society*

A part of the Pierce County forest was reserved for another purpose. In the mid-1920s conservationist and East Coast lumberman Charles Lathrop Pack donated funds to the University of Washington to purchase land for an experimental forest. "This should be situated on one of the big highways that is much traveled," he wrote to Dean Hugo Winkenwerder of the College of Forestry. "It would be one idea to have a small amount of large timber, some timber of various ages; also a place where there would be some regeneration particularly of Douglas fir. After this forest is purchased, it should be put into shape to sell forestry." The university selected a site near Eatonville and dedicated the Charles Lathrop Pack Demonstration Forest on January 9, 1926.

The Depression and New Deal era also saw significant changes in lumber production as well, although their effects were not clearly apparent until after World War II. Plywood, pulp and paper manufacturing began to replace sawn timber as the primary output of the mills. Retooling for the new production methods, however, was expensive and few mills could afford the change. One by one those lining Tacoma's Commencement Bay shoreline ceased operations. The Dickman Lumber Company was the last to close its doors in 1977.

The fate of the St. Paul and Tacoma Lumber Company was slightly different. In 1957 the company's stockholders agreed to merge the firm with the St. Regis Paper Company, whose Kraft Company had maintained a pulp mill adjacent to the older concern since 1936. "There was sadness in Tacoma at the disappearance of the name St. Paul and Tacoma," maintained Murray Morgan in his corporate history. "The creation of the company in 1888 had spurred the greatest boom in the city's history. The steadiness of its management during the Panic of 1893... held the framework of the community together... To many in the city, St. Paul and Tacoma seemed as much a part of their lives as the mountain, the bay, and the tideflats."

Timber clearly provided employment for thousands of workers in Tacoma, but not all were employed in lumber manufacturing. Mills attracted other industrial firms, businesses and service professionals to the city. Industrialization and urbanization also brought men and women who labored for others. They, in turn, brought with them traditions of union organization forged back home.

As early as 1903, the Tacoma Chamber of Commerce tried to get the U.S. Army to create a military base at American Lake. When the United States entered the "Great War" in 1917, the organization renewed its efforts and succeeded. *Tacoma Public Library*

Tacoma's Workers and Their Unions

Unionization came early to the City of Destiny. The Tacoma Typographical Union 170 was the first when it organized on September 30, 1883. Locomotive engineers and firemen followed the next year. These organizations, and the many other unions that followed, represented one facet of labor history in Washington state. "No confrontations ushered in these unions," maintains a history of Pierce County labor. "Immigrants brought with them their unions, as well as schools and churches, as they pushed west to build new settlements." After 1886 these unions were commonly associated with the American Federation of Labor (AFL), a national organization created in 1881. "The drive for shorter hours of labor dominated the movement," the local history continues, "as workers demanded more leisure time to spend with their families and improve their lives."

There was, however, a second labor trend in Washington history. Just as the more traditional unions arrived early in Tacoma, so too did more radical voices responding to an emergent industrialization. Class conflict was a theme underscoring the movement, one that gave the Pacific Northwest a reputation for strongly influencing labor radicalism nationwide. "Something in the society of the region polarized it more dramatically than other places," explains historian John Findlay. Part of the reason originated in the logging and mining base of the local wage-earning industries. Then too there were dramatic shifts in an economy dependent upon corporate decisions made by East Coast firms. Unemployment could be only a heartbeat away. And when it came, local workers oftentimes found it impossible to identify who was responsible for their misfortune.

The first encounter with labor radicalism was with the Knights of Labor during the expulsion of the Chinese in 1885. The union failed to survive the 19th century, however, and workers turned to the AFL for national leadership. The change divided the local labor movement. Tacoma's labor history makes this point when summarizing the events surrounding Tacoma's 1919 general strike:

In the 1890s, the Northern Pacific moved its repair shops from downtown to what became South Tacoma. A new neighborhood was formed and the shops became a magnet for other industries locating in the future Nalley Valley.
Tacoma Public Library

"Ideological differences among labor activists flared up in the emotional atmosphere of World War I. Patriotic demonstrations, wartime censorship, federal prosecution of antiwar groups, the industrial union movement in the AFL, and other issues divided the unions. Activists chose sides, tagged as radicals or conservatives. The split reached a climax in 1919 over the issue of a general strike to support striking shipyard workers... Amid protests from a conservative minority of delegates, the [Central Labor Council] ruled the strike was on for February 6. The press headlined the strike as a Bolshevist plot and described with relish the division in the union movement. Lacking support, the general strike was ineffective and ended in three days."

Tacoma had an organized police force early on in its history. Mayor Jacob Robert Weisbach appointed himself the city's first police chief in 1885.
Old Town Photo Studio

Railroads revolutionized the forest industry by allowing loggers to go deeper into the woods.
Old Town Photo Studio

A cut in wages was one motivation for the strike, but so too was the broader issue of the right of workers to organize themselves. World War I had seen the federal government support private industry's insistence on the open shop and company-formed unions. Locally, the so-called "American Plan" was used to eliminate radical labor organizers, particularly those recruiting on behalf of the Industrial Workers of the World.

"We hate their rotten system more than any mortals," sang the Wobblies. "And what we'll have for government when we're finally through is one big Industrial Union." William (Big Bill) Haywood, who once visited the Home Colony on the Longbranch Peninsula, organized the IWW in 1905. For him, labor was engaged in a violent class struggle that would only end when capitalism was destroyed. The philosophy proved especially attractive to loggers and lumber mill workers in Washington state. John Findlay explains why:

"Life in the lumber camps was miserable. Most loggers worked in the cold of winter and resided in company camps with poor sanitation and safety, little recreation, minimal family life, and poor meals.... Loggers sought escape in the seamier side of towns where they would spend (or lost) all their money.... To these workers, the union could promise many economic and workplace benefits. But it also provided a society, something to do, a place to go and people with whom to associate. The IWW provided a substitute for home life and family."

Tacoma had two IWW locals. And while the city avoided the fate of Everett, where in 1916 Wobblies were killed when supporting a shingle weavers' strike, the local IWW could not survive federal intervention during World War I.

Matters came to a head in July of 1917 when timber workers, striking for improved conditions and an eight-hour day, shut down the industry in Western Washington. "Lumber workers paraded through the streets of Seattle and Tacoma," according to Robert Ficken, "joining with striking teamsters and streetcar employees to create an atmosphere of public support for the walkout." By autumn, however, U.S. Army soldiers were in the woods, and the logging firms had created the Loyal Legion of Loggers and Lumbermen as a company union to replace the IWW. Federal assistance went further. Agents raided meeting halls and deported foreign sympathizers. One can still find newspaper references to the IWW following Tacoma's 1919 general strike, but for all practical purposes events during World War I "almost — but not entirely — killed off radical unionism."

The Northwest Council of Sawmill and Timber Workers called for a strike in May 1935. Rioting broke out in the streets of Tacoma when Gov. Clarence Martin called out the National Guard. *Old Town Photo Studio*

Stifling the IWW and the creation of the 4-L kept labor organizers in the lumber industry at bay until the New Deal, when the 1935 Wagner Act gave labor the right to organize and bargain collectively. The Northwest Council of Sawmill and Timber Workers called for a strike in May of 1935, when it became clear that mill owners planned to resist union recognition. By the middle of the month 30,000 workers were walking picket lines throughout the region. The results in Tacoma were particularly brutal when Gov. Clarence Martin in June sent national guardsmen and the state patrol "to prevent strikes from interfering with the reopening of the mills." Robert Ficken describes what happened next in what is known as the "Battle of the 11th Street Bridge":

"Rioting disrupted the city of Tacoma in the final weeks of June 1935. The national guard, backed by state patrolmen, blocked access to the tideflat sawmills, preventing pickets from interfering with limber production. Turning their attention to the office of the Loyal Legion of Loggers and Lumbermen, frustrated strikers surrounded the building and threatened to assault its occupants. 'For several hours,' wrote a frightened 4L official, 'we were not sure what was going to happen to us.' In early evening, the guard and patrol finally arrived to disperse the demonstrators, tossing tear gas bombs and spewing gas from the exhaust pipe of a police vehicle. 'It sure scattered the crowd hell-west and crocked,' reported a relieved J.A. Ziemer following his rescue from the Legion office. That night and the next day, soldiers occupied the streets of Tacoma to prevent pickets from gathering and patrolled the city's residential areas to intimidate workers."

By August the ordeal was over, but mill owners were forced to admit that "the clear result of the strike was the fastening of organized labor on the lumber industry." As for the Loyal Legion of Loggers and Lumbermen, its days were numbered by 1935, for the Wagner Act also outlawed company unions.

The lumber strike was the last major union altercation to affect Tacoma and Pierce County between the two world wars. It was not the first where violence — or the threat of violence — underscored the conflict between management and labor. A guard killed a young Croatian worker during a labor demonstration at Tacoma's ASARCO smelter shortly after the end of World War I. During the 1920s, when John L. Lewis and his United Mine Workers were a force, miners in Wilkeson struck over a decrease in wages. They permanently lost their homes and jobs in the process as mine owners forced them to leave. The companies then imported scabs. Unemployed miners who stayed in the area went to South Prairie and formed a tent city called "Union Hill." In Wilkeson itself, writes Nancy Hall, "'Up-town' [the mining section] and 'Down-town' became hated enemies. Each day at a certain time of the day all the people from 'Down-town' would walk to the mine areas and curse the new miners... The Company stood pat and so did the miner's Union. There was not a chance of reaching any agreement."

Tacoma's founding mothers and daughters were: (top row, left to right) Gertrude DeLin, her daughter Grace, and Anna Judson (both families were the first to file Donation Land Claims in Tacoma); (bottom row, left to right) Julia McCarver and Marietta Carr, wife of M.M. McCarver and daughter of Job Carr, the two founders of Tacoma City.
From Tacoma, Its History and Builders by Herbert Hunt

Tacoma's longshore union proved more successful in keeping scabs away from the city's shoreline following a strike of West Coast ports beginning on May 9, 1934. As before, the lines were clearly drawn during the 12-week ordeal. For the workers, explains historian Ron Magden, "the stoppage was a struggle by workers to achieve job security through the closed shop and union hiring halls." Management maintained "that the strike was a Communist plot and longshoremen were being duped by radicals." Tacomans formed a Citizen's Emergency Committee dedicated to the opening of the port by force, if necessary, and petitioned the city council for police officers. But, unlike the lumber workers' strike the following year, Tacoma was able to avoid the violence seen at other West Coast ports.

The strike, one that saw San Francisco's Harry Bridges emerge as a dominant force, ended on July 21, 1934, when longshoremen agreed to arbitration. "Overall, the 1934 strike was a major victory for the marine and longshore unions," concludes Magden. "Not only had they won most of their demands, but the men had also gained a sense of power and solidarity during the strike that carried their unions to further victories in future negotiations."

Timber workers and longshoremen represent the glue — lumber manufacturing and commerce — that held Tacoma's economy together during the early years of the City of Destiny. This discussion of the city's workers remains incomplete, however. While the next chapter will discuss in greater detail how important harbor development was to Tacoma, one must now consider how women contributed to the world of work.

A Woman's Work is Never Done

Women were always an important part of the history of Tacoma and Pierce County, initially because a married couple received double the amount of acreage allowed for a Donation Land Claim in the 1850s. From the very beginning, families settled the many communities, and farming required the work of women as well as men. But women's labor went beyond just that to teaching in the rural schoolhouses and serving as postmasters in the smaller communities. They managed grocery stores and boarding houses and ran local missions. In Tacoma, city directories show women as nurses, midwives, seamstresses, hat makers, stenographers, realtors and photographers, as well as members of local unions. Of course, women were homemakers as well, and their wish to provide a good urban environment for their families governed much of what they did on behalf of the community.

One way to explain the role of women in the history of Tacoma and Pierce County is to look at the institutions they created and nurtured, beginning with the establishment of Annie Wright Seminary, a girls' school named in 1883 for Charles B. Wright's daughter. The institution was to be a place where the daughters of pioneers would "develop from strength to strength, contributing to the righteous upbringing of the great country."

Other organizations expanded on the importance of education. The Nesika Club was formed in 1892 to allow women to undertake their own research on science, art, literature and current affairs. Ten years later the wives of prominent businessmen created the Aurora Club "to promote the literary and social culture of its members," while the Aloha Club concentrated on the arts. "In November 1899," a club history reports, "a plan was adopted to purchase pictures to be exhibited" in the Tacoma public schools. "Reproductions of paintings ranging from old masters to the contemporary were purchased... for the next forty years."

Even though some women found themselves in the forefront of historical events, others contributed their creativity in other ways, as this 1941 portrait of Mrs. Nellie Van Arkle illustrates. *Tacoma Public Library, Richards Collection*

A woman's sewing circle — ladies interested in promoting education and reading in what was still a frontier community — began the Tacoma Public Library. Mrs. Grace Moore, wife of a prominent attorney, along with other women lobbied the city council into taking over the responsibility for the library after they demonstrated its value to the community.

By 1909 there were some 30 women's clubs in the city of Tacoma. However, their interests had changed by this time. While education remained a constant theme, community service and the improvement of social and civic conditions emerged as an overriding concern. The Young Women's Christian Association, formed in 1905 in Tacoma, was one example of this shift in focus. "The first official act of the new group," its history says, "was to place a matron at the Northern Pacific train station to aid women travelers." The Altrua Study Club and the Council of Jewish Women, formed in 1908 and 1920, were other examples of organizations committed to social betterment.

Following World War I, there is proof that women were clearly entrenched in occupations traditionally

The Puyallup and Sumner Fruit Growers Association viewed women as ideal workers in its cannery. *Washington State Historical Society*

considered the work of men. In 1929, for example, the Soroptimist Club of Tacoma organized as a service organization for all professional businesswomen. Those in the insurance industry formed their own association nine years later. Even though tied to their professions, these groups saw community service as their primary function and most of the work they did was connected directly to improving family life.

Tacoma did not hold a monopoly on the organizations formed by women to further their own interests. It was noted earlier that Granges included women as equal partners with their farmer-husbands. Some Pierce County communities, however, went beyond that notion to create organizations truly their own. The Ohop Ladies Aid, started in 1895 by Olava Kjelstad and Tora Larsen, sought to relieve the isolation women faced in southeastern Pierce County. Social gatherings became the impetus for community work, including the construction of a mission house for religious instruction. In 1907, Gig Harbor women created the Fortnightly Club to promote both education and service in the peninsula areas of the county.

By the eve of World War II, women were active partners in the world of work. As seen in the case of Nettie Asberry and her role in creating the NAACP, women were also active in local politics. Their role as lobbyists for reform legislation must never be forgotten. Indeed, the President's Council of Women's Organizations grew from a Pure Food Council formed in 1908 "to clean up the unsanitary conditions prevailing in the preparation and handling of foods." A legislative agenda grew from this initial concern to include everything from women's suffrage and Prohibition to the working conditions of wage earners. Women had yet to be elected to a major public office. But that situation would clearly change in the future.

This chapter has shown how the world of work helped shape the history of Tacoma and Pierce County, one where agriculture and the timber industry were the early foundations for the region's economy. Both activities, however, were helped by and extremely dependent upon Tacoma's status as a major commercial city on Puget Sound. As the next chapter reveals, the development of a harbor on Commencement Bay was crucial to the growth of the City of Destiny.

CHAPTER FIVE

THE MEDITERRANEAN OF THE PACIFIC

In the late 1860s, when Jay Cooke was deciding whether or not to finance the construction of the Northern Pacific, he sent his trusted colleague Sam Wilkeson to take a look at Puget Sound to see if the endeavor was worthwhile. "I brought to this archipelago of harbors an extraordinary measure of the water and the security of the anchorage," he reported in his notes published in 1869. To prove his point, Wilkeson cited from Isaac I. Stevens's railroad survey report:

"Nothing can exceed the beauty and safety of these waters for navigation. Not a shoal exists within them; not a hidden rock; no sudden overfalls of the water or the air; no such strong flaws of the wind as in other narrow waters... And there is in this region so many excellent and most secure ports that the commercial marine of the Pacific Ocean may be here easily accommodated."

"Both time and space fail to catalogue the ports on Puget Sound with their soundings," Wilkeson continued. He made it clear in his report, however, that this "Mediterranean of the Pacific" had the deep waters needed for the harbor development planned by the Northern Pacific.

Wilkeson emphasized another point as well. San Francisco Bay and Puget Sound were the only potential harbor areas on the West Coast, he maintained. And of the two, the latter had the greatest commercial advantage:

"The economy of the shorter line from Asiatic ports to Puget Sound will give to Puget Sound the commerce of transhipment [sic] from China and Japan. But the Northern Pacific Road will not take the transcontinental commerce between Asia and Europe unless its line is shorter in time and cheaper in freight charges than the Union Pacific. The time is not far off when the saving of one day in the circuit of the globe will be deemed of importance. In railroading,

(Opening photo)
In 1877, two years following the discovery of coal in eastern Pierce County, the Northern Pacific had constructed and then enlarged the bunkers designed to export the fuel.
Old Town Photo Studio

distance governs. The shortness of the degrees of longitude under the route of the Northern Pacific Road gives this line an advantage over all those south of it, which cannot be overcome or even resisted. If this advantage shall be thrown away in the location of the road, controlling empire in commerce and boundless wealth will be thrown away."

These two themes — deep harbor and Asian trade — governed to some degree the Northern Pacific's decision to establish its terminus on the south shore of Commencement Bay. Indeed, for railroad officials the terminus was the commercial wharf begun in 1873, more so than the town that grew in its wake.

The history of Tacoma's harbor up to the turn of the 19th century is therefore primarily a story of how the Northern Pacific constructed the city's first port west of the Puyallup River. Even so, the railroad's endeavors are only one part of a continuing saga telling how Tacoma's harbor expanded eastward across the Puyallup River delta. Here the Tacoma Chamber of Commerce and Commercial Club planned a new harbor development during the early years of the 20th century. Then, by the end of World War I, Pierce County voters approved the creation of the Port of Tacoma to expand harbor and industrial development far beyond that envisioned by the Northern Pacific in 1873.

The Northern Pacific and Tacoma's First Harbor

Until 1889, when Washington became a state, the federal government owned the tidelands surrounding Tacoma. Courts defined the area between low and high tide as water, not land, meaning that the Northern Pacific terminus and Tacoma's first harbor were created on property that the company did not initially own. By statehood the railroad had made substantial progress along the shoreline and into the future Thea Foss Waterway. In the process engineers had dammed one arm of the Puyallup River (now the Wheeler-Osgood Waterway) to control persistent flooding. They also began the dredging and filing operations needed to create the Thea Foss. The company had also expanded its terminal wharf, adding a lumber mill and coal-bunkers in the process, and filled land needed to form the Half Moon Yard.

Corporate officials also lured the Army Corps of Engineers to the City of Destiny in 1875 when Congress directed local officials to determine if federal funds should be used in local harbor development.

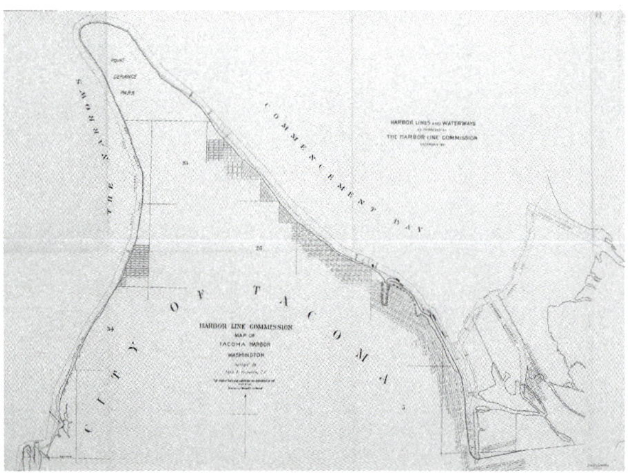

Harbor lines and waterways as proposed by the Harbor Line Commission, 1891
MSCUA, *University of Washington Libraries, map collection*
Surveyed by Fred G. Plummer

In 1918 voters approved the creation of the Port of Tacoma.
Old Town Photo Studio

(Far right)
The river delta was part of the Puyallup Indian Reservation before its development into a port-industrial area for Tacoma.
Old Town Photo Studio

The Puyallup River delta before its transformation into a harbor
Thomas R. Stenger Collection
Photo by Davidson

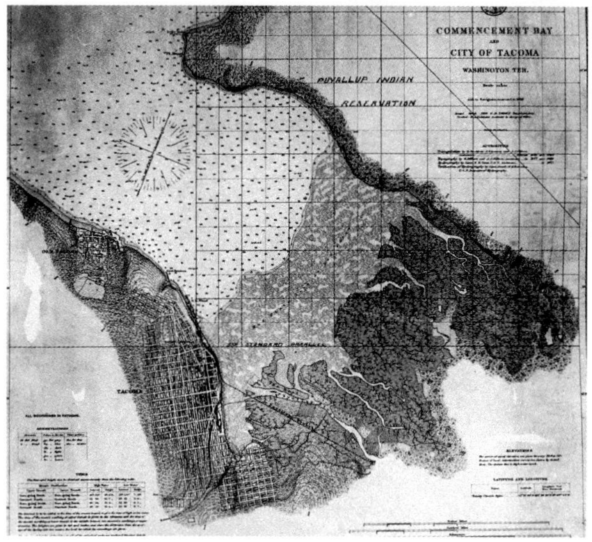

Tacoma harbor in 1888
United States Geological Survey

The Half Moon Yard in the early 1880s
Old Town Photo Studio

It took almost 30 years for Congress to finance the work on the Thea Foss, Corps engineers felt that federal monies were being used to protect the railroad's monopoly along the shoreline. In 1902, however, Congress ignored the Corps' concerns and appropriated funds to continue the waterway dredging, a project completed in 1905.

The Corps' misgivings were in response to the Northern Pacific's concerted effort to purchase all the tidelands fronting the city of Tacoma. Washington state's Constitution as well as subsequent legislation established the means whereby the tidelands were to be surveyed, platted and sold. And by 1897 the company had purchased from the state close to 127 acres of tidelands adjacent to the terminus. At the same time the Tacoma Land Company — a subsidiary of the railroad — purchased the tidelands extending into the Thea Foss Waterway and proceeded to transfer ownership of its Tacoma shoreline to the Northern Pacific.

Land purchases from both the state and other private owners continued beyond the immediate terminal area to include all the tidelands from Point Defiance to the head of Commencement Bay. The acquisition "will have a most important effect upon its [the railroad's] future welfare," wrote E.H. Henry, chief engineer, to Northern Pacific President Edwin W. Winter in 1897, "as there will never again be an opportunity to acquire, at reasonable cost, any considerable area of these tidelands... and it should endeavor to take advantage of the occasion, to secure all the land which it will have possible use for, even though such use may be remote." By the fall of 1900 the railroad was the single owner and private developer of four miles of tidelands along Commencement Bay.

As a commercial and industrial development, the Northern Pacific's port was a complete success. By the turn of the 20th century, corporate officials had designated uses along the shoreline, including a two-mile stretch reserved for lumber and flour mills anchored on the north by the Tacoma Smelter. The city's pride and joy, however, was a mile-long complex of commercial facilities fronting the townsite along the Thea Foss Waterway that local boosters called "the longest wharf in the world." Foundries, fuel depots, shipbuilding concerns, and a wide array of other industries encircled the waterway as well.

Tacoma's municipal government looked upon this development with dismay. The city was cut off from any direct access to the harbor because

The terminus of the Northern Pacific Railroad Company was located below the New Tacoma townsite just north of the Half Moon Yard.
Old Town Photo Studio

In 1911, following years of negotiations, the Northern Pacific transferred ownership of one of its warehouses to the city for a municipal dock. It became a local safe haven for the Puget Sound mosquito fleet.
Old Town Photo Studio

Northern Pacific's plans included no public wharf or a direct transportation link between the town and the shoreline. As a remedy, City Attorney James Wickersham submitted a bill to the 1895 state Legislature that would have allowed cities to own their own tidelands. If the Legislature had approved the measure, Tacoma could have acquired all the Northern Pacific development along the shoreline, creating a public port in the process. Wickersham's bill failed in 1895, but the proposal did open the door to the concept of public ports and the passage of the Port District Act in 1911.

That same year also saw the dedication of the Municipal Dock on the Thea Foss Waterway. Tacoma's Mayor Angelo Fawcett was credited with the ability to convince the Northern Pacific to relinquish a part of its harbor development for the facility in 1911. "The opening is taken to signal a new industrial epoch in Tacoma," proclaimed a newspaper writer at the time. "Tacoma now leads many cities in a variety of ways. She owns her own electric light plant and now she owns her own dock. She was the first to have an advanced commission form of government and is ready to adopt any other matters of civic advancement."

The Municipal Dock really was a symbol of significant change in the City of Destiny. Within two years, in 1913, construction workers had completed a new 11th Street Bridge connected to the public dock but leading as well across the Thea Foss Waterway toward the undeveloped Puyallup River delta. Those who told everyone to "Watch Tacoma Grow" envisioned a new harbor development across this bridge expanding beyond the original Northern Pacific terminus onto former Puyallup Indian Reservation lands. By 1911 the vision also included the possibility of a new Port of Tacoma.

Expanding Tacoma's Harbor

Ever since 1853 an unseen line at the 5th parallel separated King and Pierce counties. This division rested roughly at the mouth of the Puyallup River, meaning that all the lands east of the waterway — the present-day Port of Tacoma — were beyond the control of local government. Therefore, as whites acquired the Puyallup Indian Reservation and began to plan a new Tacoma harbor they also sought to move the county boundary eastward. A court order in 1901 was required to overpower King County's objections, but the subsequent election led to a new boundary paralleling reservation lands. Only those owning property in the area to be annexed to Pierce County could approve or reject the proposal. Since the majority had a Tacoma harbor in mind, the vote really was a foregone conclusion.

In later years Frank C. Ross claimed credit for the election, and he no doubt played a significant role. When he compiled his biography for Herbert Hunt's history of Tacoma, he portrayed himself as an urban planner because of his scheme to create a "Greater Tacoma" on his Puyallup reservation lands. In 1916, two years before voters created the Port of Tacoma, he even prophesied "that within twenty-five years [Tacoma's] retail business center... will be two miles east of [its present location]," in areas immediately adjacent to his tidelands property along Hylebos and Wapato creeks. He planned to lure people completely away from Tacoma and the Northern Pacific terminus into a new town, making the City of Destiny a mere suburb of his grand scheme.

The plans of Ross, along with his partners, James Ashton and Allen C. Mason, never materialized. Finding financial backing was a major difficulty, but so too was their inability to get local support from

Wharves along the Thea Foss Waterway before the construction of Dock Street
Old Town Photo Studio

There was little development along the shoreline north from Old Tacoma in the latter years of the 19th century.
Old Town Photo Studio

either the other property owners within the delta or from those businessmen deeply rooted in Tacoma's downtown. Indeed, the Chamber of Commerce had harbor designs of its own and during the early years of the 20th century emerged as the primary planning agency for shoreline development east of the Puyallup River.

By 1905, lumber mills lined the shoreline between Old Tacoma and Point Defiance. The city became the "Lumber Capital of the World."
Old Town Photo Studio

The Chamber began its work in 1902, the same year Congress authorized funds to dredge the Thea Foss Waterway. In November of that year, according to the *West Coast Trade,* its membership appointed a committee to make "a thorough investigation of waterfront improvement projects, with a view of presenting a comprehensive plan for future government appropriations for the various city waterways." A month later the Chamber introduced a $1.75 million project for dredging four of them. The Corps of Engineers, however, refused to recommend an appropriation for the Chamber's comprehensive plan because in its view the development of new waterways did not benefit the public or serve any national purpose.

When Congress agreed with the Corps' recommendation, the Chamber shifted its emphasis from public funding to one where private financing would pay the tab for harbor development. Members, however, still insisted on retaining their role as harbor planners. By 1911 this meant hiring Virgil Bogue to create a harbor plan for the entire shoreline stretching from Browns Point to Steilacoom. When in December of that year Bogue introduced his recommendations to the public, explained Murray Morgan, he emphasized the importance of improving the tideflats for industrial use:

"Tacoma has the advantage of cheap coal and coke of good quality and cheap electric power, and with her enormous area of tideflats, which reach all the way to Puyallup and beyond, opportunity for industrial enterprises practically unexcelled... With the courage and help of the people, Tacoma will become one of the great ports... Without that courage and help, development will at best be slow and uncertain."

Bogue's prophecy rang true for the immediate future. His plan, Murray Morgan continued, "subsided into a swamp of citizens' committee studies, never to reappear in its original form."

The problem wasn't so much the plan as the price, and the Chamber's belief that private owners of the harbor land could fund harbor development. Businessmen were so sure of this course that the Chamber officially refused to support the creation

Flour milling was crucial to Tacoma's economy following the completion of the Cascade Line in 1887. Eastern Washington wheat was first lured to Centennial Mill's Elevator A.
Old Town Photo Studio

Tacoma's undeveloped harbor shown after the construction of the Northern Pacific Railroad headquarters building in 1886
Old Town Photo Studio
Photo by French

The Wheeler Waterway, now part of the Thea Foss, was originally a branch of the Puyallup River.
Old Town Photo Studio

of a Port of Tacoma when first put before the voters on November 15, 1912. Instead, the organization thought that the City of Tacoma should fund new public wharves — like the Municipal Dock — while leaving the rest of port development in the hands of property owners guided by the Chamber and Bogue's plan. The election was a close one, but the measure went down to defeat.

Circumstances had changed by 1918, when once again the matter of a public port was put before the voters. By then the Panama Canal had opened, easing foreign commerce with Europe. Shippers were convinced that following World War I, "the bulk of maritime commerce was going to shift from the Atlantic to the Pacific Ocean," note Magden and Martinson in their waterfront history. Since private dock companies were turning ships away, modern facilities were needed to handle the increased trade. "No man should stand against the progress of Tacoma," declared the *Tacoma Daily Ledger*. "The voters will decide between lethargy and growth; whether a portion of the Pacific trade of tomorrow shall be brought here, or whether more wide-awake communities shall wax greatly from it without competition."

This time voters rallied, approving the measure 15,054 to 3,429. Tacoma's businessmen had help from Puyallup Valley farmers, where spokesman W.H. Paulhamus maintained that "a publicly-owned warehouse and cold storage plant means more to farmers of Pierce County than to any citizen of the City of Tacoma." Longshoremen too supported the measure arguing that "a Port of Tacoma might never be the largest municipal port, but it could be the best." The first Port board represented these three interests with banker Chester Thorne, longshoreman Edward Kloss and Puyallup Valley farmer Charles Orton taking the helm in November 1918.

Private property owners formed Commercial Waterway District No. 1 and began dredging Hylebos Creek in 1914.
Old Town Photo Studio

The Port of Tacoma

Creating the Port of Tacoma was a slow process and remains an ever-changing one. When the board first met, its primary need was to acquire land for wharf construction. Magden and Martinson outline the challenge:

"The shoreline of Commencement Bay contained only a few improvements east and north of the Middle Waterway, the area [in 1982] occupied by the St. Regis Paper Company. The one exception was Todd Shipyard, located on the edge of today's Hylebos Creek area. Beyond the Middle Waterway, and along the south and west sides of the harbor, the bay was ringed with private docks. From the standpoints of both logic and necessity, the Port would have to locate east of the Middle Waterway."

Funding was also a necessity. While property tax revenues were available, commissioners knew early on that "a bond issue was necessary to acquire land, construct warehouses, and build connections to existing railroad tracks."

They hired Frank J. Walsh, who had assisted with the construction of Camp Lewis, to put a port plan together. Voters approved both it and a $2.5 million bond issue in May 1919. Land purchases and the construction of Pier No. 1 followed, culminating in its formal opening on March 21, 1921. The *Edmore* of the Pacific Coast Steamship Company inaugurated the new facility. "The loading of the Edmore was a test of the utility and efficiency of the new municipal port," reported the *Tacoma News Tribune* on that day, "and proved beyond a question of a doubt... the great advantage the port will offer inland mills of exporting lumber by water, making it possible for them to compete with the waterfront mills which have their own docks."

A second pier followed along with a cold storage plant and a publicly owned grain elevator approved by voters in 1928 and completed in 1930. Magden and Martinson note that by this time "Pier 1 had an open storage capacity for 50,000,000 board feet of lumber. Two ninety-foot cranes handled the lumber from dockside to waiting ships. And at Pier 2 the shed held 45,000 tons of all classes of general cargo... The Port of Tacoma was now a comprehensive port capable of handling lumber, wheat and perishables."

By the early years of the 20th century, grain milling dominated the shoreline between Old Tacoma and the Northern Pacific terminal wharf.
Old Town Photo Studio

The port commissioner's attention then turned to the creation of industrial sites on the tideflats. They were not alone in wanting to see the boggy areas still prevalent throughout the delta transformed into a manufacturing district. Even as the public wharves went into operation, the Chamber of Commerce began to develop a 10-year comprehensive plan covering the tideflats. In 1930 the Tacoma City Council even tried to form a "filling district." P.W. Bourgaize, president of the Tacoma Planning Commission, recommended in 1934 that this body "make a special study of a plan of development of our tide flat area as the future of our city depends to a great extent on its proper development." The Chamber responded the following year by creating a 25-member Tidelands Planning Commission and submitted its plan in 1937.

As harbor development moved eastward toward the Puyallup River, residents were encouraged to "Watch Tacoma Grow." *Old Town Photo Studio*

Below the Tacoma Hotel in the 1880s, Native American canoes shared the shoreline with Northern Pacific Railroad trains. *Old Town Photo Studio*

The document proposed to further dredge the Sitcum and Wapato waterways, filling potential industrial lands in the process. The notion underwent considerable debate during the years leading up to World War II, ones involving Pierce County and city of Tacoma commissioners, the local planning commission and Port officials. Why the thorough review was explained in the plan's introduction. The Bogue plan failed, maintained Chamber members, because neither Pierce County nor the city of Tacoma had formally approved it. The organization had no intention of repeating its past mistake.

The project seemed assured in 1940. The year before, the Washington state Legislature had enabled port districts to create industrial sites and, in response, the Tacoma Port commissioners created an Industrial Development District within the area proposed in the Chamber plan. But mobilization and war stopped all major expansion. In 1946, however, the Port of Tacoma began a reclamation project to fill the area between the Sitcom and Wapato waterways. "They hadn't completed the dredging operations," wrote a *Tacoma News Tribune* reporter in 1948, "before new industries began moving in... Acreage in the area is being sold for the cost of improvement and each purchaser must build an industrial plant within one year." Port officials expected to continue the dredging and filling along the Wapato to create even more industrial sites.

Between the two world wars, Port commissioners, along with the Chamber and numerous other allies, laid the foundation for future harbor and industrial development. Theirs was a massive engineering task, but it was not the only one to take place during the early years of the 20th century. Others were burrowing underneath Point Defiance, building bridges and highways, constructing water and power systems and attempting to control floods along the Puyallup River. All of these efforts, while reshaping the landscape, contributed to the growth of Tacoma and Pierce County and in some cases made life just a little bit easier.

CHAPTER SIX

PUBLIC LANDSCAPES

The creation of such places as the Fort Lewis Military Reserve, McChord Air Force Base, Western State Hospital, Mount Rainier National Park, or a prison on McNeil Island explain much about the history of Tacoma and Pierce County. Other public facilities might be added, such as the agricultural experimental station outside Puyallup and a soldiers' home near Orting. State and local parks are scattered throughout the county. So too are fish hatcheries. Some developments were a part of the landscape when settlement began. Others grew with time.

There is one thing that links all of these facilities together. In each instance, local residents acknowledged that government was required to fulfill an overwhelming social, cultural or economic need. Governments could achieve what people could not always do on their own, especially when it came to the costs involved. Congressional and state legislative appropriations accompanied many of these projects. But so too did voter-approved bonds and the willingness of the electorate to tax itself for specific purposes. The result was a landscape of public developments located throughout the county. It even went beyond local boundaries when the city of Tacoma began to provide hydroelectric power.

Previous chapters have explained how and why some aspects of the public landscape came to be. Tacoma's businessmen lobbied for a military fort in 1917 as a way to ensure economic growth for the city. The same held true for the creation of Mount Rainier National Park in 1899 and the repeated attempts into the 1920s to change the name of the mountain to Tacoma. Economic concerns were also behind the location of an agricultural station in the Puyallup Valley as well as the persistent attempts to control flooding along the river, a problem not

Tacoma's first fireboat, built in 1929, is now an exhibit on Ruston Way. *Ron Karabaich Collection*

The 11th Street — now Murray Morgan — Bridge was completed in 1913. Streetcars originally carried workers from their homes in Tacoma to the city's developing harbor and industrial area. *Old Town Photo Studio*

Tacoma had its own airport located near the U.S. Navy dirigible mooring mast north of Fort Lewis. Now a part of McChord Air Force Base, the development was part of the Chamber of Commerce's "Greater Tacoma" campaign. *Tacoma Public Library*

completely solved until the completion of the Mud Mountain Dam on the White River after World War II.

Other parts of the public landscape grew out of a genuine desire to improve the lives of people. Parks and playgrounds are obvious examples of ways residents reserved land for relaxation and regeneration. Legislators conceived the soldiers' home at Orting and the Veterans Hospital on American Lake as safe havens for the men whose service in the military went all the way back to the Civil War. Pierce County commissioners created a poor farm to provide for the homeless south of Sumner, and Western State Hospital grew from the awareness that the mentally impaired deserved care and treatment.

Then there were simple matters of necessity. People needed streets, roads, bridges and ferries to move from place to place. The public's role in transportation began in the 1850s when the territorial legislature required local property owners to build Pierce County's first roads. A whole realm of changing technologies affected what followed as railroads and streetcars replaced the horse and buggy and were in turn replaced by people's dependence upon the automobile. Many public streets and highways are emblematic of these changes, but the greatest symbol of them all is the Tacoma Narrows Bridge. Its initial construction in 1940 documented how the automobile was to rule the future.

More than travel was involved, however. In Tacoma, residents realized early in their history that government had to provide some of the basic necessities of life. Urban dwellers needed fresh water to drink and abundant supplies to fight fires. With time they expected inexpensive and reliable electrical

(Far right) North Fort Lewis — wars in the 20th century led to an expansion of Fort Lewis northward toward land situated between DuPont and Steilacoom. *Tacoma Public Library*

power. To meet the demand, Charles Wright in 1884 formed the Tacoma Light and Water Company. When the firm proved unable to meet local expectations, voters authorized the City Council to purchase the company. The notion of public utilities was born on that day in April of 1893.

Water and Power

The history of Tacoma is in part a story about the surveyors and engineers who imposed an order upon the urban environment. Some have already been introduced. William Isaac Smith produced the Tacoma Land Company plat for the new terminus in 1874. Nelson Bennett supervised tunnel construction through Stampede Pass and under Point Defiance for the Northern Pacific. He was also president of the Metropolitan Park Board in 1909 when efforts were under way to construct a park and boulevard system throughout the city. Virgil Bogue, another engineer, created the first comprehensive plan for Tacoma's shoreline. Countless officers of the Army Corps of Engineers shaped the harbor both before and after voters created the Port of Tacoma.

There were others who deserve attention. Clarence O. Bean, as Tacoma's first official surveyor, performed the rather thankless task of defining street rights-of-way and grades. Fred G. Plummer, whose name appeared on many city and county maps, in 1891 surveyed Commencement Bay for the Washington State Harbor Line Commission. And when Tacoma entered the realm of public utilities after 1893, the professional engineer became a given feature of municipal government.

Two men, Ira S. Davisson and Willibald A. Kunigk, were particularly prominent during the early years of the 20th century. Davisson was public utilities commissioner from 1918 to 1940. According to the utility department's centennial history, he was "a man right for the

(Opening photo)
The Stadium Bowl was carved from a gulch that bordered the new high school. Dedicated in 1910, it housed numerous pageants, visits from presidents and Tacoma's first professional baseball team.
Old Town Photo Studio

Nelson Bennett was the engineer behind the Stampede Pass and Point Defiance tunnels. He was also president of the Metropolitan Park Board when plans were under way to construct a park and boulevard system throughout the city.
From Tacoma: Its History and Builders by Herbert Hunt

The glass-walled hangar at Tacoma's airport in 1948 — known later as Oswald Field, the facility was located at Mildred and South 19th Street near Tacoma Community College.
MSCUA, *Universtiy of Washington Libraries*

times, a 'take charge' commissioner who grabbed the reigns and took off at a gallop." Kunigk became city water superintendent in 1917 and remained in that position also until 1940. "In the entire history of City Water," the history continues, "no man would have greater influence on the growth, expansion and conduct of the department."

Prior to these appointments, a generation of activity had shaped Tacoma's effort to provide water and power to residents. Any real development was delayed until the death of Charles B. Wright in 1898. For five years the city had been in the courts arguing that, in Murray Morgan's words, "Wright's company had misrepresented its assets in a way that constituted fraud." The controversy ended through a compromise settlement with the estate, but Tacoma had inherited a run-down water system in the process. "Cows continued to luxuriate in the flume that brought Clover Creek water to the reservoir" on Hood Street, explained Morgan. In the "early years of the twentieth century, new, deep wells were dug in South Tacoma tapping the aquifer below the clay and gravel. The new wells yielded water of exceptional purity, but it was not cheap. The water had to be pumped to the surface and the cost of power was high."

Obtaining cheap power along with pure water was an additional challenge for Tacoma, one that put local officials in the middle of a national debate over who should control local utilities. While there was a general consensus that cities should own and maintain their own water systems, there was no agreement when it came to electrical power. Private companies had pioneered the technology and by the end of the 19th century dominated — some would say monopolized — the major distribution systems in the country. In Pierce County, Puget Sound Power and Light controlled the industry through privately owned hydroelectric plants at Electron and Dieringer. Tacoma initially relied on this private power, but by the turn of the century high rates forced government officials to conclude that public utilities also meant public power.

Construction on the Nisqually River La Grande hydroelectric power dam began in 1910 and was completed in 1912. Here a 1924 repair crew rewinds generator No. 2. *Tacoma Public Library*

The White River hydroelectric power plant at Dieringer was constructed by Boston's Stone and Webster Engineering Corporation in 1912. *MSCUA, Universtiy of Washington Libraries, Washington State files, Pierce County*

The Green River gravity water system and the Nisqually hydroelectric project grew out of the city's first efforts. Voters approved the bonds needed to finance both in 1909, an election the *Tacoma Times* called "a victory freeing Tacoma from the grip of special interests." Work began the next year.

The construction of the LaGrande dam on the Nisqually was the first to get under way. Located some 30 miles from Tacoma, the project "was an engineering marvel with hundreds of men battling the elements, a capricious wild river and the limitations imposed by tools primitive by today's standards," says the centennial history. The hydroelectric power project went into operation on November 6, 1912. Two parallel transmission lines stretched 36 miles from the Nisqually River generators to its substation at South 25th and C streets in downtown Tacoma.

Cushman Power House No. 2 located on Hood Canal north of Potlatch MSCUA, *Universtiy of Washington Libraries*

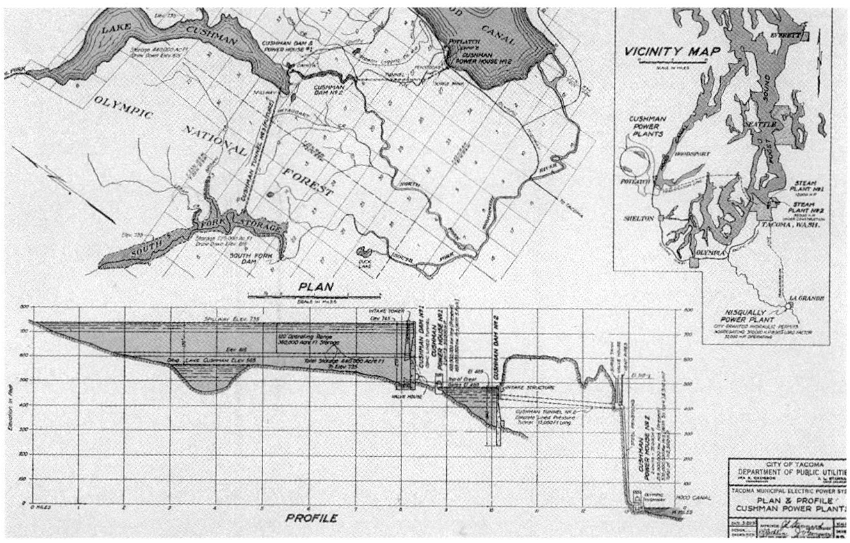

Cushman Power Plants, completed in 1926 MSCUA, *Universtiy of Washington Libraries, map collection*

The gravity water system from the Green River proved to be "the single largest municipal project" in the city's history up to that time. It entailed the construction of a headwork on the Green beginning in the Cascade foothills in King County. A pipeline then routed the water to a new reservoir above McMillin. The route crossed both the White and Puyallup rivers, descending in the process from 900 to 100 feet above sea level. The two basins of the reservoir covered 16 acres. From this point additional pipelines carried the water into the Hood Street and Alaska Street reservoirs.

Bids were first submitted on September 8, 1910, and the project "took two full years with hundreds of men employed by the several contractors. It was backbreaking work. Simply getting materials — including 60-inch pipe — 43 miles from Tacoma was a Herculean task. Several miles of roadway had to be hacked through timber and brush. When there were no railway or logging tracks, equipment was hauled by brute strength." Workers completed the project on May 29, 1913.

The water and power projects came during a period of unprecedented growth in Tacoma and a realization that supply was not keeping up with demand. This was especially true in the case of hydroelectric power, where shortages were a persistent problem. Ira Davisson's first task in 1918 was to seek new power sources when private companies "refused to sell power unless the city stopped building hydroelectric plants." The utilities commissioner's solution was to harness Lake Cushman on the Skokomish River across Hood Canal in Mason County. In 1919 Tacoma voters approved a bond issue to purchase water rights and land. Construction began five years later.

This was how *City Light* described the construction scene:

"All day and all night, and all summer long, steam engines were puffing, trucks speeding, carpenters building forms, riggers manning the concrete tower

When Tacomans were faced with a power shortage late in 1929, the *U.S.S. Lexington* provided the needed electricity from an anchorage at the Baker Dock.
Old Town Photo Studio

and chutes at dizzying heights — and always the grinding of the mixer and the steady flow of concrete. Five hundred men toiled ceaselessly but would not be denied."

Impounding of the waters began in October 1925, followed by a formal dedication ceremony in May of the next year. "Tense was the waiting and joyous were the shouts," reported Ira Davisson, "as the electrical energy freed by President Calvin Coolidge as he touched the key which sent current pulsing from Washington, D.C. into the Olympic Mountains and set the huge turbines whirring."

George M. Savage Company's kiln for paving bricks
MSCUA, *Universtiy of Washington Libraries, industries and military file*

The Cushman project did not end Tacoma's public power development. In fact, the search for new sources of electricity continued way past World War II, involving a second dam on the Nisqually as well as additional projects on the Cowlitz and Wynoochee rivers in Lewis and Grays Harbor counties. Each project entailed massive changes to the rivers involved. But the development of utilities was only one way that the natural environment was transformed into a public landscape. In northeastern Pierce County engineers changed the course of a river.

Flood Control on the Puyallup

When settlement first began in the upper Puyallup Valley in the 1850s, the geography was different from what one sees today, especially in the vicinity of the Stuck River near Sumner. This waterway was actually a slough of the White River, whose historic course flowed northward through King County toward the Duwamish at Seattle. Flooding around the slough was a persistent problem early on. During periods of high water the White would flow into the Stuck, causing tremendous floods both in the Puyallup Valley and throughout the delta at Tacoma. Normal weather would return the White to its traditional course through King County.

The Stuck and White rivers became a battleground for King and Pierce County farmers during periods of high water. Early on, farmers along the Stuck constructed a dam to keep the White River waters flowing north. King County farmers in response blew up the barrier in the hopes of keeping the floods from ruining their crops. The whole matter of flood control along the river system dominated the news of the day and remained an overriding concern of both valley farmers and Tacoma businessmen far into the 20th century.

Matters came to a head in 1906 when a logjam near Auburn in King County blocked the White River's flow into the Duwamish. Seven years of litigation followed as both King and Pierce County officials tried to divert the White into their respective opponent's territory. But the dispute did not relate only to the county farmers. The flood of 1906 doubled the flow of the Puyallup just as the Army Corps of Engineers had begun to dredge the river's mouth for a commercial waterway at Tacoma. Three years later new flooding completely destroyed the work.

A compromise of sorts was reached for upriver farmers by the eve of World War I. Pierce County agreed to make the diversion of the White River into the Stuck a permanent matter by means of a dam at Auburn. Because this alteration to the river's course also affected the amount of water fed into the Puyallup confluence at Sumner, King County agreed to help pay for flood control measures in Pierce. The Washington state Legislature sanctified the compromise by creating an Inter-County River Improvement District, an agency that into the 1920s began the arduous task of straightening the respective rivers and constructing the levees designed to keep them within their engineered channels.

While all of this work was under way, Congress began to wonder about the future of the commercial waterway at the Puyallup River's mouth in Tacoma. The Corps of Engineers recommended the complete abandonment of the project as one too expensive to maintain as long as flooding persisted. What could save the project was an idea put forth by Hiram M. Chittenden. He was at the time one of the West's most prominent engineers, known specifically for his design of Seattle's ship canal and locks, for his support of public port districts in Tacoma and Seattle, and for a road system he designed in Yellowstone National Park.

LaGrande entrance to Nisqually Canyon, 1910 MSCUA, *Universtiy of Washington Libraries*

He proposed to divert the Puyallup River through a man-made channel leading directly into Commencement Bay from either Hylebos or Wapato creeks. In this way the Army engineers could finish dredging the Puyallup Waterway without the threat of future floods. Unidentified "local interests," claimed Chittenden, had agreed to fund the river's diversion. It still is not known who those interests were but the event never happened. With congressional approval the Corps abandoned the project — at least for the

Supporters of the first Narrows Bridge saw it as a way to lure new settlers and shoppers into Tacoma.
Old Town Photo Studio

Construction of the Narrows Bridge also meant a new road to Gig Harbor. Here is the beginning of present-day State Highway No. 16.
Old Town Photo Studio

time being — and flooding continued to plague property owners where the Puyallup still meandered through the delta.

The Army Corps of Engineers finally abated flooding through the construction of Mud Mountain dam on the White River east of Buckley. The project also included straightening three miles of the Puyallup River where it meandered through Tacoma into Commencement Bay, and the construction of levees to retain the water's flow. The whole project, one that also required the construction of new railroad and highway bridges, was completed in 1950.

The valley and the harbor were truly transformed not only by these two feats of engineering but also by those transpiring for the half century before 1950. Flood control was not to be achieved only through the works of man. A national park around Mount Rainier was needed, maintained Senator Watson Squire in the 1890s, "to preserve the mountain forests, which slowed spring runoff and thereby reduced flooding and summer drought in the lower portions of the watersheds."

Creating Mount Rainier National Park

The use of beauty as a promotional tool began early in Tacoma's history. "Parks are the adjuncts of cities of more mature years than this young giant of Puget Sound," noted one writer in 1888, "but nature has provided here that which many other cities acquire only by the outlay of much money and labor through a series of years." Among the features cited were the natural prairies located south of the city where American Lake attracted any pleasure seeker wanting to "drink in the beauties of nature, and who delights to fill his lungs with the pure air, fragrant with the odor of forest and mountain." Of all the natural advantages, Tacomans claimed Mount Rainier, which was "never seen to better advantage than from the streets of Tacoma." It is no wonder, therefore, that local businessmen joined the campaign to create Mount Rainier National Park.

According to Theodore Catton, many were a part of the endeavor:

"The campaign for Rainier was a collaborative effort by many groups and individuals. No single figure stood out as its leader, nor did any single organization coordinate it. More than a dozen scientists, many of whom had climbed the mountain, formed one component of the campaign. They were scattered across the nation... and used the opportunity of professional meetings to... prepare memorials to Congress setting forth arguments for the national park. Meanwhile, a few dozen mountaineers, most of whom resided in the Puget Sound area, constituted another component. Their infectious enthusiasm for the mountain... helped to persuade Washington's congressional delegation that the national park was a popular cause... Finally, the Northern Pacific Railway had an important and surreptitious effect on park legislation in the later 1890s."

Many were inspired and had written about the wonder of Mount Rainier, beginning in 1792 when George Vancouver first introduced the landmark to the outside world. Murray Morgan remembers that in the 1830s, Fort Nisqually's William F. Tolmie became the first known European "to reach the snowline, the first to report the existence of its great glaciers." He had American Indian guides to help him during his failed attempt to reach the summit and they evidently gave him the Indian name for the mountain. "Had a fine view of Tuchoma or Mt. Rainier, appearing in relief against the cloudless firmament," he reported at the time.

Lt. Charles Wilkes in 1841 was the first American to describe the mountain, although his brief report — it "is conical and covered about 2/3 of its height with snow" — was not exactly awe-inspiring. Other visitors and authors, however, filled the void. Theodore Winthrop, by Catton's account, saw The Mountain in 1853 as "an image of solemn beauty, which I could thenceforth evoke whenever in the world I must have peace or die." Joaquin Miller was equally awestruck in 1889 when contemplating the local scenery from the veranda on the Tacoma Hotel:

"You look straight down into the deep blue waters that tide in from the Japan seas. A common shot across, and a like precipice, with the ever crowding and ever crowning density of green. Then a little to the right the precipice melts down, and the green fir trees touch the silver sands. Then the sands sweep in a crescent about the heads of the sound; then sea-marsh; then the trees, dense, deep, tall and imperious, for ten, twenty, thirty, forty miles' Up! Up! Up!

"You start to your feet — You stand with your head uncovered; for above all this density of wood and out of and above all this blackness there gleam and flash face to face the everlasting snows of Mount Tacoma.

In 1888 Congress allowed Tacoma to create a park in the Point Defiance Military Reservation. Early development of this "pleasure ground" included a swimming pool, boathouse, restaurant and a public promenade along the shoreline.
Old Town Photo Studio

"Be silent, as I should be silent. It is an insolent thing that I should dare to dwell even for a single paragraph in the idle attempt to describe the indescribable."

The local movement to create Mount Rainier National Park (or Washington National Park, as it was first called) began about the time Miller visited Tacoma. Philemon B. Van Trump, who along with Hazard Stevens became the first to successfully climb the mountain in 1870, was an early advocate as were other early climbers. "Their involvement, concludes Catton, "underscores how much the Mount Rainier National Park idea was rooted in the physical and aesthetic experience of climbing the mountain." Both Tacoma and Seattle businessmen also supported the endeavor, although persistent arguments over the mountain's name tended to fragment local advocates. What pulled everyone together and raised the issue to the level of a national campaign was the establishment of the Pacific Forest Reserve by President Benjamin Harrison in 1893.

His action was part of a growing concern over the future of forestry in the nation. In 1891, Congress had passed the Forest Reserve Act that allowed a president to set aside timberlands within the public domain. In this way their exploitation could be better controlled. Harrison's reserve centered on the crest of the Cascade Mountains along a stretch 42 by 36 miles. But it excluded the western side of Mount Rainier. There were additional problems with the designation. Creating a national forest was no guarantee that the area around the mountain would be protected against future development, since the underlying motive of the new law was to manage — not necessarily preserve — the forests. These two specific shortcomings "fueled the campaign for a national park."

Congress required six years to agree on the appropriate legislation. For a while the legislators "could not be persuaded that it was the responsibility of the federal government to create a national park like Yellowstone in the state of Washington." Then, too, Speaker of the House Joe Cannon opposed the measure because he was sure that Congress down the road would be asked to fund improvements. Seattle businessman John P. Hartman assured him that that would not be the case. "I promise you," he recounted later, "that if this Bill is passed I will not

In 1907 W.W. Seymour gave the city $10,000 for a conservatory. Its construction was not without controversy. The Tacoma Boosters thought the money would have been better spent on playgrounds for children. *Tacoma Public Library, Richards Collection*

be here asking for money from the Federal Treasury to operate the place so long as you shall remain in Congress." Shortly after that the bill passed both houses and became law with President McKinley's signature on March 2, 1899.

Not everyone was happy with the final outcome. Preservationists lamented the exclusion of environmentally sensitive areas located in the lowlands outside park boundaries. "Just in case first impressions of the peak's worthlessness proved erroneous," Alfred Runte suggests, "Congress allowed both mining and exploring for minerals to continue." Big business was never too far away from the deliberations, in other words. The Northern Pacific Railway, whose land grant covered the mountain, asked for and received a trade of the lands "from federal property in any other state served by its tracks. Naturally the trade worked to the advantage of the Northern Pacific, which divested itself of rugged, marginally-productive land at the expense of the nation at large."

Using funds from the Works Projects Administration, Hoodlum Lake was transformed into Franklin Park in 1939 through the efforts of the West End Playground Association and the Metropolitan Park District of Tacoma.
Tacoma Public Library, Richards Collection

Family camping at one of Mount Rainier National Park's tourist camps
MSCUA, Universtiy of Washington Libraries

On the other hand, Congress created a magnificent park that Tacomans proceeded to mold into a recreational haven. Access to the wonderland was the first challenge. Road construction began in 1903 and by 1910 a primitive lane reached Paradise Valley. When in 1911 an automobile aided by a mule team successfully carried President William Howard Taft to the future site of tourist activity, local newspapers proclaimed that people could now go "from sea to snow-line by automobile in one day." The slogan almost became a mantra for local promoters of the park.

A wide array of accommodations greeted park visitors. Those using mass transit could take a stage to Longmire Springs. The Tacoma Eastern Railroad constructed the National Park Inn at this location in 1906. Paradise was a hive of tourist activity by the 1920s and 1930s. Caravans of buses brought visitors to the rustic inn. Those with automobiles of their own could stay in cabins or join other campers staying in a tent city located nearby. It was, to use a motto at the time, "home from the range," one where the urban dweller could escape the city but never be too far from its comforts.

Mount Rainier National Park was, in other words, the most public of public landscapes growing out of a desire to improve the lives of both local residents and tourists from afar. With time the federal government assumed more responsibility for the care and maintenance of this national treasure, but The Mountain — by whatever name — always was and always will be the centerpiece of the history of Tacoma and Pierce County.

EPILOGUE

THE PAST AS PROLOGUE

Throughout this history certain themes have helped to explain the Tacoma and Pierce County of today. This is not the end of the story, for it continues past World War II to fill another half century. Murray Morgan in 1984 referred to this era as a combination of the old and the new, "a time again to dream." It was also a time when residents took stock of their past and created — or planned for — ways to improve their living and working environments.

"Traditionally," Morgan maintained, "Tacomans had been inclined to think about their town as a quiet place, unafflicted with the disorders of big cities." The historian continued:

"Even after the Second World War, it was an article of faith that in Tacoma there were few traffic jams, little racial tension, scant corruption in local government, and no organized crime. True, prostitution was tolerated as bootlegging had been during Prohibition, but Tacoma was a seaport, a lumber town, still almost on the frontier — and after all, somebody had to accommodate the soldier boys after dark or they would go to Seattle."

World War II forever changed Tacoma. The sheer magnitude of the industrial effort required to end hostilities brought thousands of people to the region. Besides an expanded Fort Lewis, men — and especially women — built ships, logged and milled timber, assembled airplane parts or worked at the ASARCO smelter. On the tideflats new chemical and aluminum plants emerged, adding to the demand for more and more people. The federal government played a part in this change by building public housing while the city of Tacoma initiated its first comprehensive planning endeavor.

Federal housing became a part of Tacoma's landscape during World War II. MSCUA, *University of Washington Libraries* *Photo by Howard Clifford*

(Opening photo) For over a century, local boosters have assured one and all that "You'll Like Tacoma." *Tacoma Public Library*

Those who came and stayed altered the city's human landscape in ways still seen today. It was noted earlier how the downtown area was affected by the internment of the Japanese in concentration camps and the arrival of African Americans migrating from other parts of the country. Revised immigration laws opened the door to people of other nations and by the end of the 20th century wars in Southeast Asia, China and Korea had produced a complex of

In 1959 Tacoma and Pierce County dedicated a new County-City Building. The old was demolished to make way for the new facility. Among the victims of modernization was the Pierce County Courthouse seen here next to the Washington National Guard Armory. *Tacoma Public Library*

The heart of Tacoma by night *Caroline Gallacci Collection, a gift of Linda Geddy*

Asian neighborhoods scattered throughout Tacoma and Pierce County.

Problems accompanied the changes introduced by World War II and the Cold War. Tacomans, for example, found their commission form of government "an alliance of small fiefdoms with each commissioner seemingly more attentive to guarding his own turf than looking after the community interest." During a state Senate investigation in 195, residents also learned that local government was not only incompetent but corrupt as well. Again, in Murray Morgan's words:

"The cast subpoenaed to discuss law non-enforcement included cops of easy virtue and unusual influence; a city official who accounted for several thousands of dollars in currency to his safety deposit vault by explaining that he must have won it gambling in Alaska; and the commissioner of public safety, who described himself under oath as a practicing alcoholic and testified to a long evening spent on 'an inspection trip' to a three-story brothel operated by a lady known variously as Amanda Truelove and Lil Buckley. Miss Truelove-Buckley, duly sworn, could not describe the man she paid protection dues to because the transactions took place under a red light."

Citizens responded by approving a new form of government the next year. A council and mayor were now to determine urban policy. A city manager was to oversee the execution of that policy. A planning department was authorized through the charter, while the administration of public utilities was removed from city council control and placed in the hands of a separately elected board. The new system eliminated the worst abuses discovered in the old, but Tacomans still remained vigilant. Indeed, the populace demonstrated its displeasure of city council behavior in 1970 by recalling five of the nine members.

When Lakewood incorporated in 1996, it became one of Pierce County's newest cities. *Tacoma Public Library*

Matters were not much better in unincorporated Pierce County, although it took voters until 1980 to approve a remedy. As in Tacoma vice was the catalyst for changing a system that had been in place since 1853. Tacomans forced the bordellos out of the city and county massage parlors and topless taverns filled the void. Owners of the establishments used arson to force their competitors out of business and were helped by law enforcement officers willing to look the other way. When in 1978 a grand jury indicted Sheriff George Janovich on charges of racketeering, voters had had enough. Two years later they approved a new charter that, like Tacoma's, modernized the structure of government.

Growth pains were, of course, behind the new governments. Census statistics for the 20th century reveal that Pierce County, when compared to Tacoma, was growing at a faster rate. These figures were a numerical manifestation of suburbanization, especially following the dedication of the second Narrows bridge in 1950. Up to this time Gig Harbor and the surrounding peninsulas were still linked to the Pierce County mainland by ferries and the pace of settlement was rather slow. The new bridge led first to a population explosion and then, by the end of the 20th century, to demands for growth management. Symbolizing the tension between these two trends were plans for a second bridge over the Narrows, a project not yet under way in the fall of 2001.

After World War II, in 1947, the Army air field at McChord became part of the new Department of the Air Force. One plane was christened the "City of Tacoma." *Tacoma Public Library*

Suburbanization also occurred elsewhere in the county. The new towns incorporated after World War II show where people congregated at this time. Besides Gig Harbor on the peninsula, which formed its own government in 1946, Bonney Lake and Fife followed suit in 1949 and 1957, respectively. By the

In exchange for providing funds to construct an international airport near Bow Lake in King County, Tacoma's mayor, Harry P. Cain, insisted on the name of Sea-Tac as a way to acknowledge the city's contribution. *Tacoma Public Library*

1990s, Edgewood, located north of Puyallup, as well as Lakewood and University Place, both southwest of Tacoma, had all formed cities. Other towns expanded their boundaries to capture the new residential districts or — as in the case of Northwest Landing at DuPont — to build a completely new planned community.

Social turmoil also accompanied growth and change in the latter decades of the 20th century. Here Tacoma was not alone, but joined cities throughout the country seeking to come to terms with the pressures of the Cold War, the demands for racial and gender equality and the acceptance of diversity as a significant component of American life. The Vietnam War and the protests against it are two symbols of this era, but in Tacoma the seeds had been planted years before.

One area of discord centered on the so-called "red scares." There were two of them, the first following World War I when in 1920 U.S. Attorney General A. Mitchell Palmer rounded up those considered supporters of the Bolshevik Revolution in the former Soviet Union. Locally, the Palmer Raids were an excuse to deport men who had migrated to Puget Sound from southern Europe and Russia. By the 1950s the nature of the red scare changed. Led by Senator Joseph McCarthy, Congress was determined to locate all possible communist sympathizers in the United States. Jean Schuddakopf, a graduate of Stadium High School and an employee of the Tacoma School District, found herself a victim of this modern-day witch hunt in 1954.

Social tensions brought retribution and reconciliation in Tacoma. President Gerald Ford, for example, signed a congressional bill in the late 1970s designed to compensate Japanese Americans for their loss of land, businesses and possessions during World War II. In the year 2000 plans were under way to construct a "Reconciliation Park" on a site close to Old Tacoma and near where some of the Chinese lived in the 1880s prior to their expulsion. Park planners see the project as a way to point to urban diversity and to apologize for the local treatment of Asian populations in the past.

The Puyallup Tribe of Indians was able to reclaim the rights granted to them by the 1854 Medicine Creek Treaty, although it took some 120 years to achieve this goal. Their endeavors began with fishing, a right given to them by treaty.

Following years of settlement and government regulations that kept the American Indians from fishing in their accustomed places — a right given to them by treaty — Puget Sound Indians took the matter before federal district court judge George Boldt in Tacoma. His decision in 1974, one that allotted 50 percent of the harvested fish to the American Indians, was a tremendous victory for all the recognized tribes in Pierce County.

Other successes followed, including the reclamation of original tribal lands along the southeastern border of Tacoma. The property included the cemetery where Chief Leschi is now buried. Then in the 1980s, following a concerted effort to document the loss of reservation land within the Puyallup River watershed, the Puyallups successfully negotiated a settlement with a wide array of governments and property owners. The result made the tribe a guaranteed partner in all future land use planning and economic development decisions made throughout Tacoma and Pierce County.

Planning and economic development dominated the post-war decades, especially following the 1944 publication of *Tacoma the City We Build*. As noted earlier, this document was the result of a demonstration project initiated by the National Resources Planning Board. Mayor Harry P. Cain also requested an additional report, compiled by Colonel E.P. Antonvich, itemizing the costs of a whole series of public works projects. The Colonel explained the reasons for the endeavor in his introduction:

"In order that the City of Tacoma might have a calculated program of public improvements ready to launch upon the termination of the war, you have asked me... to study the needs of the city, to review the various projects that have been considered by Tacoma citizens in recent years and to determine which projects should be given priority as most needed in the immediate post-war period."

The three most important projects were new schools along with sewer and street improvements. Port development, a civic auditorium, recreational facilities and a new city hall were also high on the list of recommendations. Before the war was over, voters had approved a $7 million bond issue to begin the construction.

Tacoma's urban renewal program emerged from these wartime beginnings. For the next three decades local residents witnessed the transformation of the downtown area through parking garages, escalades and a new County-City Building completed in 1959. The next year Cheney Stadium welcomed the Pacific Coast League's Tacoma Giants. Following the opening of the Tacoma Mall in 1965, Broadway was converted into a mall too. Not all of these projects survived the 20th century — the escalades are gone and the Broadway mall is now open to traffic — but at the time of their construction they were evidence that Tacoma's approach to urban planning was truly modern.

During the wartime planning endeavor local residents made it clear that they wanted a boulevard along Commencement Bay and a civic center. In response to the first request, Schuster Parkway was completed along the shoreline in the 1970s. Planners then extended the parkway along Ruston Way and replaced the lumber mills and other industries with a two-mile linear park. The Tacoma Dome was dedicated in 1983, providing a versatile space for both entertainment and recreation. Its opening was not without controversy, however. The following year local citizens filed a lawsuit to keep the city from installing modern neon art in the facility. When the challenge failed, voters repealed Tacoma's ordinance mandating that 1 percent of construction costs for publicly funded projects be reserved for art.

By the end of World War II, lumber mills along Tacoma's Ruston Way were closing. The 1946 Top of the Ocean signaled the beginnings of the waterfront as a people place of restaurants and parks. *Old Town Photo Studio*

Shipbuilding was once a prominent industry throughout Tacoma's harbor. The J.M. Martinac Shipbuilding Corporation still operates along the Thea Foss Waterway. *Ron Karabaich Photographer*

Freeway construction was another manifestation of the times. The interstate through Tacoma was under construction by the mid-1950s and completed north to Everett in 1967. By the end of the 20th century, other freeways linked Tacoma and south Pierce County east to Puyallup, west to Gig Harbor across the Narrows Bridge and across the tideflats into Northeast Tacoma. Also during this time, the City of Tacoma took over public transit, an action that ultimately produced Pierce Transit for both intra- and inter-county travel.

With early urban planning came the destruction of parts of Tacoma's past as buildings were demolished to make way for the new. When freeway construction threatened the original City Hall and the Northern Pacific Headquarters building at the northern end of Pacific Avenue, historic preservation was born. Local architects spearheaded the movement to create the Tacoma Landmarks Preservation Commission in the early 1970s. Community and business commitments to save the city's past — one bus advertisement read "the best way to build a city is not to tear it down" — were substantial. By the end of the 20th century a theater district, a restored Union Station and the University of Washington Tacoma campus were all clear examples of the preservation impulse.

Preservation and protest extended to the neighborhoods as well. Here urban renewal threatened not only the built environment but also the social and cultural relationships that had grown over time. However, the African American voice emerged more from neglect than intrusion. When city planners concentrated more on businessmen's concerns in the central business district rather than on demands for basic civic rights, protests followed. In 1969, for example, a Mother's Day racial disturbance resulted in the shooting of one police officer and the arrest of 35 people. But times were also changing. New mandates required citizen participation when federal appropriations were spent locally. The result was the

The 1965 dedication of the Tacoma Mall — retail businesses from the city's downtown moved to the new facility. *Tacoma Public Library, Richards Collection*

introduction of new neighborhood organizations and leaders all insisting on a voice in city affairs.

Gradually a new relationship formed between Tacoma's government officials and its citizens. Within the realm of economic development, the nature of work changed following World War II, necessitating new solutions to the age-old problem of attracting businesses and industry to the City of Destiny. Tacoma was no longer the "lumber capital of the world," a loss due more to what was going on within the industry itself than to anything the city might have done to keep local mills operational. Even so, Murray Morgan sensed a psychological malaise during these times:

"Perhaps the biggest problem of all was the old-timers pervasive 'Can't Do' attitude. After the economic collapse of 1893, skepticism concerning development proposals was ingrained; sometimes it bordered on paranoia, 'In Tacoma,' a city official once mourned, 'you could be arrested for optimism.'"

There were other possible explanations for the local business attitude. New state and federal regulations established limits beyond which industrial development could not go, with air and water pollution overriding concerns. In 1983 the Environmental Protection Agency designated Commencement Bay a hazardous waste site. The following year the ASARCO smelter closed, unable to control the pollution accompanying its operations. On the other hand, the new rules opened other economic opportunities for local businessmen. Early in the 1980s Fairchild Camera and Instruments located near Puyallup, introducing high-tech industry to Pierce County. By the end of the 20th century, Intel Corporation had opened a plant at DuPont and Tacoma was promoting itself as the No. 1 "wired city" in the nation because of its publicly owned cable and telecommunications system.

Public-private involvement, partnerships and cooperation underscored economic development after 1945 in Tacoma, as these few examples illustrate. Achieving economic success by these means was particularly crucial for the Port of Tacoma. At war's end the tidelands harbor area was only partially

The J.C. Penney department store under construction at the Tacoma Mall *Tacoma Public Library, Richards Collection*

developed with streams and the uncontrolled Puyallup River delta meandering around the dredged waterways. Here was the potential for expanded ship moorage and new industrial sites. Hylebos and Wapato (Port-Industrial) Waterways were attended to first, with dredge matter used to fill the uplands.

Some of the new land became a construction site for buildings then towed to the Alaskan oilfields originating on Prudhoe Bay. Others acquired a life of their own connected to the changing nature of maritime commerce when container cargo began to dominate the shipping industry. By using these large metal boxes of uniform size, goods could move from ship to railroad car or truck with relative ease and efficiency. However, storing, loading, unloading and transferring containers required a substantial amount of land. This Tacoma had and in the 1970s the Port lured the Totem Ocean Trailer Express (TOTE) terminal from Seattle to the City of Destiny.

Tacoma's history, therefore, ends on an ironic note. Ever since 1873, when the Northern Pacific Railroad selected Tacoma as its terminus, the City of Destiny and the Emerald City have competed for urban dominance on Puget Sound. Seattle appeared the winner following the 1897 Klondike Gold Rush because the city was able to capture the Alaskan trade. But even then some writers were not so sure about which city was best. One notes, for example, that were he to live in the region he would invest in Seattle and live in Tacoma. The Port's capture of the Alaskan trade from Seattle suggests that the equation has shifted in Tacoma's favor. However, whether Seattleites will make a mad dash to live, as well as invest, in the City of Destiny only history can tell.

partners in tacoma

Partners Table of Contents

Building a Greater Tacoma

Business, Finance & Professional Services

International Trade

Manufacturing & Distribution

Marketplace

Quality of Life

Patron Tacoma Power

Construction Enterprises & Contractors, Inc.

The buildings that shape a city help define its character and are the embodiment of the social and economic activities that make the city vital. Contributing to the development of Tacoma's economic growth, and further, seeing those efforts last, are two of the most satisfying aspects of the well-established Construction Enterprises & Contractors, Inc. (CE&C). The firm can point to more than a half-century of construction throughout Puget Sound, recalling many rewarding and challenging opportunities that have come to characterize life in the Northwest.

As did so many others, George Warter returned from service in World War II determined to build a life for himself in Tacoma. He spent a short time prior to the war as a carpenter and came directly back to construction, working for his brother-in-law, Jim Purvis. When Purvis died suddenly in an airplane accident in the mid-50s, George and his sister, Eileen Sandstedt, agreed to continue running the firm. Commercial construction became the company's primary focus, and several business locations came into existence thanks to CE&C, including the Green Firs Shopping Center and Captain Nemo's Restaurant. Under George Warter's leadership Tacoma is home to such familiar landmarks as the South End Swimming Pool, the Fircrest Methodist Church, and McIntyre Hall and Men's Group Housing at the University of Puget Sound. Most of the low-income housing at the Hillside Terrace and Salishan was remodeled by the firm.

The firm became proficient in handling concrete construction; the concrete buildings at Pierce College are enduring examples. One of the firm's most challenging projects was the large group lecture hall at Evergreen College just outside of Olympia, which was built from concrete poured in place. This project required creativity on the part of the team, which designed forms to produce the required deep V-shaped ribbing that makes up the outside walls. An important finishing step for the exterior also included careful exposure of the aggregate and resulted in an engaging visual and tactile finish. The staff at CE&C demonstrated in this project that they could transform architects' intentions clearly as the work moved from one-dimensional blueprint to a functional three-dimensional structure. Thousands of college students have used this distinctive facility in the building's 30 years of life.

Crawford's Seafood, built by CE&C in 1949, was a landmark in Tacoma for many years.

Shelton Civic Center is a fine example of CE&C's skill at renovation.

Maintaining its reputation for quality, the firm changed hands but stayed in the family when Gregg Warter bought the business in 1984 from his father, George. In 1990 Darrell Barnes invested in the company and became Gregg's business partner. In the last 10 years they have found that their most rewarding projects involve renovating commercial or public buildings, and more than once they have worked on buildings the firm built decades ago. Some of the more recent projects completed by the firm locally are the multipurpose addition at the King County Aquatic Center, additions to Foss High School, the new Renton City Jail, new Ptarmigan Ridge Elementary School in Orting, the thoroughly renovated Shelton Civic Center, and upgrades and additions to Sound Ford in Renton. The company is a presence in the greater Tacoma area, both in remodeling and in the strength and functionality of some of its earliest construction.

Remodeling of commercial or public buildings necessarily involves an added dimension, one of public safety, which is a more critical issue than in new construction. So, during the firm's upgrades to Highline Community College in Des Moines, for example, the safety of the students who used the facilities, as well as the employees, was of primary importance. CE&C's excellent reputation for safety is well known, which may be one reason it has completed work for just about every school district from Olympia to Seattle.

In the earliest days of the business, then-owner Jim Purvis made what has become a long-standing commitment to the youth of the area. He was determined to bring the South End Boys' Club from dream to reality by donating his time and materials. This tradition has continued with fund raisers to feed the area's needy children and sponsorship of area athletic teams, which foster self-motivation as well as improved academic performance.

Water and Barnes also recognize the value of supporting community activities that provide young people with opportunities to help them become the next generation's reliable work force.

Along with a clear knowledge of today's materials, tools and safety measures, the staff at CE&C must have a creative and flexible approach to each set of blueprints in order to transform another person's ideas into a functional reality. Employees must be willing to take risks, since the construction business inherently contains many unpredictable issues such as supply and weather. Another challenge is to adapt to the changing technology of their own workplace. Computer software aids them in producing estimates with greater accuracy and speed than was possible before and enables them to track the financial aspects of a job closely as well. In addition, developing technology will allow the use of computers in the field to replace unwieldy but reliable blueprints. CE&C follows these software developments and makes maximum use of each new tool as it becomes available.

In construction, every day brings new challenges, often ones that no one could have anticipated. This endless variety, together with the creative demands of turning ideas into reality and the need for safely completed jobs, on time and within budget, requires a strong team with a vision. Construction Enterprises & Contractors, Inc. believes that being better tomorrow than it is today will take it into the future. Its commitment to clients to build quality facilities that will last for decades has provided many repeat customers. The staff accomplishes this by listening to and working with their customers to fulfill each dream. Having this kind of a commitment will carry CE&C into its 100th year of business building in the greater Tacoma area.

Corporate Casework

For Corporate Casework, reputation is everything. Formed in 1993, the company has become the Puget Sound's leader in custom cabinets and specialty countertops through its dedication to quality, service and on-time delivery.

In 1993 Lee Robison formed a partnership with his brother, Scott. Together with several local cabinetry experts, the Robison brothers studied the local construction market and decided their new organization would target a specific niche within it. They discovered that companies seeking to remodel their existing office space had trouble finding sources for custom cabinetry or individually designed work spaces such as reception counters. The larger cabinetmakers in the Puget Sound area usually avoided such specialty work, as their businesses were more focused on volume. Projects involving tenant improvements, as this niche is called, were too small and time consuming for them.

The Robisons had found their niche. They set out to capture it through an aggressive, service-oriented strategy. Almost a decade later, Corporate Casework has tripled in size and now completes 200 projects a year. Its clientele reads like a Who's Who of Northwest corporations and includes such firms as Microsoft, Amazon.com, REI, Washington Mutual and Optiva.

Reception area at REI's flagship store

Corporate Casework has two main facets to its business. About 70 percent of its work focuses on building custom cabinets for its professional clientele. The other 30 percent of its operation is dedicated to creating specialty countertops, reception desks and other high-profile work areas. Each project is unique and requires precise craftsmanship. For example, the company recently constructed one reception area for a dental office that included an aquarium in the middle of the counter.

A talented staff is what makes Corporate Casework great. Roy Thompson, one of the company's finest woodworking professionals, has 40 years of experience. James Kenmir, who along with Thompson is known all over the Puget Sound area, has 20 years of experience in the business. Together with the younger staff members, Thompson and Kenmir have come to symbolize the attention to detail and the quality of service that Corporate Casework's clients have come to expect.

Lee Robison understands that to retain such a remarkable staff, the company needs to reward their dedication. Individual achievement is always encouraged, as the Robisons have a "promote from within" policy that has proven effective over the years. General Manager Mike Kimball started in the business on the building side and has progressed to where he has a working knowledge of every function necessary to turn out a quality product on time. He is living proof of the company's policy to promote from within.

Other employees who show a serious interest in their craft are mentored by Corporate Casework's more experienced woodworkers. New employees start on the custom cabinetry side of the business, where they develop their skills. Once they have mastered this, they can move up to working on the specialized counters and work areas, which require the highest possible level of skill. In this area of the company, there is no substitute for old-fashioned woodcraft skills, as each counter is designed and built entirely by hand.

Once the cabinets and countertops are constructed, Corporate Casework uses its own fleet of trucks to deliver the finished products to the office site. The company's installers then make on-site modifications to ensure the smooth fit between the new casework and the office space for which it was designed. At times, this can be a challenging process. But Corporate Casework's employees always have a "can-do" attitude, and they frequently work long hours to ensure their products are installed accurately. From their spirit flows the company's reputation of delivering quality products on time.

Completing each project on time is a major priority for Corporate Casework's management staff. Rob Rushton, who grew up in the business and has years of experience, does more than sell. He develops projects with customers by showing how to create a look within budgets and time restraints. His part of the team is vital in coordinating between shop and field scheduling. Each project takes an average of 30 to 60 days to complete, and at any given time the company can be working on 10 to 15 different contracts. As difficult as this is to manage, Corporate Casework efficiently meets its deadlines.

Nevertheless, this is not a production-line operation. Companies that are looking for extra attention or want a distinctive look for their office areas come to Corporate Casework for its ability to blend form with function through its artisanship. When REI needed custom work done in its flagship store in downtown Seattle, Corporate Casework recycled wood from REI's original store for use in the cabinets within the new store, exactly as REI had hoped.

While the core of Corporate Casework's operations depends on craftsmanship, the company has introduced new technology to the shop floor. The company's computer-operated saw can cut wood to exact dimensions without damaging the lamination. Other machines have eliminated the laborious filing previously required on each piece of casework before assembly. High technology has made Corporate Casework's production facilities more precise and efficient. Far from replacing artisanship, automation has meshed perfectly with traditional woodworking to create an even better product.

Virginia Mason Hospital reception desk

A new reception desk for law firm Guy Carpenter

As Corporate Casework's success has grown, so has its desire to be a good neighbor. Every year the company donates 10 to 15 projects to different causes around the Puget Sound. Recently it donated either money or cabinetry to the Tacoma Food Bank, the Tacoma Rescue Mission and a nonprofit theater in Seattle. In addition to its donated projects, every August contributions are made to charities such as Juvenile Diabetes, the American Heart Association and the Make-a-Wish Foundation.

The future is bright for Corporate Casework. The niche so wisely selected by the Robison brothers years ago continues to grow as more companies remodel or expand their facilities. It is a niche that Corporate Casework has come to dominate, thanks to its talented and dedicated employees who understand that the company's reputation is based on the cornerstones of quality, service and customer satisfaction.

Holroyd Co. Inc.

Hidden beneath the majestic volcanic peaks and massive glaciers of the Cascade Mountains is one of Puget Sound's best-kept secrets and most dependable natural resources — large gravel deposits. This important component of the area's geology required a vision of a solid future before it could be utilized, and Arthur Holroyd provided that vision soon after he settled in the area in 1885. Today the Holroyd Company's familiar green trucks, long a fixture in Tacoma and Pierce County, are kept busy transporting gravel, sand and concrete for the area's continued residential and commercial growth. These trucks are the most visible sign of the family-owned Holroyd Co. Inc., which in 2006 will enter its second century of supplying foundation materials throughout the region. The early beginnings of the company illustrate how one man realized his personal American dream and bequeathed that dream to his family.

Arthur Holroyd, who founded the Holroyd Company in Pierce County in 1906, was born in Lancashire, England, in 1865 and was educated there before immigrating to Canada. After six months in the province of Alberta he moved to Washington and homesteaded in McKenna, south of Tacoma. There he established a business hauling wood in to south Tacoma and groceries and supplies back to his neighbors in McKenna. Holroyd recognized the opportunities before him and worked with determination and will to build a business. As he became more established he moved to town, founded a business dealing in building materials, and eventually purchased property in what is now Lakewood. This significant step gave him the opportunity to realize one of his most important dreams, to own land, which had been illegal for his people in England.

Holroyd soon began to supply a greater variety of building materials, at one point including sand, gravel, concrete blocks, sewer pipe, and even stucco and plaster, and the business grew. Cement used as ballast on Belgian ships was purchased by Holroyd and made available for construction in the earliest days.

One of Arthur Holroyd's four children, his daughter Alma Merle, began working with her father's business when she was only 15, helping with the books and office correspondence. Later, her husband, Thomas Miller, worked with the family as well. Alma Merle Miller is credited with strengthening and expanding the business, acquiring and developing its area gravel deposits and adding to the fleet of delivery trucks. After Arthur Holroyd's death from pneumonia in 1942, Alma Merle and her family continued to supply area builders and contractors. Her brother, James Arthur, worked successfully to expand sales and was active in the business until his death in 1980.

Arthur Holroyd and his son-in-law, Thomas I. Miller, work at the counter that was the nucleus of the business in its early days.

In 1953 current president Margaret Nielsen, a third-generation Holroyd and daughter of Alma Merle, became a partner and continued her mother's practice of daily hard work and close involvement in the business. Margaret remembers the biggest vertical pour of that time, in 1974, as one of the company's more memorable jobs. The company's distinctive green trucks provided the concrete for the landmark grain elevators on Ruston Way, hauling and pouring concrete 24 hours a day for nine days. The entire Holroyd staff worked on the project, filling three shifts around the clock, and today there is a great sense of satisfaction knowing that the grain terminal is still an active, working part of the port and a landmark on the Tacoma skyline.

Arthur Holroyd looks over the work ponds in the 1930s with his granddaughter Margaret, who is now president of Holroyd Co. Inc.

Holroyd Co. Inc. is able to maintain a steady staff of around 100, including four office workers and four sales representatives. Each employee receives valuable on-the-job training and is qualified to do a variety of different jobs within the company. Sporadic drug testing assures both staff and the community that all Holroyd drivers are safe and responsible. Although construction work is often seasonal, astute management at Holroyd's is able to provide year-round employment and its steady payroll helps support the community. Benefits include solid medical protection for employees and their families as well as 401(k) retirement plans. Families are included in the yearly picnic, traditionally held at Titlow Beach Park. Holroyd employees are a stable part of the community.

One of Holroyd's strengths has been its ability to adapt over the past 100 years to the changing needs of the community, and it has been an active participant in maintaining the Northwest's enviable quality of life. Washington citizens are proud of the state's clean air and water and have demonstrated repeatedly that both can be enjoyed while also sustaining business and community growth. The family contributes by meeting all environmental requirements for their business. At each of their concrete batch plants they have washing facilities, which allow them to essentially recycle concrete. The sand and gravel are washed and, whenever possible, recycled. The company works to be a good neighbor.

Durability is important in foundations and is also a noticeable trait of the family members who are the heart of Holroyd Co. Inc. When times were hard, the business was reorganized and restructured but never defeated. At one point, when access to one of their gravel deposits was obstructed, the family hired a helicopter and shipped gravel in boxes to be washed. From the dream Arthur Holroyd brought with him, to the mother and daughter who were successful in a field rarely visited by women, endurance and perseverance have become recognized family characteristics.

Today Margaret Nielsen, her husband, David, and two of their sons, Stephen and Mark, own the company, and Stephen and Mark represent the fourth generation to work daily in the business. Holroyd Co. Inc. estimates that company-owned gravel aggregate supplies will last another 100 years, and it plans to continue supplying building materials for the area economy. If the last 100 years of service are an indication, Northwesterners can continue to rely on solid foundations through the lives of their own great-grandchildren.

Madsen Electric

Established by Carl T. Madsen in 1948, Madsen Electric began as Carl T. Madsen Electrical Installations Company of Tacoma. The company's first job was the second, safer Tacoma Narrows Bridge, nicknamed Sturdy Gertie, which opened in 1950 and remains in use today. Sturdy Gertie replaced the first bridge, known as Galloping Gertie because it rolled and undulated on windy days, finally collapsing in a strong windstorm.

The Tacoma Narrows Bridge assignment became a model for Carl T. Madsen Electrical Installations Company's focus on unique and difficult projects, which included schools, public works and wiring of Distant Early Warning stations in Alaska. While Alaska projects ended in the mid-1960s, public works projects expanded to include street lighting and military contracts. In 1954 the company became a 1040C corporation with new ownership, and changed its name to Carl T. Madsen, Inc., then CTM Electric in 1970 and finally Madsen Electric.

The company also became a leader in the new style of business known as "bidder design," which replaced traditional plans and spec work. An early design project was the Wells Fargo building on Pacific Avenue, a 21-story landmark that defined the Tacoma skyline in the early 1970s, later followed by St. Joseph Hospital Tower.

Large public projects such as the County City Building were the mainstay of C.T. Madsen Electric during the 1950s and 1960s. These projects included the Highway Licensing Building in Olympia, barracks at Fort Lewis and major schools throughout the area. The 1970s brought the addition of major private works contracts, including the Wells Fargo Office building, the St. Joseph Hospital Tower, Mary Bridge Children's Center and USA Insurance building in Federal Way.

REI's Seattle Flagship store is one of many retail facilities completed using the design-build method.

The Wells Fargo building continues the tradition of building major projects in the Northwest.

A Tacoma landmark receives a renovation that maintains its historical nature.

The increase in private contracts also included a major focus on heavy industrial work that continues to this day. A major builder of sawmills in the 1980s, Madsen Electric established itself as the premier electrical contractor for specialized industrial work. From rolling mills such as Kaiser Aluminum, to paper processing at Simpson Tacoma Kraft Company, sawmills like Por-Tac, bottle lines at CNC Bottling, ovens at Baxter Manufacturing, oil refining at U.S. Oil, microelectronics at Matsushita and plastics at Dyno Overlay, Madsen has both expertise and experience.

By the late 1980s Madsen Electric recognized that customers wanted their contractor to do more than simply build a project and move on to the next. The owners and building users wanted continued support in the maintenance and alterations to their existing buildings. To meet this need, Madsen Service provides 24-hour electricians on call. Fully equipped trucks and specially trained manpower provide each service call with everything needed, on a moment's notice, around the clock.

Today Madsen Electric designs and installs wiring, lighting and electrical systems for new and existing structures, in a wide variety of styles from health care to high-rise office buildings, and industrial to retail, and it provides 24 hour service for each.

An example typical of the company's distinctive and challenging projects is the Recreational Equipment, Inc. (REI) Flagship Store in downtown Seattle. The building team — owner, architect and general contractor — evaluated electrical and mechanical contractors based on experience, design capabilities, ability to work as a team, financial stability, project safety record and quality of on-site supervision. Madsen Electric was selected for its proven track record of design-build projects, design innovation and sub-system abilities. The company's proposed lighting system for the signature climbing rock, called the "REI Flagship Store Pinnacle," won recognition for outstanding achievement in lighting design from the Illuminating Engineering Society of North America. Using a system of colored lights and an astronomically correct time clock, the rock fades from daylight to sunset colors as dusk approaches.

Office space built for a specific tenant, using the design-build method

One of the many major medical facilities completed in the Greater Northwest

The first major project completed by Madsen Electric, which started a tradition that has shaped the look of Tacoma.

Whatever the project, Madsen Electric provides efficient teamwork, advanced technology and superior customer service. As a member of a Peer Review Group formed in 1991, Madsen Electric participates in a peer review process as a way to bring additional value to the customer and the construction process. The Peer Review Group consists of eight electrical contractors located in different geographical regions of the United States. Each contractor is a union employer, dominant in its field and an established leader in NECA (National Electrical Contractors Association). Each participant opens its business, including books and internal practices, to the other group members for periodic review and recommendations. The peer review process improves company practices and policies, boosts employee morale, and builds a reliable network of experts across the country.

Through its managers and employees, Madsen Electric's community support has grown with the company's business growth. A charter member of the National Electrical Contractors Association of Southwest Washington (NECA), Madsen has participated in the Model Cities Program, The Municipal Authority, The Electric 21 Council, Academy of Electrical Contracting, Boys and Girls Clubs, YMCAs throughout out the area, rebuilding of the Job Carr home in Tacoma's Old Town and sponsored countless youth baseball teams throughout the years.

For over half a century, Madsen Electric, part of the CTM Group of companies, has met the electrical needs of commercial, industrial and service customers in the Puget Sound region and has built a solid reputation for designing innovative and versatile electrical systems, on time at a competitive price. The company slogan remains as true today as it was 50 years ago: "If it's electric, it's our business."

Potelco, Inc.

Everywhere in the Northwest, when people pick up the telephone, log on to the Internet, heat their homes, watch television, turn on the lights and cook dinner, chances are Potelco, Inc. has enabled them to do so. As a full-service utility contracting firm, Potelco, Inc. installs the infrastructure that makes much of contemporary life possible. If the need is power lines overhead or gas lines below ground, traffic lights or telecommunications, Potelco, Inc. is the contractor that private companies and government agencies turn to when they need a big or small job done expertly and efficiently. In a world where rapid change is the norm, the combination of experience and innovation has kept Potelco, Inc. ahead of the game for 40 years. And the company just keeps growing.

Potelco, Inc. is a family-operated business. It was founded in 1961 to service the telephone and power utilities in and around Tacoma. The company's name was created by combining the words "power" and "telephone," the communications utilities that were the basis of the business. Joe Tucci, Sr. joined Potelco, Inc. shortly after its founding and headed the company until 1988. The company started small, with just a dozen or so employees, but every year saw accelerated growth. In 1978 Joe's son, Gary Tucci, joined the company, after graduating from Washington State University with a degree in business. Ten years later, the elder Tucci retired, leaving his son at the helm of Potelco, Inc.

Crews from Potelco, Inc. perform trolly line installation with minimum disruption of traffic.

Equipment from Potelco, Inc. preparing trenches.

With the emergence of new technologies, Gary Tucci saw infinite potential for Potelco, Inc. When he joined Potelco, Inc., the company's annual earnings were $5 million. By 1998 the business had grown to $18 million annually. That was the year he decided it was time to make the leap to the national stage. With three partners, he helped organize Quanta Services, Inc., a public company under whose umbrella smaller utility contractors unite to form "sister" partnerships to tackle big jobs coast to coast.

The concept for Quanta was simple. Tucci knew that across the country there were many small, family-owned utility contracting firms whose original founders were at or near retirement age and worried about the future of the companies they'd worked a lifetime to build. Those firms wanted to stay in business, and Quanta wanted to acquire them. Joining the Quanta family allowed some 70 firms to keep operating, while Quanta was able to expand its services to literally become a "one-stop shop" for every client. The strategy benefited everyone, including Potelco, Inc., whose business increased more than ten-fold in the three years since Tucci and his partners founded Quanta. In 2001 Quanta was a $2 billion company, while Potelco, Inc. employed 800 people and saw its earnings skyrocket to $120 million.

While Potelco, Inc. is based in Sumner, having moved the five miles east of Tacoma in 1980, its assignments take it throughout the Northwest to Washington, Oregon, Idaho and Montana. Clients include the private companies and public agencies that build and maintain the utility, communications and transportation infrastructure on which society relies. Power companies, gas companies, telephone and cable companies, mass transit systems, state highways and military installations all call on Potelco, Inc. Federal, state and local agencies rely on Potelco, Inc. to install heavy highway lighting, traffic signals, ramp metering systems and mainline communications. The company's many services include installing natural gas lines, power lines, traffic signals, cable replacements, fiber optics, underground construction, and both aerial and underground telecommunications.

Power lines are installed and maintained by Potelco, Inc.

The firm's approach to every project is based on teamwork. Because the company has long-established partnerships with other contractors, it offers a skilled team to tackle all aspects of every job. Experts from several disciplines work together as one crew, so a client never needs to worry about duplication of services or delays due to conflicts with scheduling. When the Potelco, Inc. team is on the job, interference with service is kept to a minimum, lessening the impact on neighborhoods. The company's construction services also include the use of specialized pieces of equipment, which are owned by Potelco, Inc.

Not many contractors can offer such a complete, one-stop package to their clients. Potelco, Inc. is a "design-build" contractor with its own staff of engineers that provides all its clients with comprehensive plans, including construction design and cost estimates for both materials and labor. The engineers, as comfortable in the field as they are in front of a computer, design each project with an understanding of both its immediate building needs and its future maintenance requirements. Once the plans are approved, Potelco, Inc. can handle all aspects of construction. This complete service package saves clients money because it eliminates the need for costly subcontractors.

Potelco, Inc. is a leader in innovative construction strategies. It is the only contractor in the area using the Linemaster Robotic Arm, a specialized piece of equipment that allows a crew to work on overhead power lines without shutting down customer service. Joint trenching is the construction technique that opens one trench to hold multiple utility carriers, causing minimal disruption at the construction site. When performing street light maintenance, the firm's procedures limit power outages to just one to three days, a real plus for public safety. To lay gas lines, Potelco, Inc. equipped some of its own Caterpillars with special off-set plows and chutes so that crews can lay roughly half a mile of pipe per day. Digging ditches can be a dirty, disruptive business, but Potelco, Inc. uses an innovative system of wheel trenching, a cleaner, more efficient procedure that is also more environmentally friendly.

Construction sites can be hazardous, which is why Potelco, Inc. stresses safety above all else. Safety training is an ongoing part of the company's business, and all employees routinely receive the training they need to perform their jobs in a safe and efficient manner. Every week, Potelco, Inc. crews meet for safety meetings, and daily discussions about the issue occur on a regular basis. Both in-house trainers and outside consultants develop and coordinate the Potelco, Inc. safety program.

Potelco, Inc. is a company committed to meeting the utility needs of the Northwest. Its spectacular growth in the last decade, backed by the firm's proven track record and reputation for quality and innovation, created a firm foundation for the future. After 40 years of solid success, there appears to be no limits to its future growth.

Tile Technology Roofing Company, Inc.

At Tile Technology, ownership and employees share something special, something elusive to most other businesses. A rare phenomenon in the labor-intensive roofing industry, Tile Technology delivers promises on time. Commonly referred to as S.P.O.T. (sales promise on time) around the conference table, in the hallway or on the job site, everyone knows it's this company's secret recipe for success.

Owners Don Vose, Bob Deaton, Glen Paine and Douglas Vieselmeyer

"Do what you say you're going to do when you say you're going to do it" was the common thread between two high school pals who eventually combined their assets under the corporate veil of Tile Technology Roofing Company Co., Inc. Glen Paine Jr. lent his 1962 black premier flatbed pickup, sparse set of tools and roofing know-how. Douglas Vieselmeyer brought his college degree in business administration/marketing, experience in business management and collateral for their contractors' license bond to the partnership.

The stage was set. These two 25-year-old men were committed to taking the entrepreneurial plunge. Getting started in November of 1987 gave the partners a short first year to warm the engines before their first big fiscal race.

When all the accounting was complete, the firm's first full year spelled success. Tile Technology recorded $750,000 in roofing sales and a net profit after tax. Every new call for service originated from a satisfied customer. The company had no phone-book listing or any other form of advertising for the first few years. By the third year, roofing revenues reached $2.5 million, and still the company did not even have phone numbers advertised on its trucks.

A corporate culture was emerging in harmony with an identity that put the competition on the ropes. With the growth in revenue came the need for more people. This meant new challenges, new paradigms and a new level of commitment. A simple and proven philosophy, obvious to the founders of Tile Technology, would become increasingly difficult to anchor in employees' minds.

With more than 100 employees and sales nearing $8 million annually, Vieselmeyer and Paine had to find a way to keep delivering their promises to each customer. Professional sources helped turn the organization upside-down, putting ownership at the bottom of the pyramid. Key people were strategically placed to ensure proper transition of information and delegation of responsibility. Unparalleled compensation packages were offered to attract the industry's elite work force. Strategic internal and external marketing plans were designed to merge the concept of an organization that could "walk its talk." Finally, new blood was invited into the ownership circle.

First, Bob Deaton, a highly respected professional with vast knowledge of the roofing industry, doubled the sales efforts of any other individual. Deaton's loyal relationships and growing focus on leadership had an immediate and lasting effect on the organization's ability to deliver its promises. Donald Vose, an owner of his own roofing firm in Eastern Washington, came aboard when ownership initiated negotiations to merge his talents and assets into the Tile Tech family. With nearly 20 years of experience managing dispatch and scheduling for a large roofing firm, Vose's impact in these areas was felt overnight. Customer confidence ratings, historically tracked in-house, were assessed by independent third-party review. Did the company actions really match ownership's words?

Tile Technology Roofing endured a rigorous four-step rating process to earn the prestigious ValueStar Certification from the nation's top rating organization of local service businesses and professionals. ValueStar's Certification shows that Tile Technology's legal status, licenses, finances and insurance are in good standing, and that the company has passed ValueStar's high customer satisfaction survey. Tile Technology Roofing Co., Inc. then by agreement maintains high customer service satisfaction levels and adheres to ValueStar's Customer Bill of Rights, ethical business practices and a number of other related requirements.

Rigorous requirements present no problem to a corporation with high internal standards. The company subscribes to an innovative "corporate fish" philosophy borrowed from the world-famous Pike Place Fish in Seattle. Unlike often cumbersome and overwhelming management philosophies, this simple yet effective four-step philosophy empowers employees to make conscious choices, have a good attitude, enjoy their work, keep their minds focused on the task at hand and make each potential customer feel special, whether or not he or she decides to purchase a new roof. The result was profound: satisfied customers and happy employees.

Tile Technology also sponsors special events and contests, invites guest speakers, holds seminars and maintains a library of personal improvement tapes and books. Office walls are adorned with motivational quotes and photographs. The PRIDE (Professional Results Inspired by Dedicated Employees) Grand Prix was designed to build pride in work, home and social life. Employees are encouraged to participate in community service, remain drug free and recognize the efforts of co-workers. Points are awarded for each achievement, and in 1999 two contest winners each received a new car, one bright red and one yellow Corvette. Prizes and contests always change to keep employees focused on the goals of achieving individual potential while working toward the team's objective.

The "World Famous" Tile Technology Roofing fleet of vans now services the entire Pacific Northwest.

Despite the necessary focus on business, Vieselmeyer and Paine's roots remain in Tacoma. The two experienced nearly parallel family dysfunction, divorced parents, welfare assistance and early entry into the working world. One thing they consciously made time and money for was the community that gave to them. Like so many in the business world, their focus was and is the children.

Tile Technology Roofing remains an active donor of money and time to Big Brothers Big Sisters, the Boys and Girls Clubs, Northwest Harvest, a variety of youth sports clubs and individual citizens in need like Lorraine Gustafson, a 66-year-old widow living in South Tacoma in an old Victorian house with a roof so rotten, portions of it blew off in strong wind storms. Ownership received word of Lorraine Gustafson's roof problem and lack of finances from a neighbor during one of the company's most unusual marketing efforts, the "Ugliest Roof" contest. While the random drawing from a host of other ugly roofs didn't pick this one, the folks at Tile Tech along with some other industry friends came together to not only replace Mrs. Gustafson's roof but also rebuild, repair and clean up her entire house and yard.

Great employees accomplish great things. All of the employees at Tile Technology Roofing are committed to "Re-creating the Vision!"

What began as a simple vision has evolved into a tradition far greater than putting on a good roof. Although business is clearly important, making a difference in peoples' lives comes first.

Berg Equipment & Scaffolding Co., Inc.

Edward and Patricia Berg built one of the Northwest's largest scaffolding and high-reach equipment businesses based upon a simple pledge to satisfy customers. The family-owned operation now services cities stretching from Bellingham to Portland.

Berg's venture began when he left a secure position as a manager of a scaffolding company in Yakima, where he had worked for 11 years before coming to Tacoma. When Berg and his wife, Pat, opened the doors of Berg Equipment & Scaffolding Co., Inc. in June 1969, they employed only two people, their 15-year-old son, Randy, and Dwight Johnson, both of whom are with the company today. Ed and Pat provided the business know-how and Randy and Dwight provided customer service.

The early days of business did not go without considerable risk. The business was born with very little capital and most people would have had second thoughts. The scaffolding supplier — Bil-Jax Scaffolding of Archbold, Ohio — supported Berg in his efforts. "It was a risk, but we never would have made what we made if we hadn't taken a risk," said Pat Berg, who is still actively involved in the company. Berg Scaffolding now employs 80.

The Berg family got its first big break in 1970 when a contractor used its equipment to build the Holiday Inn of SeaTac. Ed Berg designed a unique fly-shoring system for that 10-story building that allowed the scaffolding to be hoisted, repositioned and secured, avoiding the usual practice of tearing down and rebuilding, and saving time and money. It was a turning point for Berg, who in 1984 opened another scaffolding rental outlet in Seattle. A few years later Berg diversified its product line to include aerial lift platforms, forklifts and a wide range of other scaffold-related products.

Berg Scaffolding has been involved in the construction or refurbishing of many famous Tacoma landmarks, including the Old City Hall, Tacoma Dome, St. Joseph Hospital, the University of Washington satellite campus, the Pantages Theatre, Union Station and several buildings at the University of Puget Sound. Berg Scaffolding was also used in the painting of Washington state's 160-foot capitol rotunda, a job that provided many unique challenges.

Berg has built his company upon salesmanship and friendliness, and it grew as a result of the word of satisfied customers. Berg's son, Randy, has worked at the company since it first opened, beginning as a 15-year-old laborer who helped service and erect scaffolding. Kathy has been involved with the business for 20 years and has been creative with new business direction. Now the younger Berg and sister Kathy run the family-owned business.

The Bergs remain committed to providing a business that still puts service and the customer's satisfaction at the top of the priority list.

Home of Berg Equipment & Scaffolding Co., Inc.

Bosnick Roofing, Inc.

If there is any place in the country where a good roof matters, it is the Northwest. Familiarity with the unpredictable weather as well as a thorough acquaintance with the city of Tacoma are both essentials in building a successful roofing business. Bosnick Roofing, Inc., with a heritage of hard work, quality jobs and a close-knit staff, has in nearly three decades earned its reputation for reliability. For those who live and work in Tacoma, chances are good they have been sheltered by a Bosnick roof. The company specializes in commercial work and has seen the world from the top of Madigan Hospital at Fort Lewis, Annie Wright School, Union Station in downtown Tacoma and even from commercial sites in Alaska.

Don Bosnick began working with his father, Millon Bosnick, on roofing jobs when he was only 6 years old. Like many of his generation, Millon served in World War II, and after being discharged at Fort Lewis, decided to settle in the area. He began working for his father-in-law, who owned a roofing business. When that business closed in the 50s, Millon continued working in roofing, taking his son up to work on roofs beside him. In 1971, with a business degree from the University of Puget Sound in Tacoma, Don and his father founded Bosnick Roofing, Inc. Since 1982, when Millon retired, Don has led the company as president and sole owner. His son, Todd, who also has a business degree from Washington State University, will eventually take over in management.

The employees at Bosnick Roofing are the heart of the business. Supervisors lead crews, totaling a staff of approximately 50 people, throughout the year. The company has numerous maintenance contracts, providing steady work through the slower winter months. Management works closely with each crew, and because employees' opinions count, turnover is low. Several people have been with the company since its beginning and, in some cases, continue working part time after their official retirement.

Don Bosnick knows from personal experience that roofing is physically demanding, and the seasonal nature of the business requires long hours during summer months. He also knows that such job demands can be hard on families, so a cornerstone of his management plan is to provide a variety of recreational opportunities for his employees and their families. The office has season tickets available for professional sports in both Tacoma and Seattle, and employees play on a softball team in the Industrial Metropolitan Park League. Equally important is the company's sponsorship of a variety of children's athletic teams. Local Boy Scout organizations know they can turn to Bosnick Roofing for help with projects.

When Don Bosnick looks back over the years he has worked in roofing, he can point out many changes. Materials have changed and improved, of course, but more important are the equipment changes that have reduced the backbreaking physical labor of roofing. Keeping up with those improvements helps keep the Bosnick staff safe and fit and makes each job more efficient. The company's repeat customers attest to its satisfaction rate. Bosnick roofs will be a familiar sight on Tacoma's skyline for decades to come.

Annie Wright School preserves its heritage with a good roof.

LUGO Construction, Inc.

Part of Tacoma's skyline has been built by LUGO Construction, Inc., a hometown firm with a regional outlook. This local construction firm has successfully completed commercial projects throughout the Western states.

Adrian Lugo

Projects include shopping centers, medical clinics, high-tech manufacturing facilities, offices, warehouses, resorts, cultural centers, churches, museums and casinos. LUGO doesn't specialize on a type of building; it specializes on a type of construction delivery system. Design build is its forte.

Whether a client brings an architect to the table or is using a favorite design team, LUGO acts in concert with design professionals to produce on-time, in-budget projects. When time and money are critical, this construction firm meets the challenge. Its many awards display a can-do attitude as well as a commitment to customers, employees and community.

Emerald Queen Casino

Julie's Landing

LUGO is an Inc. 500 company and included in its list of fastest-growing companies. LUGO, a winner of the Pierce County Chamber of Commerce's Business of the Year, is also listed in the *Hispanic Business Magazine*'s Top 500 firms and has received honors as SBA Business of the Year, Minority Business of the Year and Bank of America's Supplier of the Year.

Adrian Lugo, the owner of the company, is a believer in giving back to the community. LUGO sponsors minority scholarships and donates 10 percent of its profits to charities and community programs, including UWT scholarships, Bellarmine High School, the Boy Scouts, CCS, Tacoma Urban League, Martin Luther King Housing, the Puyallup Tribal Clinic and others. In addition, many LUGO employees voluntarily donate a portion of their wages to a fund that is collected throughout the year. At Christmas, a large portion of this fund is given to the community; at times, this fund has also been given to fellow employees who are in an emergency situation.

Why does Lugo give back so much to his community? "My father dropped out of high school at age 14 and my mother grew up in a one-room house on the Mexican border with 12 siblings," he explained. "The only difference between me and an Indian living in Mexico working in the fields is my education."

LUGO exceeds $49 million in sales. This is a far cry from its humble beginnings as a home remodeler in 1978. "My wife and I worked side-by-side when we started," he said. Lugo gave up his career in teaching to become a contractor. "It pays better," he said.

LUGO started as an experiment. "I wanted to see if you could be honest and treat people well and still make a dollar," he said. Lugo's grandmother on his father's side offered some words of wisdom: "If you treat people fairly, they'll use you for their next project." Indeed, 80 percent of LUGO's work is with repeat and reference customers.

RCI Construction Group

Northwesterners no longer take fresh, clean water for granted any more than pure air or uncrowded roadways and reliable transit. Such basics explain why people choose to live in Pierce County. RCI Construction Group, based in Sumner, contributes significantly to the enviable quality of life citizens enjoy, and its payroll helps fuel the economy of several Pierce County communities.

The remarkable growth of RCI and its nationally recognized role in the construction industry are quite an accomplishment in light of the fact that the business is only 23 years old. Mark W. Robison, CEO and sole owner of RCI, learned about construction and heavy equipment from his father, who ran a sewer and water main construction company. Working as a laborer during summers and holidays, Robison also internalized a strong work ethic, which has helped bring his company from a group of four employees, one of whom was his wife, Sheri, to more than 500 today. The company soon graduated from small water and sewer main contracts to bigger projects, ranging from planned communities and golf courses to highway contract work such as the DuPont Interchange in Pierce County.

As the needs of the community evolve, RCI is ready and quick to respond. The company provides nationally recognized expertise in hazardous waste remediation, water treatment plants, tunneling, and civil structural concrete work. Tacoma's water supply from the headwaters of the Green River is reliable thanks to the vision of the city's water division planners and the steel pipes laid and tunneled by RCI Construction Group. A total of five RCI divisions work on job sites from Hawaii to Wyoming.

Puget Sound citizens have benefited in other ways from RCI's impressive growth. The first environmental cleanups of Commencement Bay were completed by RCI, and this work continues with the ongoing restoration of sites along Tacoma's Dock Street in anticipation of the planned glass museum.

Because of the variety of projects RCI undertakes, employees are able to continually develop their skills. Many on the staff have been with the company for over 20 years. The commitment to safety, service and integrity characterizes the company's team philosophy and overflows into the communities where its employees live and work. Numerous community organizations receive steady support from RCI, among them local police guilds, food banks, the March of Dimes, DARE and Habitat for Humanity. Employees take leadership responsibilities in Rotary clubs, Master Builders' Association, and the Economic Development Council because they want to serve the community that supports them.

Road systems, sewers and water mains are seldom considered as long as they function, but are essential to the life of every citizen. RCI's work in building and maintaining this infrastructure means a better life for generations to come.

The DuPont Interchange, constructed by RCI, was completed and in use in less than a year.

Stacy Plumbing Supply Company

A homeowner wants to think about plumbing as little as possible. From the faucets to the pipes, everyone expects reliability and durability. As times change and perhaps owners, the hidden plumbing system is expected to continue to function smoothly and make few demands. After over half a century providing plumbing materials, Stacy Plumbing Supply Company has a proven track record demonstrating the same qualities of dependability and endurance.

Perhaps the biggest reason for this continued success is that Stacy's is a small, family-owned business. A picture in the modest office shows three children who now, decades later, share the responsibility of running the business. They are the fourth generation to do so and lightheartedly explain that the picture represents Stacy Plumbing's executive officers. Their early ancestor, James McAllister, was one of the first settlers in the Nisqually Delta, living in a burned-out cedar stump. At the turn of the century, another family member, Charles Stacy, established himself in Pierce County as a tinsmith, marketing handcrafted tin bathtubs. His son, Lloyd, worked with him and continued in the plumbing business, founding Stacy Plumbing Supply in 1948 after his return from World War II. The third generation was represented in late 1948 when Lloyd's son, Bob, also joined the company after his military service. Bob's three children, Greg, Deanna and Dennis, now run the business in a low-key but very effective manner, each with his or her own area of expertise. Some of their own children, now adults, also work in the business, making a total of six family members in a staff of 16. Generation after generation, the family continues to practice a strong work ethic, which translates into quality service for their many return customers.

Lloyd Stacy, founder of Stacy Plumbing Supply Company (right) with his son Bob

As a wholesaler Stacy Plumbing supplies materials for a variety of big jobs throughout the state of Washington. Its projects include medical buildings, correctional facilities, retirement homes, high-rises, and school and government buildings. Some of its most satisfied clients, however, are charitable organizations such as area homeless shelters, halfway houses and the YMCA, which benefit from materials donations. Environmental and water quality concerns are addressed by past President Bob Stacy, and his wife, Bonnie, who work together to maintain a healthy stream and spawning grounds for returning salmon runs on their rural property.

The employees at Stacy's say it is easy to come to work. The relaxed management style means they all work together to make bids, deliver products and meet customers' needs. The heart of the business is the warehouse, where virtually every new employee starts, and where an endless variety of materials would confuse most people. People in the office lend a hand in the warehouse or yard if there is a rush request from a client, and salespeople make deliveries to accommodate unexpected needs. Work on a new warehouse that nearly doubled the capacity of the business was completed in late 2000, and every available family member and families of many employees were on hand to help move into the new space. Stacy Plumbing Supply will be well prepared for another century of service.

Western Superior Structurals Manufacturing, Inc.

For over 36 years, Western Superior Structurals Manufacturing, Inc. has been a leading steel fabrication and erection company serving Washington, Alaska and Hawaii. Founded in 1965 by Gilbert Howard and Gil Herbrand, the business was originally called Western Engineering Limited and operated from a garage in the Howards' Puyallup home. A few months later, Gil Herbrand left the business and Gilbert Howard and his wife, Donna, acquired full ownership.

Soon outgrowing the Howards' home, Western Engineering moved to a larger building formerly occupied by Harold's Bottling Company on Pacific Highway East in Fife. In 1968 the former chiropractic office next door became the administrative headquarters, where the Howards built a family-owned enterprise that experienced steady growth.

Gilbert had learned how to fabricate steel while working for National Blower Company. He was a talented craftsman who could build anything with his hands. He supervised manufacturing and production while Donna served as office manager and accountant. This winning combination of skills has made Western Superior as strong as the steel it fabricates.

Western Engineering Limited was incorporated in 1969 and changed its name to Western Superior Structurals Manufacturing in 1986. In 1980, when Gilbert left, Donna took over and passed her knowledge to the Howards' four children, David, Laura, Tim and Mary Colleen, who became involved in operating the company under Donna's direction. Today Donna, Mary and Tim continue to manage the business, which is still based at the Pacific Highway location and employs 15-25 journeymen fitters and welders, depending on the workload.

A Woman's Business Enterprise (WBE), Western Superior Structurals boasts expertise in all phases of structural and miscellaneous steel fabrication and erection projects for commercial, industrial and federal agencies throughout the Pacific Northwest. The focus is on top-notch performance tailored to clients' needs and in accordance with established standards. Projects cover all types of structures including hospitals, malls, bridges, schools, banks, libraries, airplane hangars, dams, post offices and condominiums.

Major projects include the REI Distribution Warehouse in Sumner, Genie Industries in Redmond, Food Services of America in Everett, Bagley Wright Theater in Seattle Center, the Asian Tropical Forest at Seattle's Woodland Zoo, the Point Defiance Zoo Aviary in Tacoma and Toys-R-Us stores. Western Superior also made structural repairs to numerous Tacoma buildings and schools damaged in the 1966 earthquake, constructs metal catchbasins in drainage ditches, and has been fabricating steel trash debris racks for King County for over a decade.

Western Superior not only builds sturdy steel to support community structures, but also offers support in the form of financial donations to local nonprofit organizations. Yearly donations are given to the local Humane Society, the American Red Cross, environmental groups, handicapped children's organizations and the Special Olympics. Western Superior is also a member of the Fife Chamber of Commerce and the Better Business Bureau.

From building steel supports for numerous local hospitals, Walgreen's stores, churches and historic landmarks throughout Tacoma, to fashioning handrails, stairways and signposts, Western Superior Structurals Manufacturing, Inc. has established a reputation for on-time, high-quality subcontracting work. The company remains competitive in today's challenging construction environment by providing "21st century service at a 20th century cost."

Bratrud Middleton Insurance

A family's home tragically burns to the ground; an upstanding business gets hit with an unexpected lawsuit. No matter what the crisis, Bratrud Middleton Insurance is there to help. Superior customer service, a reputation for integrity, innovative insurance products and competitive pricing add up to "The Bratrud Advantage," which customers have relied upon since 1923, when E.O. Bratrud opened a small insurance agency in Tacoma.

Bratrud Middleton's officers provide hands-on guidance to the agency's professionals. Pictured are (left to right): Chief Financial Officer Steve Feltus, President & CEO Chuck Miller and Executive Vice President Bob Heilesen.

Bratrud's son, Omar Bratrud, inherited the business and merged it with Bjorn Tangney in the 1950s. Bratrud, Bjorn and Tangney merged with the Arthur H. Middleton Company and became Bratrud Middleton Insurance Brokers, Inc. in 1968. From this foundation, the firm has become the largest independent insurance agency in Washington.

The company's success led to strategic acquisitions and mergers with other independent agents throughout the state. Bratrud Middleton bought Blair Insurance Agency in Puyallup and Olympia Insurance Brokers in Olympia in the early 1980s. More mergers followed, expanding the company's client base throughout southwestern Washington. In addition to its corporate office in Tacoma, the company operates branch offices in eight Washington cities — Aberdeen, Auburn, Bainbridge Island, Bremerton, Longview, Olympia, Puyallup and Vancouver.

Now one of the 100 largest brokers in the nation, Bratrud Middleton provides insurance, surety bonds, advisory and other financial services to more than 40,000 individuals and businesses. Offerings include policies from the nation's top insurance carriers as rated by the A.M. Best Company, a leading insurance rating agency. Bratrud Middleton is also the largest Northwest producer of six major insurance companies and generates more than $100 million in premiums and $18 million in revenue annually.

Named one of the top "Best Practice" insurance agents in the country, Bratrud Middleton is a member of Intersure, a consortium of leading insurance agencies exchanging ideas through an international network. Member companies must demonstrate financial strength, a long and stable history and a progressive approach to client services.

For Bratrud Middleton, this progressive approach means working in partnership with customers to develop an insurance package to fit their unique coverage requirements. The company's philosophy is to know its communities and to know and serve customers well. According to President and CEO Chuck Miller, Bratrud's only goal is superior customer service, rather than growth for the sake of growth.

Miller believes the company's success is a natural result of "being better." Strong relationships with many of the finest and most respected insurance carriers in the industry give clients a competitive edge in the insurance marketplace. Due to Bratrud's considerable leverage with insurance companies, clients receive prompt and preferential treatment.

Ultimately, customers decide if Bratrud is performing to their standards. Statistics show that customers trust Bratrud Middleton. In Pierce County, for example, the agency writes a majority of all contractors' insurance. Bratrud Middleton keeps apprised of legislative, contractual and coverage changes so clients are well informed and "ahead of the game." Due to its premier position with over 20 of the largest sureties in the nation, Bratrud can secure the bonding needs for construction, banking, court, fiduciary or any other risk.

Vice President and Personal Lines Manager Sue Knobeloch (right) meets with customer Terese Grady Moon to review her personal insurance package.

Bratrud Middleton's success is also based on its ability to attract the best aggressive talent — individuals who view themselves as the future of the firm. Each professional joins Bratrud only after developing a successful track record in the industry. With experience in management, loss prevention and control, underwriting, finance and other services, new members of the team bring in-depth understanding of commercial and individual coverage needs. Professionals then use their risk management expertise to evaluate and modify insurance to take advantage of cost-containment programs such as self-insurance and assumption of risk.

As owner/shareholders, branch managers remain committed to the company and maintain close ties with their respective communities. Miller states that Bratrud's intent is to "give back to the communities that have been so good to us." Bratrud gives back by generously supporting organizations throughout the region, including the Independent Insurance Agents and Brokers, Professional Insurance Agents, Associated General Contractors, Home Builders Association, Rotary, Boys and Girls Clubs, and the American Heart Association. Bratrud volunteers dedicate their time to the March of Dimes Walk America, Salvation Army, the Battered Women's Shelter, Northwest Harvest, American Cancer Society, Junior Achievement and many others.

From several locations throughout southwest Washington — including its corporate office on 19th Street — Bratrud Middleton offers a broad spectrum of coverage choices that can be customized for any business or individual.

Community involvement, quality service, competitive pricing, professional staff, value-added services, custom-tailored programs and national recognition all add up to "The Bratrud Advantage," which customers have come to depend on. Still, Miller says, "Simply put, 'The Bratrud Advantage' is our people."

Davies Pearson, P.C.

The founders of Davies Pearson, P.C. made a deliberate decision to establish their new law firm in Tacoma more than half a century ago because they saw a community with both heritage and a destiny. The services they offered the community then are still available today, yet the firm also reflects the progressive nature of the individuals who are its core. The staff of Davies Pearson values the firm's role in the vital future of the community.

Claude Pearson and Alvin Anderson established a law office in downtown Tacoma in 1949, doing primarily insurance defense work. Claude's brother Vernon joined them in 1950. With determination and a growing network of school and military friends who contributed to their talents and drive, the firm soon established itself as a reliable name in the community. Jim Davies, a Seattle attorney, joined forces with the growing firm in the early 50s, and over the years other attorneys contributed their names and skills to expand the business. Davies Pearson was incorporated in 1972, and today 20 attorneys practice together with a staff of 30 employees. Each attorney was chosen for his or her own strengths, and thus the promise of the original founders, to provide individual attention to each client's needs, is fulfilled.

Known for its longevity and approachability, Davies Pearson, P.C. has a solid reputation as a forward-thinking law firm. Its attorneys practice in fields as diverse as mergers, acquisitions, real estate, probate, estate planning, medical malpractice, family law, personal injury (both plaintiff and defense) and employment law. Because the firm is big enough to handle larger clients, referrals come from other attorneys in neighboring counties and from across the state. With its substantial size and multiple talents, the firm can handle clients' needs throughout the country.

Continuous technological innovations are changing the practice of law, and Davies Pearson, P.C. regularly incorporates new methods to serve its clients. Interactive displays and laptops may be used in a courtroom to provide quick access and sharing of information, and the firm's Web site allows prospective clients to quickly evaluate the variety of services offered. Clients can gather information from the Internet about situations similar to their own, and recognize more fully that they can participate in resolving legal issues. This mindset empowers clients to work more closely with their attorneys, who find that educating a client about the law is a necessary and valuable component of each case. Attorneys at the firm appreciate their clients' awareness and involvement, since open and honest communication is central to a healthy client-attorney relationship.

It is important as well that clients understand the concept that law can be a living force. Law practice involves studying established precedents to anticipate future rulings, and thus attorneys at Davies Pearson find some of their most interesting work in the realm of the unknown. A client who develops software, for example, may need legal help to define business responsibilities and limitations about private communications; yet, because the field of intellectual property undergoes constant change, there are

Davies Pearson, P.C. represents stability in all legal matters.

no clear laws to support potential issues or challenges. The attorney's job involves providing advice about the best options for a developing business.

The landmark federal courthouse in downtown Tacoma

Even a brief conversation with an attorney from Davies Pearson, P.C. reveals the passion for the law that drives a successful firm. Attorneys must know the law, know the current needs of their clients, and anticipate the future needs of the community as well. The practice of law must be rooted in principle, yet must also be flexible enough to recognize analogous patterns so that future questions, as yet unimagined, will be given a balanced legal perspective.

Davies Pearson, P.C. recruits top attorneys and encourages them to make their homes in the Tacoma area. Many members of the staff have a solid record of longevity in the firm and know their neighbors and the needs of the community well. Their service to greater Tacoma has often extended beyond the law offices. Attorneys have served on the board of Tacoma Community College and as leaders of the Lions, Kiwanis and other service clubs, the Pierce County Bar Association and many other community organizations. In a notable example of the firm's quality staff, one of its founding members, Vernon Pearson, was appointed to the Washington State Court of Appeals, Division II, in Tacoma, and later served on the state Supreme Court. The individual members' variety of public service exemplifies the standards of the firm, to serve the community in more than just a business capacity.

Longtime citizens of Tacoma remember with Davies Pearson, P.C. how many changes and challenges the city has faced. The last decade of the 20th century has shown the city's capacity to create its own renaissance, with the rebuilding of the downtown core and the addition of centrally located corporate and educational facilities. The growth of the City of Destiny promises to continue, thanks to its affordability and central location. Davies Pearson, P.C. can see that future growth, including the expansion of sophisticated technology firms, will have a continuing need for a variety of legal services, and is poised to grow with those businesses.

Davies Pearson, P.C. believes in the future of the City of Destiny.

Frank Russell Company

From its headquarters overlooking Commencement Bay in downtown Tacoma, Frank Russell Company pursues its mission to improve financial security for people worldwide — an undertaking that has helped the company become a globally successful investment services firm.

Russell specializes in offering goal-oriented investors a full range of tailored solutions. A leader in global investment strategy, Russell advises clients on more than $1 trillion in assets and delivers investment programs to more than 1,000 clients in 40 countries. Russell manages $66 billion in assets in a variety of manager-of-manager funds, including mutual funds, retirement plans, commingled institutional funds and private accounts. Now in its sixth decade of operation, Russell also enjoys a global reputation for the quality of its money-manager research, multimanager investment funds and industry-leading performance measurements such as the Russell 2000® Index.

Frank Russell Company's Chairman George Russell and President and Chief Executive Officer Mike Phillips

Russell provides full-range investment services to retirement plans, foundations, endowments and investment plans of all types. Clients include the pension plans of global corporations such as AT&T, Hitachi, BHP and General Motors. More than 40 million individual investors have access to Russell's services through a network of alliances that includes many of the world's top banks, brokers, insurance companies and independent investment advisors. In the United States, these services are provided through A.G. Edwards, the country's sixth-largest brokerage firm, and Northwestern Mutual, one of the world's largest life insurance companies, and many others.

In January 1999 Russell became a subsidiary of Northwestern Mutual but retained its name, management, office locations, staffing and investment approach. In addition to its corporate headquarters in Tacoma, the company has major offices in New York, Toronto, London, Singapore, Paris, Sydney, Auckland and Tokyo.

The firm began in 1936 when Frank Russell left his Wall Street career and opened an office in his hometown of Tacoma. In 1958, upon graduation from Harvard Business School, George F. Russell Jr. joined his grandfather's company. Upon his grandfather's death a short time later, George took over the company and became its first president. He has been the visionary behind Frank Russell Company ever since and is responsible for the company's global expansion.

Currently, Russell employs more than 1,300 associates worldwide, including 950 people in Tacoma. During the past decade, the number of Russell jobs in Tacoma has increased 70 percent.

Many of the firm's client relationships span decades. For example, J.C. Penney, Russell's first institutional client, has retained Russell continuously for more than 30 years. Since then, Russell's global institutional client base has grown to include half of the largest U.S. corporate pension funds and four of the five largest retirement plans in Japan.

Branching Out to "Full Service"

In 1980 Russell expanded its offerings from investment advice to include a full range of investment services, including mutual funds and products for retirement plans. Russell's clientele, traditionally Fortune 500 corporations, was broadened to include investors of all sizes. Through independent financial professionals and strategic alliances, individual investors with as little as $5,000 now have access to Russell's investment approach.

Russell offers a complete range of investment services for individuals, retirement plans, foundations,

Frank Russell Company's corporate headquarters in Tacoma, Washington, offers a spectacular view of 14,410-foot Mount Rainier.

endowments and other organizations. In addition, the company provides specialized brokerage, private equity and real estate services to institutional and private investors.

A Culture of Strong Values

Russell built its business reputation on a corporate philosophy of unbending integrity and a complete commitment to the company's employees. CEO Mike Phillips and Chairman George Russell believe Russell associates are the firm's most valuable assets. They take special care of their employees who, in turn, take special care of Russell's clients.

This devotion to associates and clients has earned the company national recognition. In 1999 and 2000, *Fortune* magazine ranked Russell 13th on its annual list of "100 Best Companies to Work for in America" — currently the highest ranking among all Pacific Northwest companies. The company has garnered other accolades in recent years as well, such as the 2000 City of Destiny Award from the city of Tacoma and the 2000 Pacific Northwest Philanthropy Award in the Outstanding Corporation category.

Russell associates enjoy extensive employee benefits, which include tuition reimbursement, profit sharing and paid time off for community volunteerism. To further build morale and reward years of service, the company provides employees with a two-month paid sabbatical after 10 years of employment. This year, Russell also broke new ground in the compensation arena when it rolled out a cutting-edge equity ownership program that includes every associate, both full-time and part-time, around the globe.

Camaraderie among staff members is strengthened by the many social events the company sponsors. Frank Russell picnics are often spirited events, involving several hundred associates and their families. The annual picnic has been held at Cheney Stadium and, most recently, at the Puyallup Fairgrounds.

Commitment to Community

Russell is also committed to improving the quality of life in every community in which it does business. Much like the company's business objectives, Russell's philanthropic efforts aim for maximum impact. For example, Russell is a leading supporter of United Way of Pierce County, raising more than $300,000 in employee contributions this past year.

Russell associates contribute nearly 30,000 volunteer hours each year, approximately 25 hours per employee, to their favorite organizations. The company encourages participation by allowing associates to support community-related programs during part of their work week. Some 100 Russell associates donate time each week to serve as tutors in local schools.

Russell is especially committed to building community vitality through the arts. The company has a long history of financial backing for theater and other fine arts programs. Russell also is involved with development of Tacoma's Glass Museum. The facility opened in 2001 and showcases the work of renowned glass artists from around the world. The $57 million project features a multimillion-dollar pedestrian bridge constructed by international glass artist Dale Chihuly, creating a striking new entrance to downtown Tacoma.

Whether it's spearheading advancements in the investment industry or focusing on increasing the community's quality of life, Frank Russell Company has a steadfast dedication to improving lives in both the workplace and the community.

Pilkey-Hopping & Ekberg, Inc.

Buying insurance is an invisible and sometimes uncomfortable necessity. An individual maintains coverage on the premise that it won't be needed, that there will be no house fire or car accident. However, dealing with an insurance firm whose record demonstrates reliable service and integrity makes insurance decisions easier, and when the company has a century of experience behind it, as does Pilkey-Hopping & Ekberg, Inc., it's no surprise that clients come back.

Steve Ekberg, president of Pilkey-Hopping & Ekberg, Inc., has grown up in the insurance business. His grandfather, Frank, established the Frank Ekberg & Company Insurance Agency in 1896 after first working in Tacoma as a police officer. Frank's son, Dave, joined the business in 1940, remaining involved until 1997. In 1902 W.P. Hopping & Company also began offering protection to the citizens of Tacoma and later became Pilkey-Hopping Insurance. In 1979 the firms merged, benefiting from Don Pilkey's four decades of insurance experience, and became known as Pilkey-Hopping & Ekberg, Inc. Now, under the leadership of Steve Ekberg, the company offers a full line of personal, commercial and professional insurance. The firm is the oldest family-owned-and-operated insurance brokerage in the area and serves third- and fourth-generation customers. In Steve Ekberg's eyes, his grandfather's service to the community as a police officer was a good foundation for the coverage now offered by the insurance brokerage.

Frank Ekberg in 1895

Steve Ekberg is quick to praise the employees, who have their own specialties, perhaps in estate planning, or tailoring medical coverage for businesses, as well as property and casualty coverage. The office has little turnover; every employee has been with the brokerage for at least 10 years and several are approaching a 20-year anniversary. Flexible hours, job-sharing and a sense of partnership translate into company loyalty. Clients benefit from this, since they can deal with the same staff member consistently and can rely on being offered the best insurance coverage available.

Pilkey-Hopping & Ekberg, Inc. does more than keep its customers. Staff members take leadership roles in the local community. Don Pilkey served as chairman of the local United Way, and Steve Ekberg is an 18-year city council member in the small neighboring town of Gig Harbor. Both men have provided leadership in industry organizations over the years. Some staff members are involved with Boy Scouts, others as youth sports coaches, and many work to support various nonprofit organizations. Families of staff as well as customers are valued; new babies might spend time in the office if day-care arrangements fail, and children freely pop into Steve Ekberg's office once they know which file drawer has all the toys.

Any business that lasts over a century must be flexible. This certainly describes the individuals at this insurance brokerage, who are committed to the growth and stability of the region. They listen to their clients' needs, knowing that lifestyles continually undergo change, and that new developments constantly occur in industry, manufacturing and business as well. Pilkey-Hopping & Ekberg, Inc. works to anticipate these new demands and finds responsible ways to protect each client.

Port of Tacoma

Not even an elated F.H. Pettit could have envisioned such a robust future on that historic afternoon in 1918 when the Port of Tacoma was first formed.

After two failed elections, voters from Pierce County finally threw their support behind the construction of the port. At the time, Pettit, who'd become the port's first commissioner, sold voters on the idea that a port would help farmers sell their crops. He couldn't have known that the harbor would one day grow into North America's sixth-largest container port.

The Port of Tacoma's Sitcum Waterway is a hub of maritime transportation activity.

Washington United Terminals at the Port of Tacoma — Hyundai Merchant Marine's home on Puget Sound

The port's success hinges on its access to water, rails and roads. Today more than 70 percent of the cargo that moves through the harbor originates in, or is bound for, markets outside the Pacific Northwest. Imported televisions, cars and clothing that are headed for Salt Lake City, Denver and Chicago enter into the United States in Tacoma. Machinery made in Milwaukee and Detroit passes through the port on the way to Japan and China. The port, which operates on 2,500 acres of tidal property, is an important link to cities around the world.

The Port of Tacoma's North Intermodal Rail Yard, built in 1981, was the first modern on-dock rail facility for containers on the West Coast. This rail yard helped boost the number of containers handled by the port by nearly tenfold in the 1980s. More than 35 trains now move through the harbor each week and more than 1,820 move through in a year.

The port's ambitious five-year, $300 million expansion plan that began in 1999 is helping enhance transportation links. The port plans to invest $54 million to expand and improve the road and rail network, building numerous overpasses to improve truck and train access.

Also in Tacoma's future are the massive 1,138-foot container ships that carry as many as 6,600 20-foot containers, which is 50 percent more than what most container ships carry. The enormous *Regina Maersk* made its first visit to Tacoma in September 1999. To increase this large container ship business, the port needs longer piers, deeper waterways, larger cranes, longer trains, more trucks and additional back-up acreage.

Four of the world's largest container shipping lines currently call at the Port of Tacoma, and there's room for more. The port has 300-plus acres of land that can be developed or redeveloped for container terminal operations. For the first time in the existence of the harbor, wood products were not among its top five exports in 1999. Machinery ($.43 billion), meat ($.37 billion), grain ($.35 billion), plastics ($.27 billion) and auto parts ($.27 billion) were the top five exports. Electrical equipment ($2.52 billion) was the leading import that year, and Japan ($7.26 billion) and Alaska ($3.48 billion) were the top trading partners. The value of two-way trade with China, Tacoma's fastest-growing trading partner, increased by almost $500 million in 1999.

Just as in the days when Pettit watched local farmers bring their crops to be shipped, the Port of Tacoma continues to play a vital role in today's economy and will remain as the city's gateway to the world for generations to come.

Totem Ocean Trailer Express

On September 10, 1975, the 790-foot ship *Great Land* set sail on her maiden voyage from Seattle, Washington, to Anchorage, Alaska — the first such trip for the newly formed Totem Ocean Trailer Express (TOTE). Formed as a means of bringing the world to Alaska, TOTE now operates three ships and makes regular journeys, bringing necessary goods to "The Last Frontier."

TOTE began as the brainchild of Paul Atkinson, then president of Sun Shipbuilding of Pennsylvania. Sun Ship already operated a successful shipping run from the East Coast to Puerto Rico, so an expansion of that business to Alaska seemed natural, particularly as the construction of the Alaskan pipeline meant a significant increase in the materials being sent northward. *Great Land* wasn't like other ships that delivered goods to Alaska, as it was a roll-on/roll-off vessel that had been developed for use by the military. Instead of hauling goods in crates and other containers that had to be loaded and unloaded, *Great Land* hauled semi trailers that could be driven on and off easily and quickly. Cargo such as steel beams or giant machinery that didn't fit into containers could be carried much more conveniently on a trailership. TOTE's method of delivering goods was considerably faster, making TOTE competitive even after the pipeline project was completed.

In June 1976 TOTE moved its Seattle base of operations down to Tacoma where dockworkers had been specially trained in the techniques of loading and unloading trailerships. Two more ships were added: *Westward Venture* in 1977 and *Northern Lights* in 1991. In 1982 TOTE's then-president, Robert B. McMillen, along with a group of Pacific Northwest businessmen, bought the company from Sun Oil, and TOTE has been locally owned ever since. In 1984 the Port of Tacoma moved the company to a larger, state-of-the-art $10 million terminal facility on the Blair Waterway. With the addition of "hustlers," machines that push trailers on board, TOTE was able to reduce the turn-around time needed to unload and load a ship in port to 10 to 15 hours. Good relations with unions and highly skilled workers keep TOTE afloat.

Since 1975 TOTE's ships have carried nearly everything: perishable goods, military vehicles and helicopters, construction materials, department store merchandise, cars, zoo animals, even parts of the Alaskan pipeline. Private individuals can haul recreational vehicles, eliminating the 2,400-mile drive from Alaska to the continental United States. And from May to September, TOTE ships will even carry passengers who bid for one-way passage in the owner's stateroom — money from the auctions goes to charities.

Northern Lights is tugged in as the sun sets over the Olympic Mountains. *Photo by Davelle Halliburton*

Totem Ocean Trailer Express was never expected to succeed. Detractors predicted the company would fail as soon as the Alaskan pipeline was completed. On the contrary, TOTE is thriving. Two new ships are scheduled to replace the existing three vessels, and these Orca-class ships are nearly 40 feet longer and 20 feet wider, allowing them to carry more than the current capacity of 380 40-foot trailers. Watertight holds will protect 75 percent of the cargo from the elements. With all this continuing success and growth, TOTE looks forward to many more years of smooth sailing.

General Plastics Manufacturing Company

General Plastics was founded by L. W. Schatz in 1941, and has been a pioneer and innovator in the plastics industry for six decades. The Company has experienced steady growth in producing specialized plastics materials and parts. It serves many manufacturing industries, including aircraft, defense, nuclear, marine, construction, environmental graphics and others as well. Now over 130 skilled professionals work at General Plastics' Tacoma production facility, where for six decades workers have built an excellent reputation for supplying exceptional products to demanding customers.

The Leadership Team of General Plastics with over 160 years of collective experience providing a broad range of products for exacting customer specifications.

There have been a number of "firsts" in General Plastics' 60-year history. General Plastics entered the plastics industry in 1941, producing preservative coatings. During World War II business expanded to include phenolic-resin plastic laminates, the first materials in what is now known as "the composites industry." These plastics were sold into aircraft and consumer-products markets. Also during the 1940's, the Company made acrylic plastics (Plexiglas®) into aircraft windows and commercial signs, another "new" plastics product industry.

In the 1950's, in a decision critical to future success, prime mover L.W. Schatz pursued new polymer technology, pioneering development of a family of rigid and flexible polyurethane foam products. Coining the trade name LAST-A-FOAM®, General Plastics formulated polyurethane foams with a wide range of physical properties for many applications. Addressing market needs, flexible polyurethane foams were made for cushions, pads and mattresses, with rigid foams for light-weight floatation and improved thermal insulation.

Through the 1950's and into the 1960's, increasing demand for strong, light weight plastics with greater fire safety provided General Plastics opportunities to develop unique LAST-A-FOAM® materials for nascent aircraft interior applications accompanying the dawn of the Jet Age. A new flame-resistant, high-density LAST-A-FOAM® became the preferred replacement material for spruce wood-cores used in aircraft passenger compartment composite "sandwich" panels.

Ongoing research and development supports a substantial technology based business at General Plastics, maintaining its market leadership. Additionally, a top-rank Quality Assurance program permeates General Plastics' operations. Approved by several aerospace companies and the U.S. Department of Defense and Nuclear Regulatory Commission, this technology-quality combination enables General Plastics to forge long-term partnerships with aircraft/aerospace industry giants including The Boeing Company and Lockheed Martin.

Beginning in the 1970's, General Plastics supplied flexible foam for protecting missiles in underground silos and in nuclear submarines. These unrivaled LAST-A-FOAM® products, with specially engineered cushioning properties, efficiently absorb great amounts of impact energy at controlled rates, protecting missile payloads from damage. General Plastics is a sole-source supplier in these applications, with an outstanding record for quality and on-time delivery.

Also during the 1970's the Company adapted rigid LAST-A-FOAM® for protection of radioactive materials in transport containers. Should an accident occur during shipment, LAST-A-FOAM® installed between a transport container's inner and outer shells allows the payload to withstand impact damage, insulating it from heat in potential fires. This reduces the risk of hazardous substances being released into the environment.

Expanding its LAST-A-FOAM® capability, General Plastics manufactured improved core materials used in mass-market, high-technology consumer products like K-2 Corporation skis, as well as in snowboards, water skis, and surf boards. LAST-A-FOAM® also works as structural core material in portable dance floors and in "sports flooring" used over ice rinks (as in the Tacoma Dome).

In the late 1980's General Plastics introduced SIGN-FOAM® now the worldwide standard for durable and "environmentally friendly" alternatives to redwood and cedar for making outdoor signs. SIGN-FOAM® is easily crafted into final form. When painted, SIGN-FOAM® signs show outstanding weather resistance while maintaining eye-catching appeal.

Another LAST-A-FOAM® product, PRUF-STOK®, is used widely in the pattern, model and prototyping industry to replace wood. PRUF-STOK® is compatible with CNC-machine processes and tooling resins, providing labor and material savings.

Boat building applications for LAST-A-FOAM® comprise core materials in recreational watercraft and yachts, where it is used in laminated fiberglass composite structures in decks, hulls and transoms.

Over the last 30 years, construction industry use of LAST-A-FOAM® grew extensively. Applications include high-strength insulated supports for roof-columns in frozen-food warehouses and for liquid transmission lines like the Alaska oil pipeline project.

In 1987 L.W. Schatz, now Chairman of the Board, appointed his son, Henry, as Company President. Henry has maintained his father's conservative business philosophy, creating an efficient operation with low overhead and developing a strong, reasoned doctrine to support carefully managed growth.

Henry Schatz states, "We attract and retain customers by providing the best value in our distinctive LAST-A-FOAM® products and fabricated parts. Inherent in our mission is maintaining excellence in General Plastics' chosen markets and keeping focus on customer expectations while recognizing employee needs for rewarding and fulfilling careers."

Commitment to quality and service is the cornerstone of General Plastics' philosophy. Extensive testing facilities and equipment, plus years of experience, assure product quality and performance.

Pursuit of these ideals has resulted in accolades from several customers. In 1990, General Plastics won the prestigious Small Business Sub-contractor of the Year award from the U.S. Small Business Administration (SBA) for the Northwest Region. "The Company was eligible for this SBA Award because of the fine job done by the workers of General Plastics," says Henry Schatz. "Everyone here is dedicated to producing high-quality products for each of our customers."

The Company was recognized again in 1991 for becoming the first certified zero-defect "Just-In-Time" supplier to Boeing for on-time product delivery. For this, General Plastics received the Boeing Commercial Airplane Company's President's Award.

"General Plastics has remained strong and healthy through 60 years of economic cycles by identifying new markets and developing innovative products to serve them," says Henry Schatz. General Plastics expects to continue its 60-year tradition of manufacturing excellence for many years into the future.

General Plastics Manufacturing Company's 140,000 square foot manufacturing facility located in South Tacoma. Technology, quality and service form the foundation of General Plastics' successful 60-year history.

Milgard Manufacturing, Inc.

Puget Sound is famous for its gray days, but locals know that other days, summer and winter, often provide spectacular blue skies and sunshine. Due to great variations in weather and because of so many breathtaking views, good windows, both in businesses and homes, are essential. Milgard Manufacturing, Inc. knows the importance of reliable windows, and for nearly 40 years it has provided the West with the highest-quality windows available and the service to go with them.

Maurice Milgard and his son, Gary, established a glass shop in Tacoma in 1958 and soon added a line of aluminum windows to their business. Working within the industry gave Gary the entrepreneurial spark to start a business of his own, and he founded Milgard Manufacturing in 1962. A few years later Gary's brother, Jim Milgard, joined the company, and under the leadership of the two men, Milgard has grown steadily each decade since. Although its corporate headquarters remains in Tacoma, 14 Milgard manufacturing facilities now produce top-quality windows in Washington as well as in Oregon, California, Colorado, Nevada, Illinois, Utah and Arizona. The family-owned company now has over 3,300 employees across the country. Yet the firm enjoys many benefits of a small business, and Gary Milgard knows many of the 800 employees at the Tacoma facilities by name.

Milgard windows can be found in many buildings on the University of Puget Sound campus.

In the late 70s Milgard Manufacturing was one of the first window companies in the United States to offer vinyl windows, and today vinyl continues to be its most popular product line. Each window is custom-made to the buyer's specifications, and homes and businesses all over Puget Sound incorporate the latest window technology, with Milgard's help, during remodeling or renovation. Regular product testing ensures that each window meets the highest possible standards for durability and insulation value. Milgard is unique in the industry for its lifetime guarantee on its windows, which includes parts and labor. For this reason the firm expands into new territory only when it knows its high standards of service can be maintained. Gary and Jim Milgard would rather be known for producing the best, not the most, windows, and they regulate company growth with that standard as a guide.

Another feature that sets this business apart is its sister company, Milgard Vinyl Extrusions. Most window companies purchase window components that have been formed elsewhere, but with its own extrusion facilities Milgard can control the quality of each component in the vinyl. Another branch of the company, Milgard Tempering, includes divisions in Tacoma and Dixon, California, and supplies architectural glass that has been used in buildings from Hong Kong to New York. Milgard Tempering provides such niche items as NBA backboards, while families benefit more directly, knowing that their Milgard patio doors are tempered for safety.

Although vinyl windows form the greater part of Milgard's production, the company also offers a product called WoodClad™ that combines the durability of fiberglass with the beauty and versatility of wood. Newly developing technology involves fiberglass and promises home and business owners even greater choices and better tolerance for regional temperature extremes. Such progress is possible in part because Milgard's own lab maintains high research and testing standards.

Employees describe Milgard as an exciting place to work, where they are encouraged, challenged and respected for their contributions. Ongoing training programs to keep employees current with the best manufacturing, marketing and sales approaches help each employee develop his or her own skills. This respect for each employee's talents is reflected in the company philosophy. Displayed on signs in every work area, the philosophy consists of three parts: respect for the individual, the best service possible for the customer, and consistent pursuit of excellence and superior performance.

Unique windows are an integral part of architectural creativity.

The results of this philosophy are apparent in the longevity of many Milgard employees, many of whom have more than 20 years with the company, and in the numerous awards the window manufacturer has earned. Milgard was selected by *Builder Magazine* readers as the producer of the "Highest Quality Vinyl Window in the Nation" in 1998, 1999, 2000 and 2001. The company is ranked as one of the top three manufacturers, by volume, of vinyl windows in North America. For Gary Milgard the acknowledgment of superior quality is more important than volume; he wants every customer to have the best window possible.

Quality and service are at the core of the firm's philosophy and extend throughout each community where Milgard has a facility. Employees are the driving force in established and responsive community action teams in each of the 14 sales offices, which assume responsibility for service programs suited to that particular community. Regular visits from staff and family from the home office in Tacoma assist each action team as they determine local needs and projects. Friendly competition between sales offices is fostered during these visits, but even more important is the development of a sense of shared community. Thus employees enjoy many activities that also benefit their communities. Projects range widely in scope and purpose. A recent golf tournament raised $25,000 for the Make-a-Wish Foundation, which in the past has benefited from other Milgard fund-raisers. Tacoma's Festival of Trees, the Salvation Army, and litter pick-ups are other examples of Milgard's varied service. Donations to area food banks foster the community involvement that is at the heart of each action team. Milgard's payroll and its giving employees contribute daily to the vital economy of greater Tacoma.

Milgard Manufacturing, Inc. intends continued expansion into new markets. Its unique business plan, combining a high standard of service with top-quality products, means deliberate and thorough planning so that each new market will be well served from the outset. This standard of quality originates with the dynamic Milgard family at home in Tacoma.

Q-Media Services

By listening to the advice of his son, Brian Dammeier watched his small family-owned print shop grow into Washington's third-largest commercial printer and the state's largest turnkey business.

During the software industry's boom of the early 1990s, the Dammeiers took a close look at a changing market. They saw a buffet-like industry where computer companies had to pick from a variety of businesses, going to one supplier to have manuals printed, another to have floppy disks duplicated and yet another to package disks and manuals. Kurt Dammeier, then the company's 34-year-old sales and marketing manager, went to his father in 1991 with a plan to merge all those steps under one roof.

It was an agonizing decision for Brian Dammeier. The choice was to continue to run the commercial print shop traditionally, as his father had since opening it in 1902 when the company was known as Dammeier Printing. He could expect annual growth of 10 percent. Or he could risk it all, betting on new but chancy technology, which would result in enormous returns or huge losses. The elder Dammeier listened to his son and the dice were rolled.

Almost overnight, Brian Dammeier saw the family-owned company that employed only six when he joined it in 1959 grow into a major player in the publishing and turnkey industries, employing 500 by the end of 2000. Just seven years after making that risky decision, the Dammeiers sold the business to Quebecor, and today it is owned by Q-Media Services Corporation.

The expansion into high-tech publishing was a risky venture for the Dammeiers, requiring an $8 million investment in equipment and building expansion. It was then that the Six Sigma portion of the company was built in 1991, giving the Dammeiers the ability to duplicate floppy disks and replicate CD-ROMs for the first time. The payoff was immediate. Sales ballooned from $18 million in 1991 to $41 million in 1992 as it was the area's only compact disc mastering and replicating plant. It's a success story based on insight and foresight. Rather

A Technician works on fully automated CD-ROM replicators, which are housed in a clean-room environment that is sterile and dust-free

than printing manuals that would eventually be written on discs, the Dammeiers took the giant leap forward and became the one-stop shop for their computer clients like Microsoft and Gateway.

At that point, CD-ROM technology was only 10 years old and not yet even a modest threat to traditional paper documents. The industry was just coming of age and the Dammeiers were quick in recognizing the change.

In 1984 a boom in business allowed the Dammeiers to relocate from an old plant in downtown Tacoma to Fife, enabling the family to double its manufacturing space to 38,000 square feet. Just three years later, $2.2 million were spent to modernize equipment and another $1 million went toward expansion of the plant to 65,000 square feet. Within six years this once sleepy company was among the largest publishers in the country.

When Print Northwest started the Six Sigma portion of its company, a separate 60,000-square-foot facility was built to house Six Sigma, putting Print NW/Six Sigma on the information highway. In the next four years, the business soared, with its employment jumping from 132 to 450 to become the largest employer in Fife. In 1994 the company accelerated CD-ROM production from 15,000 discs a month to 30,000. In that same year, Print NW/Six Sigma won the contract for replicating the maintenance manual for Boeing's then-new 777 jetliner. It was the first time a Boeing manual was made available on a compact disc, condensing 22,000 pages of procedures and descriptions onto one disc.

In 1993 the company changed its name from Print Northwest to Print NW/Six Sigma — a recognition that 90 percent of its growth was coming from computer work. By then, Microsoft software duplication, printing of manuals and packaging was the company's primary focus. The company grossed $57 million that year, ranking it first among U.S. printers in dollar growth and third in growth percentage. That same year, the Dammeier family sold 51 percent of its company ownership to Quebecor Printing, a Montreal-based publishing giant with 82 facilities in six countries. By 1998 the Dammeiers were no longer associated with the company, having sold out to Quebecor Printing Inc., the world's largest commercial printer.

The Fife company's biggest technological changes in the 1990s occurred in CD-ROM replication, where $1 million machines quickened the process with full automation. The company now has 10 reproduction lines for CD-ROMs, significantly increasing the company's capacity.

This company went through another change in August 2000 when Quebecor sold its software manufacturing operations in Fife and Westborough, Massachusetts, for $63 million to Q-Media Services Corporation. Q-Media provides manufacturing services for software companies. The deal between the two Canadian companies involved $59 million in cash and $4 million in stock.

Despite the enormous growth in CD-ROM replication and packaging, the Fife company•still plans to turn more attention to the printing portion of the business, doing jobs like brochures for hotels and travel guides. Additionally, Q-Media wants to stay in the forefront in the Web-based fulfillment for technology and publishing. A portion of the company will remain a traditional commercial printer, employing nearly 300 in printing alone.

Besides its employment impact, Q-Media also has an impact on local charities. Each year, the company is involved in United Way fund-raisers and also donates printing jobs for businesses involved in charity projects. The current company owners pledge to continue that community involvement.

Since the Dammeiers first opened their print shop in Tacoma in 1902, the business has undergone many changes, going from what was once the new technique of "hot type" to a whole new world of "information distribution." Its printing presses have been running for 100 years. While Q-Media stays in step with advancements in technology, it remains a link between the past and future as it begins another century.

Brian Dammeier and son, Kurt Dammeier, saw their family-owned business grow into a high-tech publishing company.

Simpson Tacoma Kraft Company and Simpson Timber Company's Commencement Bay Operations

Simpson Tacoma Kraft Company and Simpson Timber Company's Commencement Bay Operations trace their roots back to 1890, when Sol G. Simpson formed S.G. Simpson Company in Matlock, Washington. By practicing sustainable forestry while protecting natural resources, Simpson is now in its fifth generation of family ownership and one of the oldest continuously operating forest products companies in the Pacific Northwest.

Simpson Investment Company of Seattle, formed in 1980 as a holding company for the Simpson enterprises, established the Commencement Bay Mill Company with the purchase of the Champion International Stud Mill on the Tacoma Tideflats in 1986. In addition to upgrading existing operations, Simpson built a new, "high-tech" lumber manufacturing complex, which replaced the old mill in May 2001.

The new facility incorporates the most technologically advanced sawmill in North America, along with a high-speed planing mill and six dry kilns. It produces lumber in a variety of lengths through a computer-controlled "push-button" process. Digital scanners assess incoming logs to determine the highest yield, and then position equipment to make appropriate cuts. Employee graders find knots and natural defects that the computer can not detect. While the old mill employed 120 production workers plus staff in a 30,000-square-foot facility, the new mill covers 200,000 square feet over 75 acres and employs 150 production workers plus staff in three shifts. Employees receive ongoing training to upgrade their skills and knowledge and improve safety and productivity.

Commencement Bay Operations' log crane operators sit 90 feet up while the grapple moves stacks of logs into the infeed where they are conveyed into the sawmill.
Alan Craft Photography

Low-cost, high-recovery, environmentally responsible operations keep the company competitive in the global marketplace. A 90-foot bridge-shaped portal crane transports logs, which reduces wheeled log handling machinery, resulting in lower costs, less noise, elimination of dust caused by wheeled equipment, and effective storm water containment, control and treatment. Computer-generated operations improve the yield of solid lumber from each log, while wood residuals are chipped and delivered next door to Simpson Tacoma Kraft Company, a subsidiary of Simpson Paper Company, for its pulp and paper operation.

Simpson purchased the Tacoma Kraft Mill from Champion International in 1986. Built in 1928 by the Union Bag and Paper Company to process wood waste from the St. Paul and Tacoma Lumber Company, the mill belonged to St. Regis Paper Company until 1984, when Champion International acquired the mill. Now under Simpson Paper Company ownership, the paper and pulp mill employs over 525 men and women, including 400 union members, on a 63.5-acre site next to Commencement Bay Operations, bordering the Puyallup River and St. Paul Waterway.

Production capacity exceeds 435,000 tons of pulp annually. The paper mill manufactures unbleached kraft pulp, containerboard grades — both mottled white and natural — along with bleached and natural paper grades. These products are used in the manufacture of packaging products such as boxes for fresh produce, grocery bags and multiwall shipping sacks.

As is true for Commencement Bay Operations, Simpson Tacoma Kraft Company takes an innovative

approach to environmental conservation, voluntarily improving operations beyond the legal requirements. Odors from the plant have been reduced by 99 percent, wastewater outflow was upgraded and moved at a cost of $5 million, tidelands were cleaned and marine habitat in Commencement Bay restored. The beach and inter-tidal area in front of the mill is now filled with marine life. A new power boiler was installed in 1990, reducing particulate emissions by 50 percent. Steam plumes were eliminated and the largest smokestack removed. An upgraded bleach plant cut dioxin emissions to nondetectable levels and eliminated chlorine emissions by 90 percent.

In 1994 the mill announced a $59 million recycling project, at that time the largest capital project in Simpson's history. The new Recycle Plant allows the mill to recycle 500 tons of waste cardboard per day. The use of fewer wood chips has reduced sulfuric odor by over 65 percent and preserves natural resources. Improvements also include installation of a unique, custom-built $16 million machine called the Beloit Bel-Liner, an enhanced paper machine which produces white linerboard, a superior sheet ready to accept detailed, high-resolution graphics. All Rainier White grades, used for products such as computer boxes and wine cases, now have improved smoothness thanks to the Bel-Liner.

Simpson has received national recognition and numerous awards for its groundbreaking technology and environmental conservation efforts. Simpson Tacoma Kraft was awarded the Governor's Environmental Excellence Award in 1988 for the first tideland and habitat restoration project in the nation, and Simpson Investment Company received the Association of Washington Business Environmental Award of the decade in 2001.

Both Simpson Tacoma Kraft Company and Commencement Bay Operations employ state-of-the-art equipment and a well-educated work force to maximize value to owners, employees and the community over the long term. Staff specialists advise managers on technical and legal environmental protection requirements, and ongoing education programs keep employees informed about responsible practices in the forest and manufacturing operations.

Simpson extends its long-term view to being a good corporate citizen, donating time and money to support local and national charities and nonprofit organizations including the United Way, the American Red Cross, Pt. Defiance Zoo & Aquarium, the Bloodmobile, and the YWCA Women's Support Shelter.

Since 1992, Simpson Tacoma Kraft has sponsored a two-week internship program, where high school students participate in specific technical projects under the direction of a team leader. Students hone engineering, math and presentation skills and are exposed to many aspects of the pulp and paper mill business. As a result of the internship program, average students become high achievers and gain new enthusiasm to pursue career options that they never dreamed possible.

For over 110 years, Simpson Investment Company has been a pioneer in sustainable forestry, a practice that extends to revolutionizing the sawmill and paper processing plants, developing manufacturing processes to conserve electricity and water, and recycling both paper and wood into useful products. For Simpson Tacoma Kraft Company and Simpson Timber Company's Commencement Bay Operations, business is about preserving resources and the environment for future generations while bringing nature's bounty to millions of people around the world.

Simpson Tacoma Kraft paper machine operator controls the computer consoles that decide the paper grade and mix while carefully observing the process. Papermaking starts out with 99.5 percent water and .5 percent pulp, and ends with 5 percent water and 95 percent paper.
Alan Craft Photography

Young Chang America

Far from the busy environs of Lakewood, Washington, one company rose from humble origins in South Korea to spread its wings across the globe. Over the past 40 years, Young Chang America has grown to include thousands of employees in countries all over the world. Today Young Chang products can be purchased in almost 50 nations, ranging from Canada to Israel, America to China, Germany and Switzerland.

Founded in 1956, three brothers came together in Seoul, South Korea, to establish their nation's first musical instrument manufacturing facility. Jai-Young Kim, Jai-Chang Kim and Jai-Sup Kim built their fledgling company into a worldwide supplier of pianos and keyboards by making quality their highest priority. The brothers used only the finest Sitka spruce for their instruments and developed specialized metallurgical techniques that have made Young Chang pianos famous for their rich tones and beautiful styles.

Young Chang craftsmanship: a perfect harmony of art and music

Over four decades later, Young Chang America helps connect Lakewood to the international community. In 1998 Young Chang moved its American headquarters from Southern California to Lakewood, Washington, to be closer to the Tacoma lumber mill that supplies its factories with specially sculpted wood for its line of pianos. The Lakewood facility serves as the headquarters for all marketing, distribution and sales operations, and the spacious warehouse behind the corporate offices functions as one of the repair and parts facilities for the United States as well.

Young Chang recognizes the importance of high technology in the music industry. In the 1980s the company acquired Kurzweil, an East Coast firm that specialized in electronic keyboard design. Today, Young Chang's growing line of Kurzweil keyboards now represents almost half of the company's business. Using the latest forms of digital audio technology, Young Chang's electronic keyboards have attracted such artists as Billy Joel, Stevie Wonder, Pink Floyd and Manhattan Transfer. Plans for the future include a new line of home-use keyboards that have the same audio quality as the systems used by professional musicians.

New steps are also being taken to integrate Young Chang's traditional pianos with its new digital audio technology. Recently, a player piano line was released that incorporates such technology into a baby grand, allowing a wide range of tones, instrumentation and prerecorded songs to be played along with the piano itself. It is a remarkable blend of past and future, creating a versatile hybrid instrument that appeals to young and old alike.

Young Chang America has made it part of the company's mission to become involved in its new community. Since moving to Lakewood, it has provided instruments for the Tacoma Symphony, as well as pianos, keyboards and other musical supplies to local and national schools and universities. It is Young Chang's way of sharing its love of music with its neighbors.

With its future melding with its past, Young Chang America continues to grow while never losing sight of its original goals set forth four decades ago. Quality and beauty are the timeless traditions that created the perfect harmony of art and instrument Young Chang's international customers have come to appreciate.

Schneider-Simpson Sheet Metal and Blower Co., Inc.

For more than 50 years, Schneider-Simpson Sheet Metal and Blower Company has been meeting custom sheet metal needs throughout the greater Puget Sound area. Formed by Elmer Schneider as Schneider Sheet Metal in 1946, the company first operated from the heart of Tacoma's industrial district on Tacoma Avenue South, near the library, before moving to its current location on South Tacoma Way in 1954.

Schneider, a sheet metal worker at a local shipyard, earned the nickname "Yump" because he jumped over benches instead of walking around them. He applied the same enthusiasm to his growing business, and by 1951 he brought on two partners, Robert Simpson and Lynden Allbaugh, and changed the company name. All three owner-operators devoted their lives to building a respected shop that originally specialized in blowpipe work for the wood industry. Over the years, as the demand for wood-related products declined, the company evolved to become a leader in custom-designed sheet metal projects in stainless steel and aluminum.

Today Schneider-Simpson has 25 employees including estimators, union journeymen and apprentices, an office support staff and a maintenance coordinator/driver. Expertise ranges from design and fabrication to full installation in the industrial, marine, hospital, and restaurant and food industries — making and installing conveyors, chutes, hoppers, hoods, shrink-wrap guides, platforms with stairs, guards, tanks and exhaust systems. The company also performs retrofits mainly for the wood, pulp and foundry industries, which are required to update their exhaust systems in accordance with new air quality standards.

Skilled in welding, forming, shearing, rolling and punching, Schneider-Simpson's journeymen are also designers who envision and then build a finished product from a customer's general concept. Many clients come to Schneider-Simpson — where every product is made to order — because they are unable to obtain quality, custom-designed products in time anywhere else. No project is too challenging, whether it involves rolling a sheet of metal into the shape of a giant lampshade for a local artist, or fashioning stainless steel palm trees, as tall as telephone poles and adorned with four-foot long steel fronds, for a local transit station. From making stair treads or flashing for glass to shaping spiral staircases, Schneider-Simpson has built a reputation for top-notch specialized work.

Schneider-Simpson Sheet Metal has been in Tacoma for the past 54 years.

In the modern age of large, impersonal corporations, Schneider-Simpson stays small to remain creative in the marketplace, control quality, and provide fast, reliable service. The corporate philosophy is to hire good people and let them fulfill their potential in a supportive environment. The company extends this generosity to the community by giving to local charities such as the Tacoma Humane Society and Mary Bridge Children's Hospital.

As the demand for custom sheet metal products continues to change in the greater Puget Sound area, Schneider-Simpson Sheet Metal and Blower Company will evolve to meet the community's needs. Whether welding pots for restaurants or fabricating mechanical arms for egg machines, the company will continue to provide quality products with the speed and reliability that customers have come to expect.

Selden's Home Furnishings

As a 1923 graduate of Tacoma's Lincoln High School, Syd Selden worked his way up from stock boy to assistant manager of the carpet department at Schoenfeld's Furniture. In the early 1930s he left Schoenfeld's to become manager of home furnishings at People's Store. It was in April 1940 that Syd opened his own floor-covering store.

When the business began in 1940, Selden's employed five people and had a back room stocked with rolls of linoleum, window shades and carpeting. However, when World War II began, shades and linoleum became priority items. The nation's carpet mills stopped producing carpet in order to weave blankets and other wartime essentials. For nearly two years, Selden's was without any linoleum or carpet to sell to residential clients.

Careful delivery service has long been a hallmark of Selden's. Here the fleet of delivery vehicles sits in front of Selden's downtown Tacoma store, *c. 1950.*

Attentive audiences flocked to Selden's in the 1950s for shows featuring design ideas. The store continues to offer quality design services to customers.

Customers, though, were anxious to buy blackout blinds, and that was the aspect of the business that pulled the company through what could have been a tough economic time. At one point in 1942, Selden's had orders for 30,000 wartime housing shades. The company hired extra workers and ran its shade assembly operation 16 hours a day, six days a week, producing a window shade every 16 seconds.

Soon Selden's was called into work on government projects at locations around the Northwest including Fort Lewis, McChord Air Force Base, Bremerton Naval Station, Alaska and Coulee Dam. During 1944 the company delivered and installed 96 railroad carloads of asphalt tile in government buildings, becoming the West Coast's largest floor-covering outlet by volume.

Selden's also had a wartime contract with the Navy to apply battleship linoleum to the floors of 77 Liberty ships. Installation had begun on the seventh ship when orders came to remove all the floor coverings; officials had discovered the flooring was combustive under bombing conditions. Left with more than 11,000 yards of linoleum it couldn't sell without authorization, the government eventually paid Selden's for the flooring. Syd shipped the linoleum to a Seattle warehouse and then repurchased it after the war.

As the war ended, Selden's found itself adjusting its inventory to meet the needs of a changing postwar housing era. In 1957 the family decided to offer a full-service home furnishing center. It purchased Kegel's Furniture in downtown Tacoma and moved into that store's larger location at the corner of 11th and A streets. Meanwhile, Selden's opened branches in Longview, Olympia, Lakewood, Moses Lake, Kennewick, Federal Way and Alaska.

During the 1960s, control over the far-flung branch stores became exceedingly difficult. Excellent customer service requires hands-on ownership supervision. A valuable lesson was learned, leading to today's philosophy of Selden's one-stop destination home furnishings center.

In 1974 the Kegel's building was torn down and the decision was made to consolidate all operations into the Lakewood store. Just seven years later, the business had outgrown the Lakewood facility. In 1980 Selden's moved to a larger building at 27th Street West and Bridgeport Way in University Place.

The opportunity to become the nation's 15th Thomasville Furniture Gallery arose in 1984. Subsequent growth and the acquisition of key furniture lines necessitated more space and a more accessible location. The decision was made to relocate to a larger building specifically designed to meet the company's needs; in 1990 Selden's moved to its current location adjacent to Interstate 5 in Fife.

Selden's destination location was constructed in 1990. A Thomasville Home Furnishings showroom was added in 1997 and a Bassett Furniture Direct gallery was built across the street in 2000.

In 1997 the Selden family added a 36,000-square-foot Thomasville Home Furnishings showroom and entry atrium that is connected to the main store. A gourmet deli, children's play area and design work center are included.

In fall 2000, the business expanded again with the construction of a 65,000-square-foot Bassett Furniture Direct gallery and warehousing/service center facility across the street from the main Selden's store and Thomasville Gallery.

Selden's has grown from a staff of five when it first opened its doors in 1940 to more than 100 now, including salespeople, designers, and warehouse and delivery staff.

Home visits by the store's interior designers have always been part of the above-and-beyond customer service shoppers have grown to expect from Selden's. Staff designers work with customers, builders and architects to address space-planning issues and to assist with everything from selecting window coverings, flooring and cabinets, to choosing the perfect furnishings and fabrics to pull it all together. Additionally, designers use high-tech software programs to show customers what a custom sofa or chair will look like before it's ordered. The software allows customers to view countless frame and fabric options.

The Fife-based stores specialize in quality and feature furniture and accessory motifs for every lifestyle and taste, from French country and Far Eastern to contemporary and casual. In addition to Thomasville, Selden's offers many top-quality lines including Drexel-Heritage, Century, Karastan, Maitland Smith, imported handmade Medallion Rugs, Hendredon, Hekman, Hooker and Sherrill. During summer months, Selden's features a selection of patio and sunroom furniture, and children's furniture is a year-round specialty.

Selden's today is a home interiors destination providing furniture, flooring, window coverings and interior design consultation to homeowners and businesses throughout the Western United States. The store's delivery services extend nationally; Selden's has furnished homes as far away as Alaska, California and Japan.

Though Selden's provides service around the world, it remains true to its hometown roots. The company's community involvement and charitable giving is focused on education, local festivals and Tacoma-area theater and arts projects.

Now, after doing business in the Puget Sound community for more than five decades, the Selden bloodline continues to be true to Syd's vision. Son Stan is now the chairman, grandson Scott is president and general manager, and granddaughter Loni Cross is office manager.

Recent growth and prosperity have left Selden's in an enviable position as the South Puget Sound's pre-eminent home furnishings store, with offerings ranging from the high-end Drexel Heritage lines to the moderately priced Bassett Furniture Store. But none of that would matter, says Stan Selden, if the company didn't put such a high priority on excellent customer service.

As the business' mission statement says: "Selden's exists by the approval of our satisfied customers. Honesty, service and quality are every team member's responsibility and come first in everything we do."

Best Western Tacoma Inn

Nestled in a prime location just a stone's throw from downtown Tacoma, the Best Western Tacoma Inn takes great pride in offering all kinds of travelers both comfort and hospitality. With 149 rooms, two hot tubs and an outdoor pool, guests can't help but feel pampered. For 17 years, the Tacoma Inn has served as a refuge for weary business travelers, vacationing families, military personnel and even celebrities.

The Northwest Contemporary architecture style that Lonnie Wynia used when he built the Tacoma Inn in 1983 gives it a feeling of spaciousness and privacy. Owner Mike Hass, who purchased the hotel in 1985, has served as the general manager since moving from Santa Barbara in 1990. Hass maintains a staff of 75 employees who ensure that all their guests receive the personal attention they deserve.

Creature comforts abound at the Tacoma Inn. Rooms are spacious and include ironing boards, hair dryers and 27-inch televisions with free movie channels such as HBO. Many have kitchenettes, king-size beds, writing desks and private balconies. For those with special needs, there are uniquely designed rooms that provide easy wheelchair access and specially constructed shower spaces. All are offered at affordable rates. Full-menu room service is also available through the hotel's excellent restaurant, the Copperfield's. Guests can enjoy complimentary continental breakfast, a fast business lunch or a delicious steak or seafood entree for dinner. The Sunday brunch at Copperfield's has been a longstanding family tradition for many of Tacoma's residents.

The Tacoma Inn's clientele ranges from business travelers and executives to vacationers, military families, and high school and college sports teams. Well-known guests have included Marcel Marceaux, Ned Beatty, Arthur Schlesinger and even daredevil Evil Knievil. Though its guests are diverse, all come to the Tacoma Inn for the privacy it offers as well as its central location to the Tacoma area.

The inn is especially well situated for vacationing families. Located near Mount Rainier, the Olympic Peninsula and the many museums in the area, it serves as a gateway to the sites and activities throughout the Puget Sound area. The Tacoma Dome, which hosts events ranging from rock concerts to ice hockey games, is only a few minutes' drive from the hotel. The waterfront in downtown Tacoma offers fine dining year-round, plus antique and art shows during the fair-weather months. Some of the finest fishing locations in the Northwest are also within easy distance, as is Seattle and its many attractions. Tacoma also boasts numerous theater groups, parks and water recreational areas. For those who love winter sports, the ski slopes at Crystal Mountain are only a short drive away. Several Native American gaming casinos have recently opened their doors, adding to the rich variety of entertainment the area already offers.

For its business guests, the Tacoma Inn offers easy access to the many high-tech companies in the area, as well as the Port of Tacoma, which is one of the largest of its kind in the country. The Bremerton

Shipyards are an hour's drive away, as are the key firms in the Seattle area. With the area's businesses thriving, Tacoma is fast becoming one of the key commercial links in the Northwest's increasingly diverse economy.

For military personnel and their relatives, the inn is a few minutes from McChord Air Force Base and Fort Lewis. Reservists, National Guard personnel on weekend duty, and others on temporary assignments feel at home during their stays. Families of those men and women serving at the base have also found the inn to be extremely convenient.

The Tacoma Inn also plays host to large groups and organizations. Its convention facilities can seat up to 400 people for meetings and seminars, or 220 for full dinners, which the inn caters through Copperfield's. Recent events have included weddings, business seminars and special interest conventions. Not long ago, several hundred World War II aviators held a convention at the Tacoma Inn in honor of the 50th anniversary of the aircraft they flew, the Boeing B-17 Flying Fortress.

Owner Hass understands and embraces the value of new technology to his hotel and his guests. Over the past two years, he has added new computers and management programs to help streamline operations. A new satellite communications system enables guests to make reservations by calling the main Best Western toll-free number. Future plans include the use of wireless technology for the operations side of the business, as well as a pay-per-view satellite uplink system that will give guests their choice of new movies to watch from the comfort of their own rooms.

Playing a supporting role in the local community means a great deal to Hass. He especially enjoys promoting the Tacoma area through his association with the Convention & Visitors Bureau (CVB). The Tacoma Inn proudly welcomes tour and travel groups that are invited to visit the city each year by the CVB. The inn also supports local volunteer organizations, such as the Fern Hill Community Group, by giving them free access to its meeting rooms and convention hall. All together, the Tacoma Inn donates time, food, space and funds to almost 100 local charities and volunteer operations. It also takes part in yearly neighborhood clean-up programs and gives beds away to several mental health facilities.

Offering easy access to some of the best entertainment, recreational attractions and corporate operations in the region, the Tacoma Inn is truly the gateway to the "Hub of the Pacific Northwest." As tourism and business travel continue to expand in the Puget Sound area, the future looks bright for Hass and his team of dedicated employees. With its warm, personal service, its creature comforts and its business conveniences, the Tacoma Inn is well suited to provide visitors with an enjoyable, affordable experience they won't soon forget.

Holiday Inn Express Hotel & Suites

For creature comforts, a friendly smile and exemplary customer service in a home away from home, travelers need look no further than the Holiday Inn Express Hotel & Suites in Tacoma. Located just off Interstate 5 on Hosmer Street, this Holiday Inn will make customers want to return again and again, as many visitors already have done.

From the well-manicured entrance, complete with brightly colored flowers and shrubs, to the park-like atmosphere of the tranquil pond adjacent to the building, guests immediately feel at home. The Holiday Inn Express Hotel & Suites is a cheerful hotel that concentrates on all the amenities that make a big impression with visitors.

Professionalism is very important to the employees, and they try to provide each guest with a "homey" feeling during their stay. One way hotel employees invoke that homey feeling is by remembering each guest's last name. "It's one thing to address someone as sir or ma'am," says General Manager Calvin Yi. "But we've found out that it really makes a good impression if you can refer to a customer by name. Their eyes light up when you do so."

Another personalized touch at the Holiday Inn Express is the homemade cookies, baked fresh each evening. This is just another way of saying that the staff cares about its guests.

Yi also acknowledges his guests every year on Customer Appreciation Day. Recently, on March 26, 2000 — the hotel's second anniversary — the staff offered guests a free car wash plus a barbecue dinner. According to Yi, one thing the hotel constantly strives for is to exceed customers' expectations. Judging by some of the recent Holiday Inn Express guest comments, the staff appears to be accomplishing that goal.

One guest wrote that his stay was very pleasurable and that he and his family were planning to stay at the hotel again in the future. Another guest spent a holiday at the hotel. Spending Thanksgiving 1999 at the Holiday Inn Express, this traveler raved about the excellent room. He called it an extension of his family celebration and thanked the staff for an excellent holiday. This visitor also informed Yi that he stayed in the Tacoma area several times a year and would definitely return to stay again in the future. A third guest commented on the friendly and hospitable staff. The hotel was the cleanest she'd ever seen, and the continental breakfast was outstanding. The moment she walked into her guest room she was very pleasantly surprised, intimating that the room lived up to the same aesthetics that greeted her in the lobby.

When entering the Holiday Inn Express lobby area, a soothing miniature waterfall greets guests. The finely manicured furniture and stylish décor make for a warm greeting.

Likewise, guest rooms are an extension of the hotel's hospitality. Each guest room and deluxe room with whirlpool tub are beautifully designed, with numerous modern amenities. Each room comes equipped with a coffee maker, an iron and ironing board, two phone lines with a data port for personal computers and three telephones — one each on the desk, near the bed and in the bathroom. A 25-inch color television also graces every room. Pay-per-view movies are available and local faxes and telephone calls are free to guests.

To date, the hotel general manager is very pleased with the results he's garnered because of the emphasis placed on customer service. "If customers are satisfied with the service they receive, then they will probably tell two to three others about that good experience," says Yi, who became general manager nearly a year ago. "Thus, word-of-mouth advertising is probably the most important aspect of marketing our product."

Many Holiday Inn Express guests are repeat customers, with the majority on business trips. Most return because of the friendly atmosphere and customer focus exhibited by the 22 hotel employees. The continental breakfast is also quite popular.

Guests are invited to begin the day by enjoying a complimentary deluxe continental breakfast buffet. A presentation of freshly brewed coffee and a variety of foods served fresh daily is just one way the staff says "good morning" to its guests. Coffee and tea are available 24 hours a day in the lobby area. A complimentary copy of *USA Today* also awaits every guest.

In addition to the 78 guest rooms, there is also a 950-square-foot meeting room capable of handling a group meeting, reunion or weekend seminar.

For recreation, the hotel offers a heated indoor pool, whirlpool spa, sauna and fitness center. The Holiday Inn Express is the only hotel in the area that provides these services 24 hours a day. Another perk for families is that children under 18 stay for free. The company feels that offering these little extras, and offering them with a smile, provides the kind of service that customers really want.

But the hotel doesn't draw the line at excellence for its customers. In an effort to foster good relations within its community, the Holiday Inn Express participates in the Fern Community Club, which meets regularly to help improve the South End neighborhood. The group's areas of concern include safety and beautification projects as well as youth activity programs.

The Holiday Inn Express general manager has customer service down to a science, an area that he's gradually refined during his professional career. Yi graduated from the Washington State University Hotel and Restaurant Management Program several years ago, where most of the core emphasis was

placed on the technical aspects of the industry. According to Yi, customer service is a subtle aspect of the business that each manager must mold into his or her respective liking. It's also an area of the business that needs the most care and attention.

Yi explained that his staff understands that everyone is different, and everyone has a different way of looking at things. In anticipating customers' wants and needs and giving them what they want during their stay, the staff creates a memorable experience for customers, and reaps the benefits of being a productive, contributing member of the community.

Johnny's Seafood Company, Inc.

Longtime residents of Tacoma and visitors alike understand how closely tied the area's history is with its waterfront. Beautiful views, relaxing strolls and an active and thriving port are part of the Tacoma lifestyle. Just as central to the history of Tacoma is Johnny's Seafood Co., located in the heart of downtown Tacoma on the Thea Foss Waterway. In 2004 Johnny's will celebrate 50 years of providing the area with the highest-quality seafood from around the world, under the careful management of President Gary Gerontis and his partner, Vice President Robert Iverson. Although their business is now truly global, its hometown origins reveal the humble beginnings of this successful family business.

In the early 1900s, the Cologerou and Gerontis families emigrated from the same island in Greece to New York, then to Tacoma, where both raised sons named John. The two men, best friends with similar interests, decided to borrow $500 and invest their own labor and will to build a fish purveying business. They became known as Big John and Little John and soon established a reputation for high-quality fish, hard work and honesty with both their suppliers and their customers, many of whom were area restaurants. The business has continued to grow and flourish and has been a part of the waterside community on Dock Street for over 40 years, where it is sure to be an active participant in the restoration of the waterfront.

Both Big John Cologerou and Little John Gerontis, big-hearted to a fault, enjoyed a reputation for generosity, fairness, trustworthiness and integrity. They were always first to lend a hand to fellow businessmen during times of crisis. When an explosion and fire left a neighboring competitor without a shop, Johnny's gave him space in its plant so he could keep working while he got his business back on its feet. The competitor worked nights in Johnny's plant for nearly a year and was able to keep his customers supplied until he could move into his new plant.

Little John Gerontis and Big John Cologerou in the early days *News Tribune File photo/1962 Reprinted with permission from The News Tribune, Tacoma, WA.*

When another fish seller spent six months in a coma after a car accident in the 60s, Big John and Little John ran his business until he could work again. Nearly 20 years later, when this man decided to sell his business, the only offer he made was to Cologerou and Gerontis. Johnny's purchased the business and the previous owner worked part time with the company for several more years. In the same way Johnny's acquired a fish market that was established in 1932 on Ruston Way in historic Old Town Tacoma, now one of its three busy locations. Each of these business transactions was rooted in real and deep friendships that flourish today.

Although he started working at the plant when he was only 10, Little John's son Gary Gerontis still has the same kind of passion and heart that the older generation brought to their workday. His years of experience have prepared him for the many challenges that the changing industry brings. Today's environmental issues, international fishing and trade agreements and global shipping costs mean the business requires intense daily effort to remain competitive. Gerontis' partner, Iverson, contributes to the exacting high standards and quality of the company's products. The storage conditions and standards of cleanliness both in the plant and the retail stores are unquestionably the highest, consistent with the company's insistence on selling only the highest-quality fish and shellfish.

Gary Gerontis and Robert Iverson on the Thea Foss Waterway

Johnny's Seafood Co. is a respected part of the local community. It participates in many worthy activities, benefiting the community with more than a reliably fresh fish supply. Johnny's has participated in fund-raisers for Mary Bridge Children's Hospital, and many local schools and churches, such as Saint Charles Borromeo, have benefited from its participation in and donations to their many activities.

The owners know how demanding the work at Johnny's is and are proud of their employees, many of whom have been with the company for more than 20 years. One of the rewards management enjoys is visiting with some of their former employees who began as teen-agers, worked their way through college and entered professional careers. Many still return to visit the staff at the offices and plant.

The fishing industry and retail marketing, as well as consumer shopping habits, have undergone steady change during the first 50 years of business for Johnny's Seafood. Rather than become rooted in habit, the company is excited about the changes the business and the community face. A new campus with both an expanded plant and office building is in the planning stages. This will streamline its busy operations and more than triple the amount of available work and storage space. The planned building will be a part of other people-friendly development along the Thea Foss Waterway, including the International Museum of Glass. The entire area will be linked by a waterfront promenade for all to enjoy.

An Internet Web site is also under development. It will feature seafood recipes taught in cooking classes occasionally offered by Johnny's. Lifestyle changes in the modern world mean that fewer people have time to cook, and Johnny's hopes to offer its customers a unique service in the coming years. This would include prepared seafood, ready to pop on the grill or in the oven. Johnny's already ships fresh, frozen and smoked seafood to its loyal customers throughout the United States and expects to expand this part of the business through online access. Top restaurants in the area and some as far away as Hawaii continue to rely on Johnny's for fish and shellfish.

The colorful style and passion for quality the founders brought to their seafood business still enlivens the atmosphere at Johnny's. Today the owners are not only looking back but also see endless opportunities for change and growth in the future. For the next 50 years the best place in Tacoma to get fresh fish will still be Johnny's Seafood Co.

La Quinta Inn & Conference Center

Located near the heart of downtown Tacoma, the La Quinta Inn & Conference Center is known for both its warm and friendly hospitality and convenient location.

The eight-story, 158-room hotel is just an hour's drive from snow-capped Mount Rainier and a 10-minute drive from picturesque Puget Sound.

The name La Quinta Inn is Spanish for "a country home." Hospitality is something that has been stressed since the first La Quinta Inn was built in 1968. Today, the employee's manual still stresses the importance of being friendly and knowing that customer service is what La Quinta Inn is about, while providing a unique style of hospitality that the company was founded on. "We strive to exceed our guest's expectations," says James Begin, general manager of the Tacoma hotel. As part of the hotel's commitment to superior customer service, La Quinta offers a 100 percent satisfaction guarantee.

La Quinta Inn is located near Interstate 5 just five blocks from the Tacoma Dome.

Rooms were recently refurbished and now offer 25-inch televisions, dataport phones, voice mail, in-room coffee and more.

Timing its opening with the start of the 1968 World's Fair, La Quinta Inns, Inc. built its first hotel in San Antonio, Texas, just across the street from the fair that captured the world's attention. Now, 30 years later, that lone hotel built on the idea of mid-priced lodging and a unique style of hospitality has grown into a chain of 302 hotels in 28 states.

While La Quinta Inns can now be found coast-to-coast, its focus has been on the Southern states, with 100 of its hotels in Texas. In the mid-1980s, growth shifted from new construction to purchasing competitors, marking the arrival of three La Quinta Inns in Washington. The hotel came to Tacoma in 1988.

La Quinta is designed specially to appeal to all types of travelers with a variety of room choices — standard rooms, king rooms for longer stays and two-room suites for families and business travelers desiring extra space. Guests are greeted by a friendly staff and a spacious lobby with a cheerful decor and comfortable seating. Just as in 1968 when the first La Quinta opened, the business traveler remains the hotel's targeted customer. People on business trips make up 65 percent of the hotel's guests and they each average 20 visits a year.

The Tacoma hotel is the exception to the La Quinta Inn's concept. As the innovator of limited-service lodging, the chain's success is based on providing comfortable, quality accommodations at an affordable price. To achieve that, hotels were built without restaurants and meeting rooms. That helped keep costs down, as lodgers were paying only for the rent of a room, not supplementing a restaurant or convention center. But at Tacoma, the hotel offers full service at still-affordable prices. It's one of just 76 La Quinta Inns that provide full room service.

In 1994 a $120 million chainwide refurbishing began. Each of the 39,000-plus rooms in the company were recarpeted, painted and furnished with new contemporary-style furniture. The makeover included a 25-inch television in each room that provides first-run movies on demand as well as Super Nintendo video games. The Tacoma hotel's two-year, multimillion-dollar refurbishing was completed in 1998. The changes also brought computer-friendly dataport phones with voice mail and oversized desks with comfortable seating. Hair dryers, irons and ironing boards were also added.

The hotel's 6,500 square feet of conference space is available for everything from business meetings to wedding receptions.

All La Quinta Inns offer a complimentary continental breakfast, free local phone calls, in-room coffee, free HBO, card-key guest room entry, 24-hour front desk and message service, a swimming pool and hot tub. Additional guest services at the Tacoma hotel include same-day laundry and dry cleaning, room service, a fitness center, restaurant, lounge and game room.

Recognized as one of Tacoma's premier venues for meeting places, La Quinta offers a 6,500-square-foot convention center that can seat 450 people in theater and 300 in banquet seating. The convention center continues to cater to a wide spectrum of people, ranging from church groups and businesses, to military reunions and wedding receptions. Whether someone is planning a wedding for 300 or a meeting for 10, the hotel accommodates a busy schedule year-round.

Ports of Call is the hotel's popular seafood-themed restaurant.

The fitness center is one of many guest services available at La Quinta Inn.

Just five blocks from the hotel is the Tacoma Dome, the world's largest wood-dome stadium. The stadium's 16,000-seat venue is the stage for productions ranging from sporting events and business conventions to rock concerts. The Harlem Globe Trotters and the Seattle SuperSonics, as well as performers with Disney on Ice have been guests at the La Quinta Inn.

Also within a short drive are the Point Defiance Zoo and numerous museums featuring Northwest history and art. As for shopping, there is Freighthouse Square, which is a series of stores in the historic domed railroad depot just two-and-a-half miles away. People staying at the LaQuinta Inn don't have to drive far to see a part of history as it is built on what was the Puyallup Indians' reservation that overlooks Commencement Bay.

The Tacoma hotel's cuisine includes breakfast, lunch and dinner. The restaurant, Ports of Call, has a wide-variety menu with a seafood theme that includes king salmon, tiger prawns and halibut. The hotel's semiformal restaurant is also a local favorite as it's open to the community, including a Sunday brunch.

With its continual emphasis on the friendliest hotel atmosphere and the most courteous service in its market, La Quinta Inn will continue to strive to provide high-quality and comfortable accommodations at an attractive price.

National Distributing Company

As a Northwest wholesaler for Anheuser-Busch, Inc., Heineken and Corona brands, National Distributing Company provides unparalleled customer service, a superior product line and an empowering environment for employees who have always been treated as family.

National Distributing Company began in 1959 as a Washington corporation that distributed mainly Schmidt Beer and operated from a warehouse on East 25th Street in the old Milwaukee Railroad building in Tacoma. Howard Bargreen was the majority stockholder. In 1973, envisioning a long-term business opportunity, friends Bob Bennett and Herb Bain purchased the company, sharing equally in ownership of shares. National continued to operate from the warehouse with a staff of eight people including Bennett and Bain. Three years later the company moved to a South Washington Street warehouse owned by Bennett and Bain, but by the spring of 1991, National had outgrown that facility and moved to its current four-acre site on Durango Street.

Herb Bain in an article from TNT

Total sales steadily increased from $1.6 million during the fiscal year, 1973-1974, to $6.9 million for 1982-1983. During the same decade, the staff grew to 21 employees. In 1983 Herb and Betty Bain purchased Bennett's shares of the company, and Bennett purchased Herb's half of the South Washington street warehouse, which he rented to National on a 10-year lease.

Old facility on Washington Street

Doug Graf, Herb Bain's son-in-law who began working for the company as a night loader in 1975, was elected president in 1993, the same year that Herb Bain became chief executive officer. Bain's daughter worked as bookkeeper and his son was involved in the Eagle Snack side of the business. In 1994 John Walentia was hired as general manager and vice president in charge of the company's daily operations. By this time, National had 76 employees and total sales jumped to $23.5 million for a range of beer, wine coolers and nonalcoholic products.

As Anheuser-Busch outperformed other brands, National Distributing gradually closed out delivery of most other products, such as Colt 45, Ballantine's and Schmidt, as well as sodas and waters. In 1997, in keeping with a national trend toward consolidation, National Distributing Company closed out all remaining brands and packages except Heineken products and became a near-exclusive Anheuser-Busch, Inc. wholesaler.

The decision proved a sound one, as sales increased 10 percent in 1999, 13.2 percent in 2000 and continue to grow today. The company's delivery area has expanded to include Thurston, Kitsap and Mason counties and now extends from Olympia north to the Hood Canal Bridge. Sales recently jumped to second place in the five-state "Region 9," trailing only a company delivering to the Salt Lake City area.

Now with annual sales exceeding $40 million, a staff over 150 and a satellite facility in Bremerton where trucks are loaded, National Distributing Company has proven that a motivated team can carry a corporation through any hardship. Employees remain loyal, inspired by a supportive environment and generous benefits. The company provides work vehicles, clothing allowances, medical and retirement benefits, bonuses and pay for performance. It has also contributed to college funds for the children of employees, distributed turkeys at Thanksgiving and held an annual Christmas party. Long-term employees are offered the opportunity for advancement and engaging, challenging work that includes much more than distributing beer.

National markets its products, a sophisticated process that has become both an art and a science. Salespeople sell the product to customers and order displays. Merchandisers build the displays and rotate beer — which has a shelf life — and replenish supplies. Drivers maintain the accounts, working eight-to-10-hour days on a total of 38 routes to deliver products and set up the displays with help from merchandisers if necessary. Each destination on a particular route is rated for difficulty, based on factors such as accessibility — presence of stairs or hills — and leading to an estimated "time-to-sell." The driver may make eight to 11 stops in one day, a significant change from 20 years ago when a driver might have made 30 stops in a day.

No matter how many stops each driver makes, the focus remains on providing the highest level of customer service. National helps clients maximize profits and develop a plan to maintain in-stock conditions by giving additional shelf space to fast-moving products.

In addition to providing superior products and services, National Distributing Company remains committed to being an outstanding corporate citizen providing financial and material support to community organizations. The company donates funds to several charities including the United Way and The Muscular Dystrophy Association. Staff members have also served on the local Campfire Boys and Girls board. The company donates space for meetings to the local Sheriff's department and has donated a beer delivery truck to the local fire department. The truck has been painted red and converted to a rescue

New warehouse ceremony

Durango Building

unit that brings specialized equipment such as the Jaws of Life to emergencies throughout the Tacoma area.

Through its alcohol awareness program, National spends considerable time and money educating consumers about responsible alcohol consumption, an issue which is also an important focus for Anheuser-Busch, Inc. By distributing brochures and other informational materials, National increases public awareness of alcohol-related problems and provides workable solutions.

National Distributing Company remains a locally owned business that meets the beverage needs of the west Puget Sound area. With a focus on honesty, efficiency and a positive work environment, National attracts and retains employees while providing exceptional customer service. Employees not only market and deliver Anheuser-Busch, Heineken and Corona products to satisfied consumers, but they also pour their hearts and souls into building a strong, successful company and giving back to their community.

SUPERVALU INC.

From the nearly extinct general store to today's megawarehouses, consumers have long depended upon merchants to sell a variety of quality food products.

For almost 100 years, food merchants relied upon West Coast Grocery Company to supply them with everything from fresh produce and canned beverages to meats and bakery items. However, as retail demands shifted in the second half of the 20th century, West Coast Grocery saw the need for better distribution to accommodate supermarkets, warehouse superstores, and combination food and drug stores. As a result, West Coast Grocery was acquired by SUPERVALU INC. in 1985.

Those living and working in tent cities during the Yukon Gold Rush of 1897 survived largely thanks to the fact that West Coast Grocery opened a grocery store where Anchorage now stands. Miners and their families bought what they needed to survive and became big fans of West Coast Grocery's house brand of products, Amocat (Tacoma spelled backward).

SUPERVALU is a leading United States food distributor, supplying approximately 5,000 retail food stores. It's also the nation's 10th-largest food retailer with nearly 500 corporate-owned stores. The 67,000-employee company, based in the Minneapolis suburb of Eden Prairie, has seven marketing regions. The Northwest Regional Office, which services 11 states and overseas military bases, is located in Tacoma.

When SUPERVALU purchased West Coast Grocery, it bought a piece of Northwest history. Even before Fig Newtons were introduced (in 1892), the Nabisco Company baked its first cookie (1898), Pepsi Cola bottled its first soft drink (1903) and Gerber strained its first jar of baby food (1927), West Coast Grocery was in the business of supplying regional retailers with the best and freshest food available.

William J. Thompson, Charles H. Hyde and O.R. Casper founded West Coast Grocery Company in July 1891 with $75,000 capital stock; annual sales that first year were $524,000.

As West Coast Grocery grew and modernized, the world changed too. The Yukon Gold Rush in 1897 led to the construction of the Alaska railroad and the erection of a tent city where Anchorage now stands. Food and supplies were hard to come by; merchants simply hadn't yet had time to set up shop in Alaska. Those living and working in the tent city survived largely thanks to the fact that West Coast Grocery opened a grocery store there. Miners and their families bought what they needed to survive and became big fans of West Coast Grocery's house brand of products, Amocat (Tacoma spelled backward).

When others were giving up on the Tacoma area's business climate, West Coast Grocery stood true. In 1899 the company purchased a brick building along Pacific Avenue from Penn Mutual Life Insurance for the sum of $50,000. Company co-founder Charles H. Hyde wrote in his journal that an officer of the insurance company was heard to say to his agents, "Make any kind of deal you can to unload the property. Tacoma is dead and will never amount to anything — don't let him (Hyde) get away without making a sale."

Tacoma proved to be anything but dead. West Coast Grocery spent more than a half century in the downtown Pacific Avenue Building, making it a real estate transaction that company leaders still hail as astute.

World War I brought a beehive of activity to western Washington's Fort Lewis, with as many as 50,000 men stationed at the base at any given time. West Coast Grocery stepped up its business to address the need at the fort's various company mess halls. When Army-run canteens wouldn't stock soft drinks or tobacco, West Coast Grocery made them available in a store directly across the railroad tracks from Fort Lewis' main gate.

By the time the company celebrated its 50th anniversary in 1941, annual sales had reached the $5 million mark. Capital stock increased to $1 million, of which $800,000 was issued.

Just a year later, in 1942, the wartime boom hit West Coast Grocery along with most of American business. Rationing and price controls took effect. West Coast Grocery discontinued the service of its three candy and tobacco trucks due to the scarcity of rubber, gasoline and able-bodied workers and because grocery stores were no longer allowed to receive deliveries of "unnecessary" sweets and smokes. Still, annual sales continued to grow: to $7 million in 1942; $12 million by 1947; and $36 million by 1955.

The company grew rapidly during the next several decades. West Coast Grocery's acquisition of small distributors, including Willamette Grocery Company, Diamond Ice and Storage Company, and Pacific Frozen Food Company, required the construction of additional warehouse and office facilities in the 1960s and 1970s.

The tiny wholesale grocery firm of the 1891 era employed more than 1,650 people and hit the billion-dollar mark for the first time in 1982 with corporate sales of $1.1 billion.

West Coast Grocery was acquired by SUPERVALU in 1985. Today, retail stores nationwide are supplied by SUPERVALU. National and major regional customers include Buehler Foods, Byerly's, County Market, Cub Foods, D'Agostinos, Dahl's, Dierbergs, Haggen's, IGA, Jerry's, Jewel, Kroger, Lofinos, Lunds, Niemanns, Redners, Save-A-Lot, Sunflower, SUPERVALU Foods, Tidyman's, Top Foods, Ukrops, and numerous others.

In the same way that the small grocers the company supplies play key roles in their neighborhoods and communities, many of SUPERVALU's 825 Tacoma-area employees are active within their hometown. The company has focused its volunteer and philanthropic efforts on childhood education and feeding the hungry, two issues that fit well with SUPERVALU's core values and business. The world-class distribution company received Tacoma's 1999 "City of Destiny" award for its volunteer efforts.

SUPERVALU INC. acquired West Coast Grocery in 1985 and is the headquarters for the Northwest region. The Tacoma facility (pictured) along with four other facilities located in Billings/Great Falls, Montana; Denver, Colorado; and Spokane, Washington, service 11 states and over 500 customers.

The West Coast Grocery Company tradition that began in 1891 continues today under the SUPERVALU banner. What was once a local, then regional effort is now a nationwide network that remains true to a handful of basic business premises: have confidence in employees and they'll have confidence in the company; build relationships of trust, respect and admiration with brokers, manufacturers and vendors; and cherish personal and business relationships with retailers — their success will be the company's success.

SUPERVALU INC.'s sales after fiscal year 2000 were $20.3 billion. It is among the Top 100 of *Fortune* magazine's Top 500 U.S. corporations. Still, because SUPERVALU specializes in the behind-the-scenes business of grocery supply and distribution, many consumers are unfamiliar with the company. That's OK, say SUPERVALU leaders; they'd prefer customers were familiar with the independent retailers they serve. Importantly, SUPERVALU has built a presence as a food retailer, as its food retail business currently accounts for 40 percent of total company sales and food distribution accounts for 60 percent of total company sales. It is pleased when consumers take for granted that grocery store shelves will be full, produce will be fresh and the newest products will be available. That's SUPERVALU's mission, and the company strives every day to fulfill it.

B & M Enterprises, Inc.

B & M Enterprises traces its success back to humble beginnings as a one-man commercial mobile wash that served Tacoma businesses and residents. Founded in 1977 by Robbert Van Cleave as B & M Mobile Wash, the company's first home was a small carport. Within two years, the business had expanded enough to add employees and claim its own industrial park building in the Parkland area of the city. The new corporate name also acquired a distinctive tone — B & M Enterprises, Inc.

In 24 years, B & M Enterprises has come a long way from its original location in a carport to its current headquarters on Highway 512 at Portland Avenue in Tacoma.

B & M Enterprises soon became the Oregon and Washington area's authorized dealer of several nationally known pressure washer and steam cleaner brands, and built a reputation for commitment to quality and customer service. The company purchased, operated and maintained three car washes in Olympia and one in Des Moines, Washington, and established one of the first bulk-soap delivery programs in the state. The delivery program has graduated from a small truck to a large semi truck and continues to expand.

In 1992 a nationally known rental company commissioned B & M to design, manufacture and distribute a state-of-the-art pressure washer. During the next three years, the company produced over 3,000 of these pressure washers while consolidating and pursuing other business ventures, which included selling the car washes and replacing them with Waste Oil Heaters and Parts Cabinet Washers businesses. B & M also branched off into building full-service truck washes for large fleets of semi trucks.

B & M's many enterprises prospered, and in 1994 Van Cleave custom-designed a larger main facility on 18th Avenue near Portland Avenue and Highway 512. The new company location includes a full-service parts room, an expansive showroom, a huge service center and a warehouse. Several technicians work in the shop and on the road, providing quick response time, on-time delivery and prompt follow-up with customers. Recently a Ryder Truck rental department was added — which became one of the top Ryder Truck Rental Agencies in Washington state — as well as a department for renting Cruise American RVs.

Now a large, well-established business with roots in the community it serves, B & M Enterprises sells and services pressure washers, car, truck and bus wash systems, industrial vacuums, floor scrubbers and waste oil furnaces, and continues to deliver soaps and waxes. The company has built a loyal customer base all over the Northwest and does business with suppliers throughout the nation.

B & M gives back to its community by supporting local schools and youth sports teams, including boys' and girls' baseball, soccer and basketball. The company also donates time, equipment use and funds to several nonprofit organizations, donates to a breast cancer research fund every year, and has been involved in fund-raising projects with the Masonic Lodge and both Boy and Girl Scouts of America.

From its modest beginning as a small one-man business, B & M Enterprises, Inc. has grown to become a leader in manufacturing and distributing total wash systems and environmental equipment and supplies. Although the company continues to evolve with the changing economic environment, B & M still excels in what clients have come to expect — high-quality products and excellent customer service.

Commencement Bay Bed & Breakfast

Tacoma's oldest licensed Bed & Breakfast (B&B) offers more than warm hospitality in an enchanted atmosphere, more than delicious breakfasts, elegant antique décor and panoramic views. Commencement Bay Bed & Breakfast offers a precious gift — a place for new beginnings.

For owners Sharon and Bill Kaufmann, opening the B&B in 1989 marked a new beginning — a *commencement* — after the untimely death of their daughter, Lori, for whom one of three guestrooms is named.

Built in 1937 as the "ideal home" by Tacoma lumber magnate John Dower, the Colonial-style mansion remains immaculately maintained and comfortable. Lori's room is decorated in soft shades of yellow and has subtle vistas of the bay. Myrtle's room, named for Sharon's grandmother, has fantastic bay and Mt. Rainier views and recalls a bygone era, with impressive décor in burgundy, pale rose and forest green. Jessie's room, named for Sharon's mother, also overlooks Brown's Point lighthouse, the bay and Cascade peaks.

While the living-room fireplace blazes on cold days, guests enjoy the inn's own gourmet coffees, play the grand piano, relax in the hot tub or work out in the exercise room. An office area includes high-speed Internet access and other services for business travelers. Thoughtful touches make the inn truly special: plush in-room robes, complimentary espresso, on-site professional massage, bicycles and same-day dry cleaning services. Lady Di, the Kaufmanns' charming black cocker spaniel, provides added hospitality and courtesy cookie tasting.

Sharon, a retired nurse, and Bill, a retired Coast Guard officer who pursued a second career in advertising, combined skill and hard work to place Tacoma on the B&B map. The inn became the first B&B in Pierce County to receive a three-diamond status from the American Automobile Association and a three-star rating from Mobil. Featured in B&B guidebooks including *Northwest Best Places*, Commencement Bay B&B recently tied for "Washington's Best Great Escape" on NBC television's "Evening Magazine." Selected as one of the Northwest's 40 favorite getaways in the *NW Sweethearts Getaway Guide*, the inn was also four times recognized by the *National Bed & Breakfast Association Guidebook* as one of the "True Bed & Breakfasts in America."

From teaching B&B classes at local colleges to speaking at national innkeeper conventions, the Kaufmanns enjoy promoting interest in Tacoma. With the Kaufmanns' guidance, aspiring entrepreneurs have opened more than 36 new Tacoma-area B&Bs. The Kaufmanns also founded A Greater Tacoma Bed & Breakfast Reservation Service, organize B&B tours, donate B&B guide books for charity auctions and conduct community blanket drives for the homeless.

A winning blend of business savvy, hospitality and commitment to Tacoma helped the Kaufmanns create a successful B&B to draw visitors to the City of Destiny. Whether staying for business or pleasure, guests at Commencement Bay Bed & Breakfast discover an idyllic retreat and, most of all, a perfect place for new beginnings.

Commencement Bay Bed & Breakfast sits high on a quiet hillside, with breathtaking views of Commencement Bay, the Cascade Mountains and Mount Rainier.

Heritage Heating and Fuel

For nearly 50 years, Heritage Heating and Fuel has warmed Tacoma and Pierce County residents through icy Northwest winters. Started as Blakeslee Oil in 1958 by Ray Blakeslee, the company's first location was a Rialto garage in downtown Tacoma. With a 1946 1,000-gallon fuel truck that racked up three miles to the gallon, Ray proudly delivered heating oil to a loyal clientele and drove his own truck almost daily for the next 28 years. In 1986 health problems forced Ray to relinquish the driver's seat and he let two sons and a son-in-law take the wheel.

The shift in ownership brought the name change to Heritage Heating and Fuel, which symbolized bequeathing the Blakeslee heritage to the next generation while upholding the tradition of the family business. The parents of Ray's wife, Corinne, had owned the local Tribune Cleaners for over 50 years, and Ray's mother ran Blakeslee Kindergarten and Nursery School in Tacoma's north end. So it seemed only fitting that Blakeslee Oil should pass from a father to his children.

The new Heritage office was in the Blakeslee family home before moving to a small space on East 26th Street near the Tacoma Dome. Delivery services diversified to include stove and furnace oil, on-road and off-road fuel, and fleet fueling for large trucks. The service area also expanded to cover the south King and Thurston county areas. As business grew, so did the company's reputation for superior products and service.

Now owned by Ray Blakeslee and three of the Blakeslees' eight children — Jim, Joe and Claudia — Heritage Heating and Fuel boasts nearly 50 skilled employees, separate residential and commercial installation departments, and a service and repair department. After moving to a 3.5-acre site on Pacific Avenue in 1998, Heritage opened one of the largest fireplace showrooms in Tacoma. Customers enjoy free coffee while browsing through more than 20 working designer gas fireplaces and custom hearths, as well as free-standing stoves and inserts to convert from wood to gas heat.

Heritage also installs and repairs residential and commercial furnaces, heat pumps, air-conditioning systems and electronic air cleaners. Heritage is also proud of having some of the best technicians in the industry. Along with these strengths, Heritage attributes its growing business to a loyal customer base, which the company believes was built by stressing the principles of honesty and integrity, and by an emphasis on customer service.

In addition to excellent service and the many HVAC options Heritage offers to the public, the company also supports its community by sponsoring Tacoma baseball teams and donating funds and volunteer hours to a number of faith-based organizations. Heritage often provides merchandise for auctions held at a local school and wraps holiday presents for the Brotherhood Academy, a Tacoma private school for inner-city children.

With a reputation for honesty and reliability, Heritage Heating and Fuel has served Greater Puget Sound for almost half a century. Simply put, Heritage makes customers feel at home with the slogan, "We take pride in the service we provide."

Ray Blakeslee drove this 1950 fuel truck every day during the company's early years, reliably delivering heating oil to homes throughout Tacoma and Pierce County.

Liberty Distributing Inc.

When Joseph Inderbitzin came to the United States from Switzerland in March of 1914 at the age of 20, he saw something that he'd never forget as he sailed into the port of New York — the Statue of Liberty.

Just eight years later, Inderbitzin bought a herd of dairy cows just outside the city of Tacoma and named his new business Liberty Dairy because he had been so impressed by the sight of that statue on Ellis Island and the principles it stands for. Today that small dairy has become Liberty Distributing and is run by Inderbitzin's grandson, Ed Inderbitzin Jr. Liberty Distributing Inc. now supplies dairy products to a variety of customers in western Washington.

Joseph Inderbitzin, who was born February 16, 1894, in Ingenbohl, Switzerland, spent his entire life working in dairy farming, just as his father had in Switzerland. Inderbitzin's first job in Tacoma was on a dairy farm owned by the Henry Felchlin family and located near what is now Custer Road and Bridgeport Way in Lakewood. Inderbitzin later partnered with Joe Marty, a school friend from Switzerland, to begin a dairy farm. But the partnership ended when Marty moved to California and Inderbitzin temporarily went to work for Flett Dairy.

On January 14, 1922, Inderbitzin married Edna Bloom, whom he had met while delivering milk at a restaurant where she worked. Bloom was born in San Francisco in 1905 and moved with her parents to Tacoma shortly before the devastating earthquake that shook San Francisco.

Just a year after being married, Joe and Edna Inderbitzin bought a herd of dairy cows and leased a 40-acre farm near Puyallup on Clarkes Creek to start Liberty Dairy. They bottled milk and sold it primarily in the Tacoma area. In 1948 Joseph Inderbitzin rented the old Glenwood dairy farm on Brookdale Road near Parkland because the Puyallup farmland was sold. However, just a year later he died in an accident on the farm. Two of his three sons, Ed and Dick, bought the delivery routes but the dairy herd was sold.

Ed, the eldest son, owned and operated this home delivery business from 1949-1983. Ed Jr. began working in the family business as a teen-ager in 1961. In 1983 Ed Jr. took over the business and changed it from a home-delivery service to a wholesale distributorship. The business has grown to include delivery to all parts of western Washington, providing quality services by a great team of employees. At age 79, Ed Sr. continues to help out most mornings.

Ed and Sally Inderbitzin's three children, Ed, Alex and Bridgett, all have worked at the business. Alex, who began by loading delivery trucks during the summer and on weekends while attending the University of Puget Sound, has been an integral part of the business since 1994. He will take over the business when his parents retire. He'll become a fourth-generation Inderbitzin to operate Liberty Distributing, a business that has grown because of its ongoing commitment to customer satisfaction.

The Joseph Inderbitzin family in the mid-1940s — Joe and Edna Inderbitzin with sons (left to right) Bob, Ed and Dick

Ed Inderbitzin Sr. with his Liberty Dairy International truck in 1939

The Inn at Gig Harbor

Everyone remembers the old lodges of the national parks system, full of rich woods and a sense of quiet. Somehow they always looked established even when new, and although built by people, each structure seemed to be a natural outgrowth of its own rustic setting. That sense of agelessness and calm made memories for each visitor that are as hard to describe as they are to forget. The same sense of timeless serenity characterizes The Inn at Gig Harbor, and the memories gathered there are just as lasting.

The Inn at Gig Harbor is a new facility that includes a full-service hotel and a fine-dining restaurant, the Heritage Restaurant and Lounge. The new building was only finished in 1997, but its roots are much older. Decades ago, the same spot was a convenient crossroads for the small community of Gig Harbor as well as for people passing by on the state highway. This central location made it a natural spot for a restaurant where friends and family gathered or travelers stopped. For years it was known as the Classic, popular for its good food as well as for the owner's collection of fine classic cars of the 20s and 30s. In 1988, under the careful hands of the original owner and Betty Stewart, the restaurant became the Cimmaron, a popular country western spot known throughout Puget Sound. Less than 10 years later The Inn made ready to welcome the new century.

The Inn at Gig Harbor reflects many qualities of the small waterfront community that is its home. Gig Harbor has a rich pioneering history; fishing, farming and logging were typical livelihoods. The harbor itself offers colorful and relaxing strolls where visitors can see everything from fishing vessels and great blue herons to fine original artwork. People come from substantial distances for classes in both visual and literary arts. Many scenic miles of shoreline in the area provide opportunities for visitors to spot bald eagles or orcas while boating or kayaking.

The Inn plays host to many different groups and is closely involved in a variety of community activities. Service organizations such as the local Rotary International and Lions Clubs meet there weekly. Many cultural organizations are active in the area and receive the support of The Inn through the use of space there. The hotel donates a guest stay to be used in fund-raising efforts for private and nonprofit organizations such as schools and environmental groups, and charity auctions often take place there. Workshops, conferences and seminars have the benefit of comfortable accommodations in a quiet setting among tall firs.

George Edman, who with his wife, Laura, is an owner and general manager, meets guests with enthusiasm and high energy and has a progressive vision for The Inn. Co-owners Wade and Beth Perrow have been active in the business and civic community for years. Betty Stewart, manager of the Heritage Restaurant, has a strong sense of history. They work together as a seamless team to create warm memories for each guest to cherish.

Guests enjoy relaxed dining in the Heritage Restaurant and Lounge.

The Poodle Dog Restaurant

Homemade chili for 15 cents, a drink for a dime, deluxe hamburger and fries for a quarter, or a multicourse dinner for 75 cents: these were some of the menu choices at The Poodle Dog Restaurant in 1935.

Although times have changed and prices increased, The Poodle Dog remains an ageless Highway 99 landmark in Fife. Opened in 1933, the restaurant prospered as Fife developed from a quiet agricultural town into a bustling industrial center. When the construction of Highway 5 turned the city into a hub of transportation in the 1960s, The Poodle Dog's owner, Rocco "Mac" Manza, still greeted customers at the door and entertained them with stories of his childhood.

Rocco "Mac" Manza

Rocco was born in 1904 in Figline (pronounced "Fellini") in the southern province of Calabria in Italy. His father, Gaetano Manza, moved to British Columbia to work for the Canadian Pacific Railroad shortly after Rocco's birth. When he had enough money to bring his wife and four children to an Italian neighborhood in Tacoma, Gaetano ran a grocery store next to the family's home at North 17th Street and Cushman Avenue.

Young Rocco inherited his father's entrepreneurial spirit and quit school in the sixth grade to sell newspapers from a pushcart on 13th Street, make sandwiches, "jerk" sodas, sell cigars and run pool halls. Rocco earned the name Mac when he visited his brother Ralph at a mechanic trade school. The affectionate nickname "Little Mechanic" soon became "Mac" for short.

Mac saved nickels and dimes, and with a $500 loan from his father bought a hamburger stand called The Blue Jay in 1933. Originally a small barbershop, the stand had only two tables and 15 stools at a lunch counter. Mac and his business partner planned to rename the stand The Mayflower to match a $95 neon sign they had bought from a miniature golf course.

The night before opening The Mayflower, Rocco could not sleep. He kept imagining a better name for his restaurant: The Poodle Dog, which reminded him of a place he had visited in San Francisco. Finally, he called the sign company at 3 a.m. The sign had to come down, he said. The Mayflower was out; The Poodle Dog was in.

When The Poodle Dog made $100 its first week, Rocco thought he was rich. The $100 soon became a tidy profit, and before long The Poodle Dog expanded and Rocco branched off into business ventures that eventually made him a multi-millionaire.

Despite his other pursuits, Rocco continued to work at The Poodle Dog Restaurant six days a week, running the cash register, buttering toast and reminiscing with customers who fondly remember his warmth, captivating stories and generosity. His charity work included support for Bellarmine Preparatory School and Catholic Community Services.

Although Rocca Manza passed away in 1999 at the age of 94, he lives on in the hearts of friends and family and in the restaurant he owned, operated and cherished for 65 years. Although The Poodle Dog's outward appearance has changed, the Manza family runs the restaurant the way Rocco would have wanted. Customers gather at The Poodle Dog for its timeless qualities — good food, good prices and traditional hospitality.

The Puyallup Fair/ Western Washington Fair Association

With a century under its belt, the Puyallup Fair, officially known as the Western Washington Fair, starts its second hundred years bringing a blend of tradition and new activities to guests.

The Puyallup Fair is the largest fair in the state and the fifth-largest fair in attendance in the country. The 17-day event starts the Friday after Labor Day and also houses the FFA, 4-H and Junior Poultry statewide competitions.

The Puyallup Fair is a tradition in the Pacific Northwest. Over 1.3 million people "Do the Puyallup" each September.

Regional and national animal shows are a part of the Fair, as well as numerous animal contests for all ages. Since the early days, grange displays have captured the eye of farmers and city dwellers, and they continue today. A pumpkin weigh-off is held on opening day, with pumpkins in excess of 800 pounds drawing top honors.

Entertainment abounds at the Puyallup Fair. While strolling entertainers catch the attention of guests wandering by, five free stages also offer a wide range of talent. The grandstand sparkles each night, featuring top-name entertainers. Past years have included Bill Cosby, Brooks & Dunn, Frank Sinatra and Reba McEntire.

Gadgets and gizmos of all sizes make the fair a shopper's paradise. Small items perfect for the piggy bank crowd are as popular as luxury items for the more mature crowd. With over 450 exhibitors, there's something for everyone.

Hungry fair-goers are in luck. They may start the day with a farm breakfast before wandering the fairgrounds. Within hours they will have developed a hearty appetite for lunch or dinner. Onion burgers, barbecue ribs, Krusty Pups, pizza and much more will tide them over until break time. Whether it's warm scones dripping with butter and jam, ice cream dipped in chocolate and nuts, elephant ears or caramel apples, there's something for every sweet tooth in the crowd.

Those who swing by to see the floral building, quilts, baking and cooking contests, photo salon and hobby hall will be ready for the Midway. While the senior set may prefer the antique merry-go-round to bring back fond memories, the Extreme Scream and roller coaster will help create new memories for thrill seekers. Little ones aren't to be overlooked. Kiddyland offers a wide range of rides with the younger set in mind.

Costumed characters are always ready to shake a hand and nuzzle up for a photo.

Over 1.3 million people "Do the Puyallup" each year. The richness of its history blended with the tradition of making fond memories year after year make the fair a "must do" in the Pacific Northwest each year.

Sheraton Tacoma Hotel

The Sheraton Tacoma Hotel opened its doors in May 1984, beginning what was anticipated to be a new awakening for a sleepy downtown that had watched business after business leave. But the hotel's arrival did not coincide with an immediate downtown surge as had been expected.

Today the company's strategic bet to build in what had been a quiet downtown Tacoma has paid off. The Sheraton Tacoma Hotel continues to grow in reputation as it remains committed to the revitalization of the city's downtown. Since the mid-1990s, the Sheraton in Tacoma has become a hub for corporate meetings, conventions and trade shows. It has become almost a city within a city.

Sheraton Tacoma Hotel's priority is making guests feel comfortable.

The hotel's turnaround began when Kimpton Group became manager of the Sheraton in late 1991. Prior to that takeover, Kimpton owned or managed smaller boutique-style hotels. But it was Kimpton's managers, best known for adding warm and friendly touches to their hotels, that helped lure more business and boosted occupancy rates to 70 percent. When the 319-room, 26-floor Sheraton opened, Weyerhaeuser, as the primary developer, was lured by the rosy projections of Tacoma downtown. But those projections were overly optimistic and the hotel instead endured difficult times. Operating at only 50 percent occupancy, the hotel lost $4 million in both 1991 and 1992. Under Kimpton's special eye for detail, the once struggling hotel began turning a profit in 1994, allowing it to look toward expansion. Brighter times were ahead for the hotel that spearheaded a revitalization of downtown Tacoma.

In 1994 Kimpton converted the Sheraton's once stuffy, 26th-floor Rose Room restaurant into Altezzo Ristorante, a moderately priced, family-oriented eatery with an Italian theme. The downtown restaurant with Tacoma's best view is no longer just a special-occasion place to eat.

In 1998 the hotel underwent a $2.5 million renovation, giving the hotel that boutique ambience that Kimpton is famous for. The renovation gave the hotel a warmer, friendlier appeal. That appeal is most apparent in the lobby, where a cozy fireplace and overstuffed chairs add to the hotel's charm and comfort. Here, guests can enjoy their favorite latte or cocktail while listening to aesthetically pleasing music. In recent years the Sheraton Tacoma Hotel was awarded the Chairman's Award by Starwood Hotels and Resorts for its cordiality and comfort. Inspections are given twice a year and only the top performers of Starwood's 700 hotels receive the award.

In addition to Altezzo Ristorante, the hotel also offers the Broadway Grill, which serves a variety of steaks, seafood and sandwiches. The hotel also offers a convention and conference space. Whether guests are planning a grand reception or an intimate gathering, the hotel's professional staff helps everything go exactly as planned. With the hotel leading the way, a new convention center in downtown Tacoma is projected to open in 2003. After the completion of the convention center, the Sheraton is planning to build a second tower with an additional 220 rooms, giving the hotel 540 rooms.

Today the Sheraton Tacoma Hotel is setting the pace for downtown Tacoma and helping make the city a destination point.

Old Town Photo Studio

For almost 30 years Ron Karabaich has owned and operated the Old Town Photo Studio located not far from the site of Job Carr's cabin, Tacoma's birthplace. Indeed, Ron grew up in the Old Tacoma neighborhood and has considered it his home for a half-century. Of Croatian ancestry and with a deep love of the past, his business has included both traditional photography and the collection of images related to his ethnic and community heritage.

Past and present were combined with Ron's introduction to panoramic photography. His interest began after seeing the work of Marvin Boland, one of Tacoma's early photographers. In 1976 he purchased the Boland camera collection and found a Cirkut camera among his acquisitions. Through his travels around the Pacific Northwest he also discovered that panoramic photography was highly popular during the early years of the 20th century, especially for small-town street views and large gatherings of people. Paul Richards, another Tacoma photographer, took hundreds of military groups during World War I that now have a home in the National Archives.

With the Cirkut camera an image is exposed on a single negative 10 inches wide and up to 6 feet long. Eastman Kodak began selling them in 1904. To make the photograph, the camera rotates slowly on a special tripod allowing an image of up to a full circle. Miracles can happen with a camera such as this, including up-close views of the battleship *USS Missouri* and full stadiums of fans watching baseball or football games.

Used originally for school and group photography, modern uses of this special camera have expanded to embrace scenic views. And what used to be shown in black and white can now be seen in color as well. Among the best known images of the Old Town Photo Studio are local views of Tacoma's waterfront and the surrounding area, the Oregon Trail commemoration, Seattle Mariners and Tacoma Rainiers baseball, and group photographs that include weddings, military conventions, family reunions and other kinds of special gatherings.

The Old Town Photo Studio is therefore unique among Tacoma's photography establishments. Ron Karabaich has gone beyond the traditional work commonly associated with the profession to preserve the history of local photographers. By adapting older techniques to the modern world, he is creating a new historical record for the future.

Fire buff and photographer Ron Karabaich adjusts his 80-year-old Kodak panoramic camera for a group photo of about 170 fellow fire buffs in front of Tacoma's old Fire Boat No. 1 along Ruston Way, July 15, 1999. *The News Tribune Photo by Russ Marmack*

Heritage Media Collection

Medical Imaging Northwest

Physicians and staff of Diagnostic Imaging Northwest and its subsidiary, Mount Rainier Imaging, joined forces in October 2000 to become Medical Imaging Northwest. The new name represents the consolidation of existing diagnostic radiology and magnetic resonance imaging (MRI) services that are now offered in a new state-of-the-art imaging center in Puyallup. This facility is a showcase of the amazing technologies that grew from and added to X-ray film diagnosis, allowing radiologists to see inside the human body in remarkable detail.

The 10,000-square-foot clinic was planned with the patient in mind. The physicians and senior staff thought long and hard about the overall layout and its eventual impact on patient care. For example, computers were installed in every examination room to provide technical personnel instant access to patient information. Interior decorators also played a key role in softening the feel of certain rooms, creating a quieter, more relaxed atmosphere for the 140 or more patients seen each day.

Digital ultrasound produces high-resolution images.

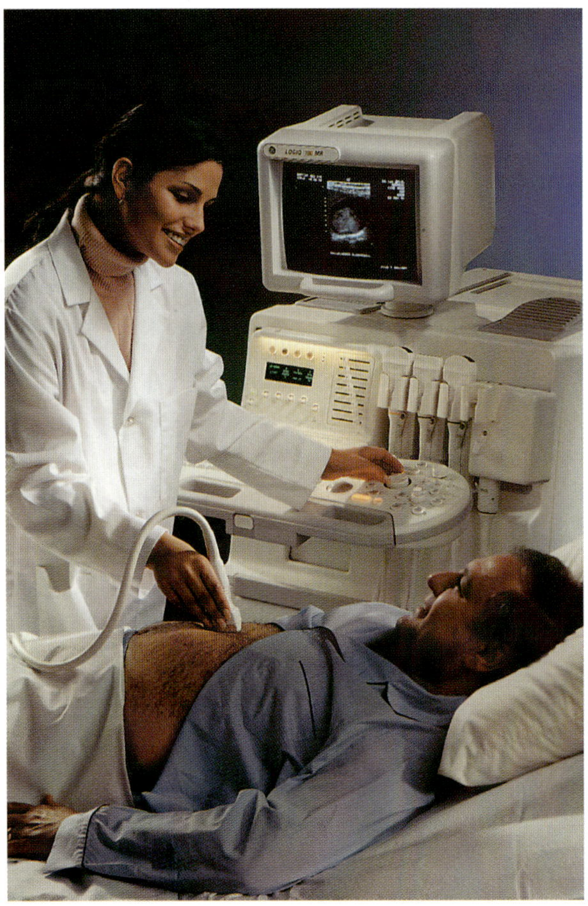

An innovative aspect of the imaging center is the installation of a Picture Archival and Communications System. PACS, an electronic substitute for film, can be used to record information from ultrasound examinations, MRI, computed tomography (CT), fluoroscopic procedures and digital mammography. It acquires, transfers, retrieves and stores images in a computer system. The major benefit of this system is that it can find and display historical, comparative images more easily than traditional film, thus providing timely patient care. Physicians in the area — or for that matter at any location — will be able to access their patients' studies on their own office computers, facilitating consultation between the radiologists, referring physicians and other specialty consultants.

These diagnostic services haven't always been available. The medical use of X-rays was discovered in 1895 by a German physics professor, Wilhelm Konrad Roentgen, and the medical community quickly began to utilize the diagnostic potential of this new method. Today, radiology employs not only X-rays but also high-frequency sound waves and magnetism coupled with radio waves to promptly, accurately and painlessly obtain medical diagnostic information. Because of rapid technologic advances in electronics and computer science that led to development of new modalities such as CT and MRI, radiological diagnostic use has more than quadrupled over the last 40 years.

Medical Imaging Northwest has been providing medical services to Tacoma-area patients since Dr. Steven Sanderson began his radiology practice in the Medical Arts Building in downtown Tacoma in the early 1940s. He was joined in 1955 by Dr. Kenneth Gross, who soon became the driving force behind steady growth of the practice that eventually became known as Gross, Larson, Whitney and Associates. In 1989 the group selected the name Diagnostic Imaging Northwest. Through all these changes the value that remained constant was a total commitment to quality service. The 14 physician-radiologist partners and 60 employees of Medical Imaging Northwest are dedicated to obtaining the most accurate possible diagnostic information in order to best serve the public.

Over the years, not only has the firm's name changed to reflect the times, but Medical Imaging Northwest has also compiled numerous accomplishments, including the following:

- Continuing to provide superlative medical diagnostic service to Good Samaritan, Allenmore and St. Clare Hospitals for more than 30 years;
- Establishing a Magnetic Resonance Imaging service in the Puyallup area in 1987 and then building an MRI center in 1990;
- Keeping pace with health care needs by expanding services over the years while introducing new technology;
- Constructing the 10,000-square-foot medical office building that houses Medical Imaging Northwest and two physician tenant offices;
- Installing the first outpatient imaging center with complete picture archival and communication system (PACS);
- Providing health care employment in Tacoma, Puyallup and Lakewood.

Community involvement is another important aspect for the staff of Medical Imaging Northwest. For the past several years, staff members have served as instructors in the Radiologic Sciences Department at Tacoma Community College. As adjunct staff members, Medical Imaging Northwest radiologists are doing their part to lessen the severe shortage of imaging professionals nationwide.

Radiologists and employees are also involved in various philanthropic organizations, including the American Cancer Society, the Council for the Arts and the local YMCA. In recent years, staff members have participated in the annual March for the Cure, a breast cancer awareness walk, and the American Cancer Society's Relay For Life fund-raiser.

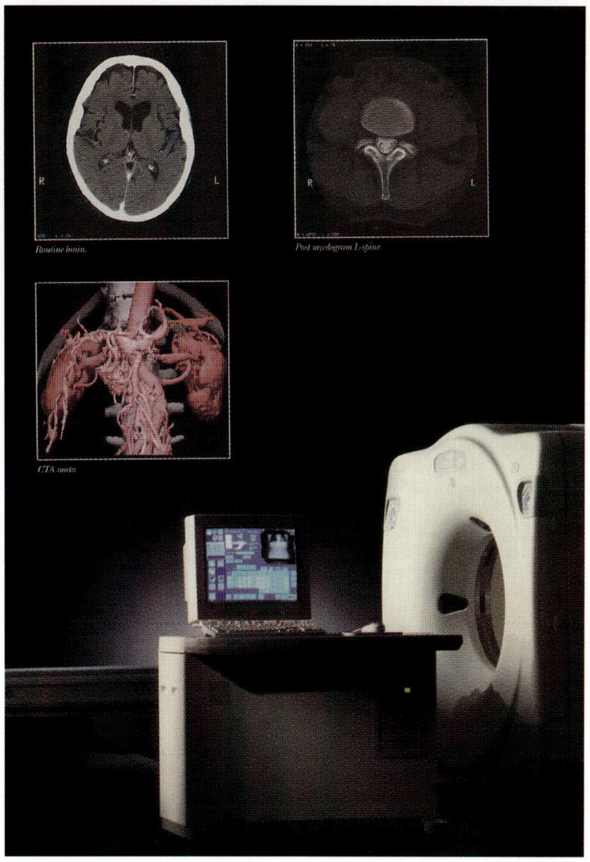

CT scanner with typical cross sectional and three-dimensional images.

Medical Imaging Northwest personnel have also participated in civic and community seminars for women, specifically focusing on mammography and breast cancer awareness. In addition, employees participate in a variety of medically oriented committees that aim to ensure the continuous delivery of excellent health care to the community.

The company's value statement imparts its intent to provide patients and referring physicians with the highest-quality service available, and to do so with sound judgment, resourcefulness, courtesy and hard work. The practice administrator sums up that declaration: "Our commitment is to provide the quality service that patients and their health care providers expect and deserve."

By recognizing and adjusting to the evolving needs of its patients, Medical Imaging Northwest has continued to serve as an integral part of the Pierce County community.

Franciscan Health System

In 1891 the Sisters of the Third Order of St. Francis founded St. Joseph Hospital, Tacoma's first Catholic hospital, dedicated to healing body, mind and spirit. The 60-bed facility launched a legacy of providing expert, compassionate care to Puget Sound residents that continues today. In keeping with the mission of St. Francis of Assisi who founded the Franciscans, the Sisters at St. Joseph ministered to all people, regardless of race, religion or financial status.

In 1899, in response to a greater need for services, St. Joseph Hospital expanded to three times its original size and added 140 beds. The modernized hospital included X-rays, electric light and ventilated wards, which were put to the test on July 4, 1900, when an out-of-control streetcar plunged into a deep ravine. Many passengers were killed, and critically injured victims poured into St. Joseph Hospital. The medical staff worked around the clock using the most advanced techniques to tend the wounded and dying. Although the 200-bed hospital was filled to capacity, the Sisters turned nobody away.

St. Joseph Hospital was hailed as one of the finest on the West Coast when it was completed in January 1899.

Tacoma citizens and dignitaries gathered at the groundbreaking ceremony for a new St. Joseph Hospital on July 4, 1913.

St. Joseph Hospital's response to the streetcar accident became a model for excellent health care that the Franciscans provided in the ensuing years. The catastrophe underscored the need for more qualified medical personnel, so the Sisters opened a new training center for nurses. Although St. Joseph Hospital — since renamed St. Joseph Medical Center — has been rebuilt four times and continues to keep up with the latest technology, the Sisters' humanitarian mission has never wavered. The Franciscan Health System continues to respond to community needs and provide broad-based care to everyone, especially the poor and underserved.

Today the Franciscan Health System includes three award-winning hospitals — St. Joseph Medical Center, St. Clare Hospital in Lakewood and St. Francis Hospital in Federal Way — as well as Franciscan Medical Group, a network of primary care physicians with six clinics; the Physician/Health System Network, a multispecialty provider network; and the Franciscan Care Center in Tacoma, a long-term care facility. Part of Catholic Health Initiatives, one of the largest not-for-profit health care systems in the country, Franciscan has over 3,800 employees and 1,000 of the area's finest primary and specialty physicians working together as a team to provide its neighbors with expert care.

Franciscan has an award-winning record, with St. Joseph rated for many years as one of the "100 Top Hospitals" in the nation for exceeding national benchmarks for high-quality medical care and cost efficiency. In 1999 all three hospitals earned the Top 100 distinction — the only health system in the nation to do so. St. Joseph Medical Center has earned its patients' trust by winning the Consumer Choice Award from National Research Corporation as Tacoma's most preferred hospital for overall quality and image.

Together the three hospitals admit more than 30,000 patients a year and provide comprehensive services including 24-hour acute care, in- and outpatient diagnostic and surgical care, and many other specialized programs. Last year Franciscan emergency rooms saw more than 110,000 patients, and more babies are born at Franciscan hospitals than at any other hospital in the south Puget Sound area.

Franciscan Health System excels in the areas of cardiac, women's services, orthopedic, oncology, diabetes and hospice care. Franciscan Heart Center offers complete diagnostic, treatment and rehabilitation services, including cardiac catheterization at St. Francis Hospital and open-heart surgery at St. Joseph. The heart cath lab at St. Joseph is a state-of-the-art showcase site for the most advanced diagnostic and imaging tools in the cardiac field today. Patients can also learn how to reduce their risk of heart disease by taking advantage of the many seminars and classes offered by the health system.

St. Joseph houses the Franciscan Cancer Center, which offers in- and outpatient cancer care, chemotherapy, and a bone marrow transplant program affiliated with the Fred Hutchinson Cancer Research Center in Seattle. St. Joseph's inpatient and outpatient diabetes program was the first in the south Puget Sound area to be recognized by the American Diabetes Association.

Women's Care services at all hospitals feature Family Birth Services, including a Level II Neonatal Intensive Care Nursery at St. Joseph Medical Center to treat high-risk newborns, midwifery services, and community programs offering support and education for women of all ages. The Women's Health Center at St. Francis Hospital offers traditional and complementary services that address the specialized needs of women, such as mammograms, osteoporosis screening, biofeedback and a chronic fatigue/fibromyalgia program.

Franciscan's mission of compassionate care throughout life includes those nearing the end. Both the hospice program, among the largest in the state, and the Improving Care Through the End of Life program offer specialized care for those with

St. Joseph Hospital, c. 1940, was newly equipped with a dial telephone system and modern pediatrics ward.

terminal illness, as well as support for their loved ones and caregivers. The End of Life program has won the American Hospital Association's prestigious Circle of Life honor for outstanding palliative care.

The Franciscan "mission to heal, promise to care" extends far beyond its hospital and clinic doors. Free or low-cost medical services include blood screening, breast exams, blood-pressure checks and immunizations through the Children's Immunization Program. Franciscan also participates in community food and clothing drives, as well as several parenting, teen-age pregnancy and violence prevention programs.

Franciscan Health System has come a long way from its beginnings as a modest hospital for Puget Sound residents. The system has evolved into an expansive network of health care programs designed to meet the community's rapidly changing needs. Yet after more than a century of service, the original mission of the Sisters of St. Francis remains unchanged: to provide outstanding, compassionate, inclusive health care and to meet the physical, emotional and spiritual needs of all people.

In 1974 a new St. Joseph Hospital towered over Tacoma as a symbol of modern medicine with a tradition of community service.

Korean Women's Association

In 1972 a small group of Korean women leaders of Pierce County, Washington, came together to address the needs of Korean wives of American servicemen. This small group of concerned women leaders founded a registered 501(c)(3) private, nonprofit organization called the Korean Women's Association of Washington State (KWA). In 1972 many Korean wives of American servicemen needed a Korean-oriented support group to help them feel at home, made up of other women who spoke their language, enjoyed their foods, shared the same culture and customs, and who could assist them in adapting to the American way of living. Domestic violence was one of the very first issues KWA had to deal with in helping many Korean wives of American servicemen.

In the early 1980s the Korean Women's Association began to expand its services to meet the needs of Asian Pacific Islander immigrants and refugees, especially those with language and cultural barriers. In the late 1980s the KWA reached out to the general public to assist the poor, elders, low-income families, disabled individuals, immigrants, refugees, and persons whose English is limited or nonexistent. Today KWA offers a multifaceted program of services tailored to minority populations, yet available to all in Pierce, Lewis, Mason, Thurston and South King counties.

The Korean Women's Association of Washington State has emerged as Pierce County's leader in innovative programs designed to enhance the quality of life for Asian Pacific Americans and other minority citizens in the Northwest. Many minorities face barriers of racism, language, poverty and vulnerability,

One of the Korean Women's Association's regular services involves ethnic food and cultural activities programs. A traditional Filipino meal is being served here.

The board of directors for the Korean Women's Association includes: (front row, left to right) Young R. Lee, Ok Sun Wilson, Sul Ja Warnick, Dr. Jay Won Kim, Maria Hwang, and Song Ja Park; (back row, left to right) Sujin Crow, Dori Synn, Young Sil Park, Tal Chun Kim, Chong Dameron, and Kyong Suk Arbeeney. Helen Kim, Mun Ju Kim and Executive Director Faaluaina Pritchard are not pictured.

and struggle with a limited understanding of and access to available services. KWA provides a helping hand, protection, and a pathway to inclusion and full participation in community life. The following is a partial list of the present programs and services provided by the Korean Women's Association:

- In-Home Care Services (Chore, COPES, Title XIX, Respite, and Private Pay)
- Alzheimer's and Dementia Care
- Asian Pacific Senior Nutrition
- Asian Pacific Senior Day Care
- We Are Family (Domestic violence, Sexual Assault, Batterer's Treatment)
- Pacific Villa (Senior Low-Income Housing)
- Naturalization Program
- Immigration Assistance
- English as a Second Language
- Legal Aid Referral Service
- Interpretation Services
- Translation Services
- Job Referral Service
- Welfare to Work Program
- Food Stamp Outreach Program
- Community Education
- Youth Services
- Support Groups
- Parenting Classes
- Transportation Services
- Feeding the Homeless

The Korean Women's Association has accomplished a tremendous amount in the 28 years since the first group of women gathered in 1972. In that time it has served over 288,000 clients of 17 different nationalities. The association has active programs in five western Washington counties and provides referral and networking services throughout the state. Its budget has grown from nothing more than what individual women could donate, in the early days, to a current amount of $5 million annually. Most impressive, however, is the amazing 4,500,132 hours of service documented, for this reflects the heart of the association — care and assistance for individuals when their need is greatest.

Korean youth are actively involved in planning and teaching various programs sponsored by the KWA.

Pacific Villa provides seniors with low-income housing.

Naturalization classes sponsored by KWA are always well attended.

KWA offers the best in ethnic-based programming, providing children through seniors with opportunities for socialization and integration with people of similar interests, backgrounds and languages. For people outside of the ethnic community, their specialized programming teaches about ethnicity and Asian Pacific cultures and customs.

Cardiac Study Center, Inc., P.S.

Built on the motto that the patient always comes first, Cardiac Study Center, Inc., P.S. has grown into one of Pierce County's largest heart care centers.

A few years after Dr. Clarence Anderson opened his practice in 1966, Drs. John P. Nagle and Gail B. Strait joined him and the clinic took on its present name. The staff has since grown to 10 physicians and four nurse practitioners, employing a total of 87 people. The clinic also has offices in Puyallup and Gig Harbor.

To meet the growing demands of the region, three physicians joined the center in the summer of 2000 and there are plans to add three more. The Puyallup office nearly doubled in size that same year. All 10 physicians at Cardiac Study Center are board certified in internal medicine with a specialty in cardiology.

As the clinic's name suggests, the physicians of Cardiac Study Center take an active interest in remaining on the cutting edge of new and innovative techniques in diagnosing and treating heart disease. Over the years, many of the physicians on staff have taken part in major studies that involved the use of new medications and devices.

The Tacoma office moved into its current location on South Cedar Street in 1982. The facility makes available state-of-the-art diagnostic equipment. As part of a complete cardiac examination, patients can expect a variety of tests to be performed including an examination by the physician, an EKG, chest X-ray, and possibly an echocardiogram or treadmill stress test.

The clinic has recently expanded its echocardiography program. This expansion has allowed the clinic to add new echo services and include stress echo and peripheral vascular studies. Cardiac Study Center also offers diagnostic nuclear medicine services on an outpatient basis. Another specialty program is the arrhythmia/device program. Patients with pacemakers or implanted cardiac defibrillators are followed to ensure that their device is functioning properly. "If there is a new treatment available, our doctors are always on top of it," says Vicki Baker, the clinic's human resource manager.

Cardiac Study Center physicians perform angioplasty and coronary stent implants at local

Dr. Clarence L. Anderson founded Cardiac Study Center in 1966.

Cardiac Study Center has been located in the Cedar Medical Center since 1982.

area hospitals. Angioplasty, a technique in which a catheter is used to clear fatty plaques from coronary arteries, is sometimes followed by the insertion of a stent. A stent is a tiny metal coil or mesh tube that remains behind after the balloon is withdrawn, preventing the artery from collapsing again. Cardiac Study Center patients requiring open-heart surgery are referred to cardiovascular surgeons.

A large part of a patient's care at the center involves education. The center believes in providing patients and their families with information regarding their condition in order to help them make informed decisions on their treatment. Critical care trained RNs talk with patients and their families about the disease process they are facing and possible lifestyle

Dr. Kingson Momah interprets a nuclear study.

changes they should make. These may include diet, exercise, cholesterol management, and smoking cessation. The nurses counsel patients who are facing hospital procedures such as cardiac catheterization. The aim of the center's education program is to help in a patient's recovery and to ensure healthier lifestyles. Cardiac Study Center physicians will continue to place emphasis on teaching patients how to live healthy lives.

Each year the employees at the Cardiac Study Center participate in fund-raising activities to benefit local area charities such as the American Heart Association and the American Cancer Society. In 1995 the center adopted McKinley Elementary School in Tacoma. Money raised through bake sales and auctions each year goes toward buying coats, shoes and school supplies for children attending McKinley. Each December, the center hosts a Christmas party for the entire school and provides donated toys.

The Cardiac Study Center will continue to expand outpatient services. To meet the growing needs of an aging society, the center's goal will be to better educate patients. This will be accomplished through the development of specialty clinics that will assist patients living with congestive heart failure, hyperlipidemia and hypertension. "Patients are living longer because of advances in cardiovascular care. The direction of the Cardiac Study Center is to give the best patient care we can."

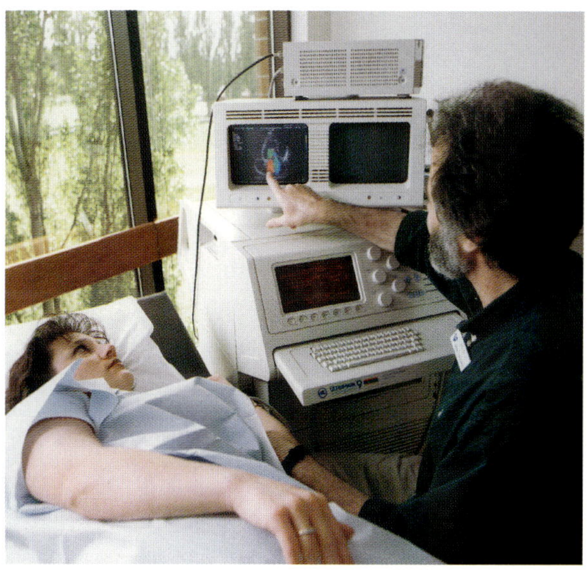

Cardiac Sonographer Wayne Allen uses color Doppler analysis to explain blood flow through the heart valves.

Metropolitan Development Council

The Metropolitan Development Council (MDC) is a nonprofit, private-sector Community Action Agency. The agency provides a broad range of innovative services in the Tacoma/Pierce County area that promote self-sufficiency and assist individuals and families in removing themselves from poverty.

The Metropolitan Development Council is an integral partner in Tacoma's renaissance. In 1964, Community Action Agencies were created all over the nation to combat poverty and to act as the local steward of a national "war on poverty" initiative. In Tacoma the Metropolitan Development Council became the primary tool to empower people in combating poverty issues. Over the years the agency has become the catalyst for change, focusing on areas that impair or block people's ability to break out of poverty. The agency takes its mandate very seriously, with ongoing efforts to develop services and to secure funding needed for their implementation.

Many of its services are as diverse as the people it serves. For example, "Jason," whose mother was drug addicted, weighed only three pounds, six ounces when he first came to the attention of the agency. He had been placed in foster care but was severely impacted by cocaine withdrawal symptoms. MDC went to the foster home, provided the immediate help needed to comfort him and then initiated a long-term support program to assist the foster family in his ongoing care. Through these efforts, Jason has now overcome the impact of his mother's drug use.

When Melanie came to the Metropolitan Development Council, she was a 100-pound, 18-year-old fireball of energy — and the mother of an 18-month-old child. On welfare when she came to MDC, Melanie entered skills training at St. Joseph's Hospital and left with hospital-based training in cytology. More importantly, she possessed within her the inner strength and will to make it on her own, free of the welfare system.

MDC has a clear focus. Its primary goal is to "provide the support so that low-income persons can remove themselves from poverty." President Linsey Hinand describes MDC as a complex social services umbrella supported by public and private funding sources. Hinand sees his staff using a holistic approach that supports healthy, long-term solutions for children, youth and families within their own community. As a result, MDC links its many programs together within its primary objectives, among them to:

- Assist youth and families to gain meaningful employment;
- Provide educational opportunities;
- Develop and maintain affordable housing;
- Combat chemical dependency;
- Provide employment and health care for homeless individuals and families;
- Support foster parenting and parent skills.

Devoted Dads is a project that combines these objectives, integrating a holistic approach to the community's needs. Research shows that children benefit from regular interaction with their fathers. Fathers are essential for healthy development, but fractured family systems often eliminate this positive impact. MDC now partners with the Division of Child Support to help dads, in practical ways, stay in better touch with their children. The office includes mentoring, legal counseling, career guidance and educational services, all available under one roof to fathers in Tacoma who want to remain responsible parents.

Traditionally, Community Action flexes to meet the community's changing needs through assessment, communication with professionals and those it serves, and participation in numerous advisory groups, including those for youth at risk of violence and the homeless. But more recently, MDC has begun to partner with the business community in providing job training and placement.

Welfare reform has changed the focus of many social services in the Tacoma area. MDC has welcomed these changes and moved to work more closely with business and labor unions. To locate jobs that provide a living wage for those without college training, MDC's employment focus has changed. For example, instead of looking solely for clerical and service work at nonunion wages from individual employers, it has found success in the construction yard where heavy construction jobs at union wages are available through an industrywide focus on training and job development.

One result of this change in focus is MDC's support of the inclusion of women and minorities in highway construction. Women comprise only 8 percent of the industry's carpentry work force in Washington state. MDC's approach has been to link creatively with contractors, trainers and carpentry union representatives. These services bridge the gap between low-income individuals and the lucrative careers they seek in highway construction. It becomes a win-win situation for everyone. MDC intends to continue its present trend toward business partnerships with construction trades.

Education is clearly one of the most critical tools available to improve an individual's standard of living. MDC case workers search for every possible opportunity on behalf of their clients. This includes activities for children from birth to 5 and their families in its early childhood programs, activities at family support centers, programs for youth violence and drug prevention, and its partnership with Pacific Lutheran University. The university has generously volunteered space for counselors to mentor, instruct and advocate for local high school students. The Upward Bound Program is a product of this partnership, assuring that children from low-income homes in which no one has gone to college may succeed in high school and complete a program of post-secondary education: out of poverty. MDC finds that once a family member enters college, others follow.

In 1999 MDC documented service to 23,500 individuals in Tacoma and Pierce County. However, the agency has found that to continue this level of service is to identify small individual steps, target goals, and then become the building block, or catalyst, in a holistic plan. The individual staff members of MDC accomplish a balancing act by confronting current challenges one at a time while seeing the future as they identify emerging strengths and opportunities for service. Because of this commitment, the children and families of today will be able to continue to look with hope and optimism to the years ahead.

MultiCare Health System

When the famous English writer Rudyard Kipling visited Puget Sound in the 1880s, he found Tacoma a booming western town. Economic prosperity and an expanding railroad spurred construction of new lumber mills and factories along the waterfront. As the city grew, a need for health care grew as well to serve an increasingly diverse population.

The seeds of a community-based health care facility — now MultiCare Health System — were sown when Fannie C. Paddock Memorial Hospital was constructed from a dance hall in 1882. The hospital opened the state's first School of Nursing in 1895 and changed its name to Tacoma General Hospital in 1915. Named for the mother of Dr. Albert Bridge, Mary Bridge Children's Hospital was established 40 years later, culminating a 35-year fund-raising effort of the Tacoma Orthopedic Guild. It is the only state-designated pediatric trauma center in southwest Washington.

The MultiCare Health System main campus, located in Tacoma, is home to Tacoma General Hospital, Mary Bridge Children's Hospital and Health Center and Day Surgery of Tacoma. It has become a major referral center for many medical specialties and sub-specialties serving southwest Washington.

Mary Bridge Children's Hospital, Tacoma General Hospital and Doctor's Hospital joined forces in 1980 to create MultiCare Medical Center, which later became MultiCare Health System, a not-for-profit corporation providing quality health care to the people of Pierce and south King counties, and all of southwest Washington. Soon afterward, Allenmore Hospital became part of MultiCare, with a focus on caring for the senior community.

The organization soon expanded to include several clinics, urgent care centers, a network of physicians, home health and hospice services, a day surgery center and three community-based hospitals governed by local boards of citizens. Tacoma General features the second-largest obstetrical center in the state, one of the area's busiest 24-hour emergency departments, adult and pediatric intensive care facilities, and serves as the region's largest referral center. In fact, more babies have been born there than at any other hospital in Pierce County.

Tacoma General also serves as the administrative agent for the Northwest Community Clinical Oncology Program (CCOP), a research program funded by the National Cancer Institute. CCOP allows patients to participate in national cancer studies and gain access to the newest cancer treatments. Tacoma General also has a special Breast Health Center emphasizing early detection.

While Tacoma General Hospital focuses on adult care, Mary Bridge Children's Hospital provides complete pediatric inpatient medical/surgical services, critical care transport, and houses the state's only designated pediatric trauma department in southwest Washington. In addition, in January 1998, Mary Bridge began offering pediatric open heart surgery for children through the Mary Bridge Pediatric Heart Center. In a family-centered care environment, parents may visit 24 hours a day, sleep in their child's hospital room or in nearby parent apartments, and use an on-site family resource center.

Mary Bridge Children's Health Center houses more than 36 pediatric specialty outpatient clinics to treat conditions ranging from developmental problems to cancer. Satellite clinics in Olympia, Covington and Silverdale serve families in outlying areas of southwest Washington. And through The Center for Childhood Safety, Mary Bridge loans out life-jackets, teaches child safety and CPR classes, and demonstrates how to wear bicycle helmets and install child car seats.

The multidisciplinary team approach and quality patient care are at the heart of the care provided at all MultiCare facilities. Many innovative and state-of-the-art programs make MultiCare a premier health care organization. Members of MultiCare Health System combine resources and expertise to bring many special programs to the community. In 1998, Mary Bridge Children's Hospital launched a full-scale pediatric open-heart surgery program that offers a full range of cardiac care — from stress testing to surgery to 24-hour on-site pediatric echocardiography.

MultiCare pioneered open-heart surgery in the state, performing the first surgeries in Washington, and continues to lead the way in heart procedures. Adult patients receive treatment at three sites: Allenmore Hospital, Covington MultiCare Clinic and Tacoma General Hospital, the regional referral center for advanced cardiac care.

At the MultiCare Center for Advanced Neurosciences, patients receive comprehensive care for diseases involving the brain and nervous system. Breakthrough technologies are available, such as frameless stereotactically guided brain surgery. Guided by three-dimensional computer imaging technology first used by the military, neurosurgeons can now reach tumors once considered inoperable. Implantations of Vagus Nerve Stimulators are also being performed to help patients control epilepsy.

A patient with visual impairment might be referred to Allenmore Hospital, where the Elizabeth Baker Kelley Eye Center provides progressive treatments for vision problems. Established in 1929, Allenmore joined the MultiCare family in 1989 and offers complete adult care, radiology and a host of special programs. The HealthWorks program focuses on prevention and treatment of job-related injuries, and the Pulmonary Rehabilitation program helps people suffering from chronic respiratory ailments such as emphysema and asthma.

Personalized care extends throughout the MultiCare system, from hospitals to family doctors. The MultiCare Medical Group, a growing network of more than 150 physicians, provides primary care and specialty services such as dermatology, urology, obstetrics and gynecology across Pierce and south King counties. When primary care physicians are unavailable, MultiCare Urgent Care centers provide immediate treatment for minor illnesses and injuries.

MultiCare complements the finest medical care with a commitment to community outreach. MultiCare Home Services brings treatment to the patient's home with services such as infusion therapy, rehabilitation and support for the terminally ill. Other community services include grief and loss counseling for both children and adults, and pediatric and hospice care.

If Rudyard Kipling were to visit Tacoma today, he would find a comprehensive health care system evolving to meet the community's changing needs. From the early stages of pregnancy to end-of-life care, from pediatric heart surgery to minor illnesses and injuries, MultiCare Health System will always remain dedicated to the lives of the people it serves.

Tacoma General Hospital was originally founded in 1882 as the Fannie C. Paddock Memorial Hospital. MultiCare's main campus was established in 1895 with this building, located on J Street.

Tacoma Historical Society

For over 100 years, Tacoma and its busy port have been key elements in the Pacific Northwest's rich economic tapestry. As the city grew and prospered, it left in its wake a rich heritage that, until 1989, received little attention. Thanks in large part to the efforts of the Tacoma Historical Society, this long-standing wrong has at last been righted. In the process, one of the Northwest's most important cities has seen its history rescued from oblivion and rehabilitated in a most modern, high-tech fashion.

Boys play baseball with the 1890s Pierce County Courthouse as a backdrop. Tacoma was able to lure the county seat from Steilacoom in 1880. *Tacoma Public Library*

The Tacoma Historical Society is resurrecting an earlier commitment to preserve the city's roots first introduced by Clinton P. Ferry in the 1890s. His vision was an art museum where Tacomans could see replicas of European masters. Soon, however, the Ferry Museum's collections expanded to include Native American and pioneer artifacts and photographs. By the early 1900s its exhibit space in the Pierce County Courthouse was packed. So too was the exhibit room in the City Hall used by the Washington State Historical Society, an organization also formed in Tacoma in the 1890s.

Under the leadership of William H. Gilstrap, who ran both institutions by this time, the two museums joined forces to construct a building on Stadium Way, with the Ferry Museum wing dedicated in 1917. But then, in 1931, the board deeded all of the Tacoma collections to the Washington State Historical Society and — for all practical purposes — Tacoma lost its first history museum.

Because of these events, much of Tacoma's own history was ignored until local citizens came together to found the Tacoma Historical Society. From its very first meetings in 1989, the society has sought to restore the city's forgotten past. Out of the early meetings the structure of the society took shape and with a strong leadership team in place, the nonprofit organization began holding general meetings every month. Talented and

Loggers and portable mills traveled the Tacoma townsite to prepare the land for streets and houses. MSCUA, *Washington Libraries, Photo by Hattie King*

committed people flowed into the society's ranks, and from them came a vision for the organization's future that was as bright as it was ambitious.

Today a healthy, active Tacoma Historical Society continues to thrive. Since its early origins, it has grown to include some 2,000 members and has become quite active in preserving Tacoma's roots. Each year it hosts the Tacoma Homes Tour, where interested people can come and learn about their neighborhoods. The city's older areas contain some beautiful historical treasures including well-kept homes that date back over a century. Proceeds from the tours are specifically reserved for a new Tacoma museum.

The society also sponsors and co-sponsors other events throughout the year. Among the most treasured of these is a Day of Remembrance held to honor Japanese-American citizens interned during World War II. The society has also developed historical photo exhibits and aided other historical organizations by lending emotional support and technical assistance. Monthly the society hosts guest speakers who give talks on a wide range of topics including everything from the collapse of the infamous Narrows Bridge, to the histories of local lumber mills and railroads, biographies of notable Tacomans and studies of the multicultural aspects of the city's roots.

As the Tacoma Historical Society grew through the 1990s, many longtime residents donated time, effort and interesting historical artifacts. The organization now has an archive that includes hundreds of newspaper editions, public documents, city directories, thousands of photographs and even a 1950s-vintage hook-and-ladder fire engine. The latter was once a part of Tacoma's fire department and was recently restored to working condition before being donated to the historical society.

High technology also features prominently in the society's future. Most recently, the board of directors has devoted much of its time to the establishment of a new Tacoma museum, its most ambitious project thus far. When the museum is constructed, the board intends to include many interactive, high-tech displays. These will be balanced with more traditional exhibits in order to give visitors both a hands-on experience as well as a fascinating glimpse into Tacoma's diverse history.

The hard-working volunteers who run the Tacoma Historical Society understand the importance of lending a hand to other organizations whenever possible. The leadership's expertise at grant writing has been shared with innumerable volunteer groups around town. Technical knowledge has also been shared, in addition to the time it devotes to promoting the community and its rich heritage.

With energy and vision, the Tacoma Historical Society embraces the new century with a renewed commitment to preserve the heritage of the previous ones. Through its cadre of hard-charging volunteers, the spirit of the past will continue to flourish and remind all Tacomans of the vibrant chapters of their city's past.

The first trains to arrive in Tacoma from Portland, Oregon, were ferried across the Columbia River at Kalama.
MSCUA, Washington Libraries

"March King" John Philip Sousa performing in the Stadium Bowl
Tacoma Public Library

READ, Inc. dba Einstein Learning Center

The Einstein Learning Center in Tacoma specializes in helping people identify their learning strengths and weaknesses. Dyslexia, the learning disability that can prevent an individual from achieving success in reading; dysgraphia, the inability to write easily and coherently; and dyscalculia, the absence of functional mathematical ability, are some of the various learning disorders that can challenge intelligent and motivated people. The center offers a thorough screening and any necessary testing by the multidisciplinary team of professionals to establish a legally defensible diagnosis. The clients then are given the tools and assistance to learn in their own distinctive way. The mission of Einstein Learning Center is to assist clients in understanding how they learn and utilize their strengths to realize academic success and function more productively throughout their lives.

The center, the only one of its kind in Tacoma, offers help to clients of all ages. Children in prekindergarten through high school are brought here by their parents, but many adults seek answers as well. One recent and inspiring client first confronted her problems with learning at the age of 63. When she saw her grandchildren facing frustrations similar to those she had always endured, she decided it was time to set a positive example and help both generations. Many clients who return for instruction after the initial screening and diagnosis have struggled for years in school and consequently deal with anger and frustration as well as low self-esteem. Thus the job of the center is complex, addressing other issues such as Attention Deficit/Hyperactivity Disorder (AD/HD), which are interwoven with learning challenges.

Individual contact between clients and staff members is the backbone of the center's success. After a thorough screening by the operations manager, the client administrator establishes close contact with parents and clients, offering reassurance when needed. Assessment and counseling are provided by the clinical psychologist, who is also involved with the testing and diagnosis. Individual teachers are passionate about each student's progress. A 62-year-old instructor agreed to learn to skateboard if her student would work on his reading. She learned to manage a skateboard, and he made progress in reading; perhaps just as importantly, the staff finally saw him smile.

Although the Einstein Learning Center has been providing services only since 1997, originally under the name READ, Inc., it is already well established as a community educational resource and carries regular contracts with area private schools for their testing.

The dedicated staff at Einstein Learning Center *Photo by Gayle Rieber*

The center would like to see a collaboration or partnership in the future among all area schools, both public and private, including colleges and universities, to identify and assist people with special learning needs. Such a comprehensive program will be supported by decades of well-documented research identifying various learning needs. Through this ambitious goal each individual will become a more productive member of the community.

Tacoma Economic Development Department

Tacoma is a city on the move. With help and planning from the Tacoma Economic Development Department (TEDD), businesses are moving in, the downtown is being revitalized, and the city is fast emerging from the shadow of big-sister Seattle.

TEDD was established by a city ordinance passed in 1999. City council members, aware that Tacoma wasn't keeping pace with the rapid economic growth of other Puget Sound communities, designed TEDD to focus on Tacoma's specific needs and market its advantages. TEDD's goals were to establish Tacoma's reputation as a highly desirable city in which to live and do business, attract outside investment, and strengthen the downtown through new construction and renovation. The department has been successful on all counts, and Tacoma is enjoying a renaissance.

Tacoma's skyline at night, with the refurbished Union Station building in the foreground

One of TEDD's strategies was to spread the word to businesses and investors: Tacoma is a dynamic place to do business. It is "America's No. 1 Wired City," thanks to its Click! Network — the largest municipally owned infrastructure for high-speed cable and telecommunications in the United States. Competitive lease rates for downtown office spaces, affordable residential real estate and a sane commute make Tacoma a smart place for entrepreneurs and their families.

Another TEDD initiative is the development of cultural institutions in Tacoma's downtown. In partnership with existing public and private programs, TEDD is working to increase public art by securing funding for art projects, expanding Tacoma's cultural exchanges with sister cities, and creating affordable spaces for artists to live and work in. One project showcases the work of internationally renowned glass artist and Tacoma son Dale Chihuly. The planned Museum of Glass will feature $12 million of Chihuly's work, including the Chihuly Bridge of Glass over which visitors will access the museum from downtown. The Tacoma-Pierce County Convention and Visitor Bureau is making residents and visitors more aware of Tacoma's tourism opportunities by publishing a visitor's guide to the city.

Construction of new spaces and renovation of old buildings is a TEDD priority. Tacoma's award-winning new downtown code — about one-tenth the size of the former code — has made investing in Tacoma simpler, and businesses and developers are responding by putting up new buildings around town. Tacoma's downtown also boasts many beautiful, historic buildings, and TEDD is working with the city to preserve and refurbish the city's past. "Adaptive reuse" is making the buildings functional again; nine buildings have been restored during the past two years. The University of Washington in Tacoma is expanding its course offerings and campus, enabling more Tacomans to receive an excellent education without commuting to Seattle. Tacoma neighborhoods are also getting assistance from TEDD, which is increasing affordable housing, offering help in the acquisition and preservation of natural areas, working to solve transportation concerns and encouraging more citizen participation in neighborhood activities and planning.

Tacoma's Economic Development Department is helping the city focus attention and resources on Tacoma's specific needs. By targeting projects that will make the city more attractive to outside investors and potential new residents, TEDD is helping to strengthen Tacoma's economic future. TEDD's Tacoma renaissance is educating others about what its residents already know: that Tacoma is a wired and wonderful place to live and work.

Bibliography

This bibliography is designed to introduce readers to a few sources on the history of Tacoma and Pierce County. Anyone who has scanned the offerings at the Tacoma Public Library's Northwest Room, the Pierce County Library system, or the libraries of other local towns and cities know that this listing barely touches the tip of the possibilities. From Gig Harbor and Anderson Island to Eatonville and Buckley there are historical societies and museums whose collections provide more clues to our heritage. Major research institutions such as the Washington State Historical Society in Tacoma, the University of Washington Library Special Collection Division in Seattle, and the Oregon History Center in Portland are also custodians of information vital to an understanding of our past. Then too there is the Internet, where many Web pages open the door to more and more history.

American Friends Service Committee. *Uncommon Controversy: Fishing Rights and the Muckleshoot, Puyallup, and Nisqually Indians.* Seattle: University of Washington Press, 1970.

Anderson, Dennis A. "Carl August Darmer: Architect for the City of Destiny." *Pacific Northwest Quarterly* 71 (January 1980): 24-30.

Andrew, Charles E. *Final Report on Tacoma Narrows Bridge, Tacoma, Washington.* Olympia: Washington Toll Bridge Authority, 1952.

Baarsma, William Henry. "A Study of Dissension and Conflict Over Council-Manager Government in Tacoma, Washington...." PhD dissertation, George Washington University, 1973.

Bancroft, Hubert H. History of *Washington, Idaho and Montana,* 1845-1889. San Francisco: The History Company, 1890.

Bates, Mildred. *A House of Mercy.* Olympia: Warren's, 1976.

Bergman, Hans. *History of Scandinavians in Tacoma and Pierce County: With Brief History of Tacoma and Early Settlement.* Tacoma: N.p., 1926.

Bjarke, Nils, "Fern Hill: The Village Where Memories Linger, 1866-1941." Fern Hill Historical Society, Tacoma, N.d. Photocopy.

_____. "The Naches Pass Highway." Fern Hill Historical Society, Tacoma, 1945. Photocopy.

Blackwell, Alice E. *Reminiscences of Tacoma.* Tacoma, 1911.

Blackwell, Ruby Chapin. *A Girl in Washington Territory.* Tacoma: Washington State Historical Society, 1972.

Bonney, William Pierce. *History of Pierce County, Washington.* Chicago: Pioneer Historical Publishing Company, 1927.

Boyland, Bernard. L. "Camp Lewis: Promotion and Construction." *Pacific Northwest Quarterly* 58 (October 1967): 188-195.

British and American Join Commission For the Final Settlement of the Claims of the Hudson's Bay and the Puget's Sound Agricultural Companies. Washington, D.C.: Lontreal Lovell, 1865-1869.

Carpenter, Cecelia Svinth. *Fort Nisqually: A Documented History of Indian and British Interaction.* Tacoma: Tahoma Research Service, 1986.

Chechopoulos, Helena. *History of Wright Park.* Seattle, 1993.

Chittenden, Hiram Martin. *Report on an Investigation by a Board of Engineers of the Means of Controlling Floods in Duwamish-Puyallup Valleys and Their Tributaries in the State of Washington.* Seattle: Loman, 1907.

Cloquet, Victor. *An Historical Sketch of St. Joseph's Catholic Slovak Church, Tacoma, Washington,* 1911-1986. Tacoma: St. Joseph's Catholic Church, 1986.

Coan, C.F. "The Adoption of the Reservation Policy in the Paicfic Northwest, 1853-1855." *Oregon Historical Quarterly* 23 (March 1922): 1-38.

Coleman, Edmund T. "Puget Sound and the Northern Pacific Railroad." *Washington Historical Quarterly* 23 (October 1932): 243-260.

Completion of the Cascade Division Northern Pacific R.R. And a Description of Tacoma the Western Terminus. Saint Paul, Minnesota: Pioneer Press Company, 1887.

Cotrano, Ross Ralph. *History of the Northern Pacific Land Grant, 1900-1952: Epic of Rails and Cities.* New York: Arno Press, 1979.

Cox. Thomas. Mills and Markets: *A History of the Pacific Coast Lumber Industry to 1900.* Seattle: University of Washington Press, 1974.

Curtis, Joan, Alice Watson, and Bette Bradley, eds. *Town on the Sound: Stories of Steilacoom.* Steilacoom: Steilacoom Historical Museum Association, 1988.

Davisson, William I. "Public Utilities in a Frontier City: The Early History of the Tacoma Light and Water Company." *Pacific Northwest Quarterly* 46 (1955): 40-45.

Edwards, G. Thomas, ed. "'Terminus Disease': The Clark P. Crandall Description of Puget Sound in 1871." *Pacific Northwest Quarterly* 70 (October 1979): 163-177.

Ficken, Robert E. *The Forested Land: A History of Lumbering in Western Washington*. Seattle: University of Washington Press, 1987.

_____. "Weyerhaeuser and the Pacific Northwest Timber Industry, 1899-1903." *Pacific Northwest Quarterly* 70 (October 1979): 146-154.

Gibson, James R. *Farming the Frontier: The Agricultural Opening of the Oregon Country 1786-1846*. Seattle: University of Washington Press, 1985.

Gunns, Albert F. "The First Tacoma Narrows Bridge: A Brief History of Galloping Gertie." *Pacific Northwest Quarterly* 72 (October 1981): 162-169.

Gray, Mary A. "Settlement of the Claims in Washington of the Hudson's Bay Company and the Puget's Sound Agricultural Company." *Washington Historical Quarterly* 21 (1930): 95-102.

Haack, Gordon W. *A Historical Study of the Tacoma Transit System*. Tacoma, 1968.

Heckman, Hazel. *Island in the Sound*. Seattle: University of Washington Press, 1967.

Haeberlin, Herman, and Erna Gunther. *The Indians of Puget Sound*. Seattle: University of Washington Press, 1930.

Heritage League of Pierce County. *A History of Pierce County Washington*. Dallas, Texas: Taylor Publishing Company, 1990.

Hall, Nancy Irene. *Carbon River Coal Country*. Enumclaw: Courier Herald Publishing Company, 1980.

Harney, Thomas Porter. *Charles Barstow Wright: A Builder of the Northern Pacific and the City of Tacoma*. Tacoma, N.p., 1956.

Hartwich, Gordon. "Early Settlements in the Puyallup Valley." Master's thesis, University of Washington, 1972.

Harvey, Paul W. *Tacoma Headlines: An Account of Tacoma's News and Newspapers*. Tacoma: The Tacoma News Tribune, 1962.

Hayes, Ralph. *Northwest Black Pioneers: A Centennial Tribute*. Seattle: Bon Marche, 1994.

Heritage, Samuel Leonard. "A Financial History of the City of Tacoma, Washington From 1890 to 1948." Master's thesis, College of Puget Sound, 1949.

Hildebrand, Lorraine Barker. Strawhats, Sandals and Steel: *The Chinese in Washington State*. Tacoma: Washington State Historical Society, 1977.

Hidy, Ralph W., Frank Ernest Hill, and Allen Nevins. *Timber and Men: The Weyerhaeuser Story*. New York: Macmillan Company, 1963.

Hunt, Herbert. *Tacoma: Its History and Its Builders, a Half Century of Activity*. Chicago: S.J. Clarke, 1916.

"Indian Summer Project." National Lawyers Guild, Seattle, 1973. Photocopy.

Johnston, Norman J. "The Frederick Law Olmsted Plan for Tacoma." *Pacific Northwest Quarterly* 66 (July 1975): 97-104.

Justice to the Maintain Committee. *Brief Submitted to the U.S. Geographic Board*. Tacoma, 1917.

"Kaleidoscope: A History of McKinley Hill, as told by 'Old Timers' for the August 4, 1988 McKinley Hill Festival." Tacoma, 1989.

Kamens, Brian. *The Tacoma Neighborhoods Index: Information on Greater Tacoma Neighborhoods, Subdivisions, Additions and Housing Projects from the Tacoma Daily Ledger (1883-1937), the Tacoma News Tribune (1938-1941) and Other Sources*. Tacoma: Tacoma Public Library, 1997.

Karlin, Jules Alexander. "The Anti-Chinese Outbreak in Tacoma, 1885." *Pacific Historical Review* 23 (1954): 271-283.

Keve, Paul W. *The McNeil Century: The Life and Times of and Island Prison*. Chicago: Nelson-Hall, 1984.

LeWarne, Charles Pierce. *Utopias on Puget Sound 1885-1915*. Seattle: University of Washington Press, 1975.

Magden, Ronald. *Furusato: Tacoma-Pierce County Japanese, 1888-1988*. Tacoma: R-4 Printing, Inc., 1998.

_____. *The Working Longshoreman*. Tacoma: International Longshoremen's and Warehousemen's Union Local 23 of Tacoma, 1991.

Magden, Ronald, and A.D. Martinson. *The Working Waterfront: The Story of Tacoma's Ships and Men*. Tacoma: International Longshoremen's and Warehousemen's Union Local 23 of Tacoma, 1982.

Magnusson, Elva Cooper. "Naches Pass." *Washington Historical Quarterly* 25 (July 1934): 171-181.

Malloy, Dick, ed. *The Tacoma Public Utilities Story: The First 100 Years: 1893-1993*. Tacoma: Tacoma Public Utilities, 1993.

Markholt, Ottilie. *Maritime Solidarity: Pacific Coast Unionism, 1929-1938*. Tacoma: Pacific Coast Maritime History Committee, 1998.

Marshall, Beverly Ann. *Woodrow School: The Heart of Waller Road*. Puyallup: Printed by Puyallup Public Schools, 1989.

Martig, Ralph Richards. "Husdon's Bay Company Claims, 1846-69." *Oregon Historical Quarterly* 36 (1935): 60-70.

Martin, Harry and Caroline Kellogg. *Tacoma: A Pictorial History*. Norfolk: Donning, c.1891.

McConnell, Ronald Lee. "The Changing Urban Structure of Tacoma, Washington." Master's thesis, University of Washington, 1965.

McCoy, Genevieve. "'Mount Tacoma' vs. 'Mount Rainier': The Fight to Rename the Mountain." *Pacific Northwest Quarterly* 77 (October 1986): 139-149.

McPhillips, Dorothy. *They Came from Manitou*. Tacoma, c.1998.

Meeker, Ezra. *Pioneer Reminiscences of Puget Sound: The Tragedy of Leschi*. Seattle: Lowman and Hanford, 1905.

Merritt, Jane T. "Fort Lewis: Evolution of a Landscape." *Columbia* 5 (Winter 1991/92): 27-32.

Morgan, Murray. *The Mill on the Boot: The Story of the St. Paul and Tacoma Lumber Company*. Seattle: University of Washington Press, 1982.

_____. *Puget's Sound: A Narrative of Early Tacoma and the Southern Sound*. Seattle: University of Washington Press, 1979.

Morgan, Murray and Rosa Morgan. *South on the Sound: An Illustrated History of Tacoma and Pierce County*. Woodland Hills, California: Windsor Publications, Inc., 1984.

Munyan, May G. DuPont - *The Story of a Company Town.* Puyallup: The Valley Press, Inc., 1972.

Nadeau, Gene Allen. *Highway to Paradise: A Pictorial History of the Roadway to Mount Rainier.* Tacoma: Valley Press, 1983.

Osness, Richard D. *From Wilderness to Suburbia: An Illustrated History of Parkland, Washington*. Tacoma: Western Media Printing, Inc., 1976.

_____. *Of Lions and Dreams, of Men and Realities: An Illustrated History of Fircrest, Washington*. Tacoma: Western Media Printing, Inc., 1976.

Pierce County Auditor. *Annual Exhibit of Finances of Pierce County: Including a Brief Sketch of Its Resources and Progress During the Past Fifty Years*. Tacoma: Bell Press, 1910.

Pierce County Labor Centennial Committee. *To Live in Dignity: Pierce County Labor, 1883-1989.* Tacoma, 1989.

Petrich, Mary Ann and Barbara Roje. *The Yugoslav in Washington State: Among the Early Settlers.* Tacoma: Washington State Historical Society, 1984.

Prosch, Thomas W. *McCarver and Tacoma*. Seattle: Lowman and Hanford, 1906.

Quiett, Glenn Chesney. *They Built the West: An Epic of Rails and Cities.* New York: D. Appleton-Century Company, 1934.

Ramsay, Guy Reed. *Postmarked Washington: Pierce County.* Tacoma: Washington State Historical Society, 1981.

Reese, Gary Fuller. "Historic Roads and Trails of Pierce County. Tacoma: Tacoma Public Library, 1974. Photocopy.

_____. "Origins of Pierce County Place Names." Tacoma: Tacoma Public Library, 1989. Photocopy.

Report on Flood Control of White-Stuck and Puyallup Rivers Inter-County River Improvement. Tacoma: Johnson-Cox Company, 1920.

Retherford, Sylvia. *Home at Home.* N.p., 1982.

Reynolds, Clinton. "The Early History of Streetcars in Tacoma." Tacoma, 1920. Photocopy.

Ripley, Thomas Emerson. *Green Timber: On the Flood Tide to Fortune in the Great Northwest.* Palo Alto, California: American West Publishing Company, 1968.

Saum, Lewis O. "William Lightfoot Visscher and the 'Eden of the West.'" *Pacific Northwest Quarterly* 71 (January 1980): 2-14.

Schwantes, Carlos A. "From Anti-Chinese Agitation to Reform Politics: The Legacy of the Knights of Labor in Washington and the Pacific Northwest." *Pacific Historical Quarterly* 88 (Fall 1997): 174-184.

Shackleford, Elizabeth. "The History of the Puyallup Indian Reservation." Master's thesis, College of Puget Sound, 1918.

Smalley, Eugene V. *Completion of the Cascade Division of the Northern Pacific Railroad and a Description of Tacoma.* 1887.

Smith, Marian W. *The Puyallup-Nisqually*. New York: Columbia University Press, 1940.

Stanton, William. *The Great United States Exploring Expedition.* Berkeley: University of California Press, 1975.

Sterns, Mavis. *Two Points of View.* Tacoma: Tacoma News Tribune, 1986.

Stevens, Carolyn. "The Tacoma Labor Movement and the First World War." Master's thesis, University of Washington, 1990.

Stone and Webster Engineering Corporation. *White River Development in the Puget Sound District of the State of Washington.* Boston, 1912.

Stover, Karla Wakefield. *A Brief History of Fern Hill.* Tacoma: Tacoma Writer's Club, 1999.

Tacoma Municipal Bulletin. Tacoma: Department of Public Affairs, Health, and Sanitation, 1911-1927.

Tacoma-Pierce County Genealogical Society. *Army Post Condemnation: Camp Lewis, Pierce County, Washington.* Tacoma, 1998.

_____. *History of Southeastern Pierce County, Washington.* Reprint, *History of Tacoma Eastern Area.* Tacoma, 1989.

Tacoma School District No. 10. *A Brief History of Tacoma School District No. 10, 1869-1940.* Tacoma, 1941.

Tacoma: Voices From the Past. 2 vols. Tacoma, 1988 and 1999.

Talbot, Clyde and Ralph Decker. *100 Years of Firefighting in the City of Destiny, Tacoma, Washington.* Tacoma: Pyro Press, 1981.

Taylor, Quintard. *In Search of the Racial Frontier: African Americans in the American West 1528-1990.* New York: W.W. Norton and Company, 1998.

Thorvaldson, Margit. "A Study of the Origin and Development of Pioneer Schools in School District 404, Pierce County, Washington." Master's thesis, University of Washington, 1961.

Tuthill, Rene. *Salishan's Place in History.* Tacoma, 1948.

Walk, George W. "Fighting Fawcett: A Political Biography." Master's thesis, Western Washington State College, 1976.

Wilkeson, Samuel. *Wilkeson's Notes on Puget Sound Being Extracts From Notes by Samuel Wilkeson of a Reconnaissance of the Proposed Route of the Northern Pacific Railroad Made in the Summer of 1869.* N.p.: 1870.

Wing, Robert G., with Gordon Newell. *Peter Puget.* Seattle: Gray Beard Publishing, 1979.

Winn, Joyce Karyl. "The Cowlitz Controversy, 1947-1962: Politics of Fish and Power." Master's thesis, University of Washington, 1977.

Winston, Dorothy E. Thompson. *Early Spanaway.* Tacoma: Graphic Press, 1976.

Wright, Judy. "History of the Puyallup Tribe of Indians." Tacoma: The Puyallup Tribal Council, n.d.

Appendix

1.
A SAMPLE OF PUGET SOUND PLACES NAMED DURING THE VANCOUVER AND WILKES EXPEDITIONS

VANCOUVER

ADMIRALTY INLET: The British Admiralty of the British Royal Navy.

MOUNT RAINIER: Admiral Peter Rainier of the Royal Navy.

PUGET SOUND: Peter Puget, the first European to explore the southern sound.

WILKES

AGATE PASS: Alfred S. Agate, expedition artist.

ANDERSON ISLAND: Alexander C. Anderson, superintendent at Fort Nisqually at the time of the Wilkes Expedition.

BAINBRIDGE ISLAND: Commodore William Bainbridge.

BLAKELY ROCK: Captain Johnston Blakely.

BRACKENRIDGE PASSAGE: William D. Brackenridge, naturalist.

BUDD INLET: Acting Master Thomas A. Budd.

CARR'S INLET: Lieutenant Overton Carr, who did astronomical observations.

CASE'S INLET: Lieutenant A.L. Case.

COLVOS PASSAGE: Passed Midshipman George M. Colvocoressis.

COMMENCEMENT BAY: The start of the survey of lower Puget Sound.

DALCO PASSAGE: No explanation given.

DANA'S PASSAGE: James Dwight Dana, mineralogist.

DAYS ISLAND: Stephen W. Days, a hospital steward.

DRAYTON PASSAGE: Joseph Drayton, artist.

DYE'S INLET: John W. Dye, assistant taxidermist.

ELD INLET: Passed Midshipman Henry Eld.

ELLIOTT BAY: Chaplain J.L. Elliott.

FOX ISLAND: J.L. Fox, assistant surgeon.

GIG HARBOR: Because it had sufficient depth for a small vessel.

HALE'S PASSAGE: Horatio Hale, philologist.

HAMMERSLEY'S INLET: Mishipman George W. Hammersley.

HARSTENE ISLAND: Lieutenant H.J. Harstein.

HENDERSON BAY: Quartermaster James Henderson.

HERRON ISLAND: Lewis Herron, cooper. Peter Puget named this Wednesday Island because of the day of the week, due to heavy storms, he was forced to spend the night.

KETRON ISLAND: William Kittson, first superintendent of the Puget's Sound Agricultural Company. Peter Puget named it Long Island because of its shape.

MAURY ISLAND: Lieutenant William L. Maury.

McNEIL ISLAND: Captain William H. McNeill of the Hudson's Bay Company steamer Beaver. Peter Puget named it Pigeon Island.

NARROWS: The narrow passageway separating upper and lower Puget Sound.

PICKERING PASSAGE: Charles Pickering, naturalist.

POINT DEFIANCE: A reference to its potential for the defense of Puget Sound.

POINT FOSDICK: Stephen Fosdick, gunner's mate.

POINT HARMON: The point of land in Commencement Bay where downtown Tacoma now stands. There was more than one John Harmon on the expedition and Wilkes doesn't say for which one this was named.

POINT HARRIS: Alvin Harris, sailmaker's mate; now named Browns Point.

POINT RICHMOND: William Richmond, a boatswain mate.

SINCLAIR INLET: Acting Master George T. Sinclair.

TOTTON INLET: Passed Midshipman George M. Totton.

WALDRON ISLAND: Thomas W. Waldron.

2.
DONATION LAND CLAIMS IN PIERCE COUNTY

LAFAYETTE BALCH (1851) • Steilacoom

HARRY BARNES (1855) • Fort Lewis (Madigan Hospital)

ISAAC BASTION (n.d.) • Between Roy and McKenna

JAMES H. BELL (1855) • Puyallup

ADAM BENSTON (1854) • North Puyallup

WILLIAM BENSTON (n.d.) • North Puyallup

LEMUEL BILLS (1852) • Steilacoom

WILLIS BOATMAN (1854) • Puyallup River

SHERWOOD BONNEY (1853) • American Lake

JOHN BRADLEY (1855) • Flett Creek

GEORGE BROWN (n.d.) • Frederickson

ANDREW F. BYRD (1853) • Steilacoom Lake

MARION BYRD (n.d.) • Chambers Creek

THOMAS M. CHAMBERS (c.1847-1849) • Steilacoom [Chambers] Creek

JOHN M. CHAPMAN (1851) • Steilacoom

MILTON P. CLUTE (1853) • Lacamas Creek

MICHAEL CONNELL (1853) • Connell's Prairie

EDWARD CROFT (1853) • Parkland

J. CRONAN (n.d.) • Fort Lewis (Madigan Hospital)

HENRY DE LaBUSHALIER (n.d.) • Spanaway Lake

GEORGE DEAN (n.d.) • Lacamas Creek

THOMAS A. DEAN (1853) • Lacamas Creek

NICHOLAS DELIN (1853) • Tacoma

WILLIAM P. DOUGHERTY (1851) • Fleet Creek

C. DOWNEY (1855) • Parkland
G.W. DOWNEY (n.d.) • Tacoma
WILLIAM R. DOWNEY (1853) • Fort Lewis
JESSE DUNLAP (1855) • Larchmont
PAUL EMERY (1855) • South Prairie
MURTY FAHY (1851) • Brookdale (Tule Lake)
JOHN FAWCETT (1854) • Clover Creek
REUBEN FINNELL (n.d.) • Connell's Prairie
GEORGE GIBBS (1854) • Clover Creek
FRANCOIS GRAVELLE (n.d.) • Between Roy and McKenna
GEORGE HAYWOOD (1854) • Stuck River
HENRY HEADLEY (1854) • South Fork Puyallup River
HENRY JOHNS (n.d.) • Spanaway
PETER JUDSON (1853) • Tacoma
L.J. KEACH (1855) • Clover Creek
WILLIAM M. KINCAID (1854)Sumner
A.J. KNIGHT (1853)Steilacoom Lake (Lakewood)
DANIEL LANE (1854)South Fork Puyallup River
LOUIS LATOUR (n.d.) • Roy
JACOB B. LEACH (1855) • Puyallup
JOSEPH LEGARD (1853) • Lacamas Creek
ISAAC LEMON (1853) • Puyallup River
CHRISTOPHER MAHON (1852) • Clover Creek (Spanaway)
ABNER MARTIN (1855) • Fort Lewis
F.A. McCARTY (1855) • McNeil Island
JONATHAN W. McCARTY (1854) • Stuck River
JOHN McCLOUD (1851) • Muck Creek
JOHN McPHAIL (1853) • Muck Creek
EZRA MEEKER (1855) • Midland
J.R. MEEKER (1855) • Tacoma
O.P. MEEKER (n.d.) • Midland
W.P. MELVILLE (n.d.) • Spanaway Creek
FREDERICK MEYER (1853) • Clover Creek
JAMES H. MINSON (1853)Clover Creek
JOHN MONTGOMERY (1853) • Clover Creek
ROBERT S. MORE (1854) • Puyallup River
PETER J. MORLEY (MOREY) (1854) • Brookdale (Tule Lake)
ABELE MORRISON (n.d.) • Stuck River
HENRY MURRAY (1851) • Muck Creek
JOEL MYERS (1853) • Nisqually
JOHN NEISON (1853)Tacoma
ROMNOUS NIX (1855) • • Puyallup River
WILLIAM NORTHOVER (1854) • American Lake
THOMAS OWENS (1854) • Puyallup River
HUGH PATTISON (1853) • Larchmont
ADDISON PERHAM (1853) • Puyallup River
HARRIET M. PERRY (1854) • American Lake
JOHN RIGNEY (1852) • Tacoma
WILLIAM N. SAVAGE (1853) • American Lake Gardens
THEOPHELUS SEARS (1953) • Fort Lewis Ordnance Depot
HENRY SMITH (1853) • Muck Creek
L.A. [C.] SMITH (1847) • Muck Creek
PETER SMITH (1853) • Clover Creek
THOMAS TALLENTIRE [TOLENTIRE] (1852) • Parkland
LEVANT F. THOMPSON (1853) • Sequalitchew Creek
W. VAN BUREN (1855) • Fort Lewis
JOHN VAN BUSKIRK (1851) • Steilacoom
JOHN WALKER (n.d.) • Steilacoom
WILLIAM WALLACE (1853) • Steilacoom opposite Ketron Island
HENRY WHITESELL [WHITSEL] (1854) • Orting
JAMES WILLIAMSON (1853) • Connell's Prairie
PETER WILSON (1854) • Muck Creek
W.B. WILTON (n.d.) • Tacoma
JOHN WITHIEL (1854) • Clover Creek
A.H. WOOLREY (1854) • Puyallup River
ISAAC WOOLREY (1854) • Puyallup River
CHARLES WREN (1849) • Muck Creek
B.F. WRIGHT (1855) • Puyallup
I.H. WRIGHT (1855) • Puyallup

3.
HISTORIC SETTLEMENTS IN PIERCE COUNTY INCLUDING THE FIRST POST OFFICES AND POSTMASTERS

LONGBRANCH PENINSULA
Delano • 1890, Mrs. Nancy E. Tarr
Elgin • 1885, Mrs. Lucinda Minter (originally called Minter)
Glencove • 1891, Warren T. Ball (originally called Balch)
Herron • 1894, Allen W. Fish (originally called Blanchard)
Home • 1900, Elum C. Miles
Key Center
Lakebay • 1882, Henry Tiedman
Longbranch • 1891, Ernest E. Shellgren
Purdy • 1886, Tabor A. Sherman
Vaughn • 1888, Mrs. Alice A. Hunt
Wauna • 1890, B.W. Bashford (originally called Springfield)
West Meridian

GIG HARBOR PENINSULA
Arletta • 1893, Mrs. Rebecca May Powell
Artondale • 1878, Miles B. Hunt (originally called Arton)
Cromwell • 1903, James Gardiner
Dobsons Wharf
East Cromwell • (also called Bay View)
Gig Harbor • 1885, James A. Tyrer • 1946, incorporated
Maplewood
Midway
Nesika
Picnic Point
Point Fosdick
Rosedale • 1887, James B. Brown
Sunrise Beach
Warren • 1904, John P. Stiles
Wollochet • 1891, Mrs. Mary S. Squires

ANDERSON ISLAND
Johnsons Landing
New Amsterdam
Vega • 1890, Bengt Johnson
Yoman • 1908, Alfred W. Willard

McNEIL ISLAND
Bee • 1895, Benjamin F. McCain
Gertrude • 1900, Charles R. Julin
Meridian • 1890, Mary A. Leighton

FOX ISLAND
Cedrona Bay • 1921, Frederick H. Nichols
Fox Island • 1890, John S. Stone
Hope • 1910, Mrs. Alma Wahlquist
Macklin • 1896, Benjamin F. Allen
Sylvan • 1891, Mrs. Gennie Carpenter

LAKES REGION AND VICINITY
American Lake • 1908, Andrew J. Englund
American Lake Gardens
Arkley
Clinton
Custer
Day Island
Dekoven
DuPont • 1909, Evan T. Neal • 1912, incorporated
Fernland
Fircrest • 1909, Francis M. Stephens (originally called Regents Park) • 1925, incorporated
Flett
Fort Steilacoom • 1849, fort established • 1881, Mrs. Eliza S. Waughop
Hunt's Prairie
Interlaaken
Ketron
Lake City • 1890, James Campbell
Lakeview • 1874, Moses Ward
Lakewood • 1996, incorporated
Lemons Beach
Leon • 1893, William M. Welch
Menlo Park
Military • 1906, for Washington National Guard • 1917, Joseph Edward Clark
Mounts
Murray
Nisqually • 1860, John A. Packard
Oakbrook
Oakdale
Ponders
Steilacoom • 1852, James Hall • 1854, incorporated
Sunset Beach • 1905, John Andrew Hoshor
University Place • 1995, incorporated
Whites
Tillicum • 1917, Harry M. Bona

TACOMA VICINITY
Browns Point
Dash Point • 1912, Mrs. Linna Churchill
Reservation
Ruston • 1906, incorporated
Tide Haven
Waverly

PARKLAND/SPANAWAY AND VICINITY
Allison
Beitz Corners
Breckon
Brookdale • 1893, Thomas Hall
Cavenders
Collins
Elk Plain
Fern Hill • 1890, Elias C. Ford
Harvard
Johnsons Corner
Larchmont • 1893, Samuel B. Taylor
Loveland
Midland • 1890, Mrs. Madeline E. McNutty
Murphy
Orchard Hill
Parkland • 1891, Walter S. Temple
Sales
Spanaway • 1890, Fred O. Hurd (originally called Lake Park)
Stevenson
Summit
Van Buren
Woodland

SOUTH PIERCE COUNTY
Greendale
Harts • 1892, William A. Sternitsky
Hewitt
Hillhurst • 1878, Hiram B. McAllister
McKenna • 1907, Adam G. Cook
Muck • 1877, George J. Dougherty
Roy • 1884, Mrs. Rebecca M. Warren • 1908, incorporated

PUYALLUP VALLEY AND VICINITY
Alderton • 1878, Leonard D. Durgin
Ardena
Berrytown
Bonney Lake • 1949, incorporated
Brookville
Cedarhurst
Cushman
Dieringer • 1888, Joseph C. Dieringer (originally called Norwood)
Edgewood • 1894, Niels Jepsen • 1996, incorporated
Elhi • 1892, Cyrus H. Thompson
Fife • 1900, James Stryker (originally called Gardendale) • 1957, incorporated
Firwood
Gardenville
Lake Tapps • 1890, Amos L. Crawford
Liddle • 1912, David H. Brown
McAleer
McMillin • 1890, A. Delbert Hale (originally called Lime Kiln)
Meeker Junction
Milton • 1905, Charles A. Hermann • 1907, incorporated

North Puyallup
Orting • 1877, Henry Whitesell (originally called Carbon) • 1889, incorporated
Puyallup • 1874, Darius M. Ross • 1890, incorporated
Rhode Lake • 1893, Thomas H. Shields
Soldiers Home
Sumner • 1860, John Carson (originally called Franklin) • 1891, incorporated
Willow Junction

SOUTHEASTERN PIERCE COUNTY
Alder • 1902, Martin Hotes
Ashford • 1894, Mrs. Cora J. Ashford
Barling • 1886, Mrs. Mary Barling Hunt
Benston • 1892, Richard Steulman (originally called Huntersville)
Berkeley
Clay City • 1908, Frederick W. Eastman
Cross
Dukes
Eatonville • 1890, Thomas C. Van Eaton • 1909, incorporated
Elbe • 1892, Cyrus H. Thompson
Electron • 1903, August W. Neubauer
Firgrove
Fisk (also called Eldridge)
Frederickson • 1920, Oliver R. Anderson
Glennis • 1893, Arthur Devore
Graham • 1903, Charles W. Ritchie
Harding
Holz
Kapowsin • 1902, Charles A. Fix (originally called Hall)
Kirby
LaGrande • 1910, Hugh L. Ross
Lakehead • 1904, Lewis A.J. Metsker
Leber • 1884, Peter L. Leber
Longmire • 1908, E.L. Burnham
Meta • 1892, Walter Baker
Morgan's Lake
National • 1910, Lynn H. Miller
Nelson
Ohop • 1910, Francis H. Skewis
Park Junction
Reliance
Stringtown
Tanwax • 1890, Mrs. Frank Hornaday
Thrift
Williamson

COAL COUNTRY AND VICINITY
Arlene Mills • 1910, Herbert S. Robb
Broomfield
Buckley • 1888, David S. Morris • 1890, incorporated
Burnett • 1888, Frank Athol
Carbonado • 1880, Eben G. Ingalls (originally called Carbondale) • 1948, incorporated
Cascade Junction
Crocker
Douty
Fairfax • 1896, Theron B. Corey
Grindstone (also called Barktown and Palace Camp)
Hillsboro
Lower Burnett
Lower Fairfax
Manley-Moore
Marion • 1883, Jere Stilley
Melmont • 1902, Henry L. Hawkins
Montezuma • 1901, Robert M. Thompson
Pittsburg
South Prairie • 1884, William E. Owen (originally called Melrose) • 1909, incorporated
South Willis
Spiketon • 1910, William D.C. Spike
Wilkeson • 1877, George D. Arnold • 1909, incorporated
Wingate

FAR EASTERN PIERCE COUNTY
Crystal
Greenwater
Parkway • 1931, John Espen

4.
THE INCORPORATED TOWNS AND CITIES OF PIERCE COUNTY

BONNEY LAKE (1949): Named for William Bonney, a settler who arrived about 1900 and whose cabin was one of the first on the hill near the lake.
Post Office: None
First recorded plat: Drawn from the Donald Fruit Tracts and approved by the City Council in 1952.

BUCKLEY (1890): Named for J.W. Buckley who was Division Superintendent of the Northern Pacific Railroad at this time.
Post Office: 1888, David S. Morris
First recorded plat: Alexander and James Wickersham, May 19, 1888

CARBONADO (1948): Possibly named for the Carbon River which runs below the town and that the river was named for the coal which was found in the region.
Post Office: 1880, Eben G. Ingalls
First recorded plat: Carbon Hill Coal Company by the Pacific Coast Coal Company, N.D. Moore and H.M. Watkins, November 6, 1937.

DuPONT (1912): Names for the DuPont Company which created the town for its workers.
Post Office: 1909, Evan T. Neal
First recorded plat: DuPont Company, W.C. Spruance and C. Copeland, November 13, 1928.

EATONVILLE (1909): Named by T.C. Van Eaton who platted the town.
Post Office: 1890, Thomas C. Van Eaton
First recorded plat: Thomas C. Van Eaton, June 2, 1897

EDGEWOOD (1996): Named because of its location on the edge of the woods that bordered the eastern part of the lower Puyallup Valley.
Post Office: 1894, Niels Jepsen
First recorded plat: multiple

FIFE (1957): Named for either William H. Fife, or his son William J.
Post Office: 1900, James A. Stryker
First recorded plat: multiple

FIRCREST (1925): Named because of the many Douglas Firs in the area.
Post Office: Regents Park, 1909, Francis M. Stephens
First recorded plat: Regents Park, Narrows Land Company, W.A. Irwin and E.R. York, May 4, 1907

GIG HARBOR (1946): Named during the Wilkes expedition in 1841 because the harbor was sufficient for small ships.
Post Office: 1885, James A. Tyrer
First recorded plat: Alfred M. Burnham, April 19, 1888

LAKEWOOD (1996): Named because of all the lakes and forests in the area.
Post Office: None
First recorded plat: multiple

MILTON (1907): Named because a mill was built here to provide lumber for constructing the Interurban tracks.
Post Office: 1905, Charles A. Hermann
First recorded plat: Milton Land Company by T.B. Wallace and C.B. Dodge, January 13, 1905

ORTING (1889):
Considered to be of Puyallup origin meaning "a prairie in the wood."
Post Office: Carbon, 1877, Henry Whitesell
First recorded plat: F.E. Eldridge, August 8, 1887

PUYALLUP (1890): Named for the Puyallup Tribe of Indians
Post Office: 1874, Darius M. Ross
First recorded plat: Ezra Meeker, June 28, 1877

ROY (1908): Named for Roy McNaught, son of the founder of the town.
Post Office: 1884, Mrs. Rebecca M. Warren
First recorded plat: James F. McNaught, June 9, 1884

RUSTON (1906): Named for William R. Rust president of the Tacoma Smelter at the time he sold it to ASARCO.
Post Office: None
First recorded plat: Howard Heights, Tacoma Smelter and Refining Company, October 5, 1891 and June 24, 1901

SOUTH PRAIRIE (1909): So named because of its location south of Connell Prairie.
Post Office: Melrose, 1884, Warren E. Owen
First recorded plat: Francis Bisson, April 6, 1888

STEILACOOM (1854): Named for the Steilacoom Tribe of Indians.
Post Office: 1852, James Hall
First recorded plats: John M. Chapman and Lafayette Balch, September 14, 1853

SUMNER (1891): Two name origins have been suggested: United States Senator Charles Sumner or Thomas Sumner, Ezra Meeker's wife's father.
Post Office: Franklin, 1860, John Carson
First recorded plat: George Ryan and John F. Kincaid, August 31, 1883

UNIVERSITY PLACE (1995): So named because it was a proposed location for the University of Puget Sound.
Post Office: None
First recorded plat: University Land Company, Ira A. Towne and G.W. Thompson, February 21, 1895

WILKESON (1909): Named for Samuel Wilkeson, Sr., who was secretary of the Northern Pacific Railroad at the time.
Post Office: 1877, George D. Arnold
First recorded plat: Samuel Wilkeson, Jr., April 18, 1889

5.

A Brief Chronology of Tacoma and Pierce County History

1833 The HBC established Fort Nisqually on the plains bounded by the Nisqually River and Sequalitchew Creek.

1839 HBC officials created the Puget's Sound Agricultural Company as a way to expand business activity beyond fur trading. One year later, Fort Nisqually became the northern headquarters for the new company.

1841 The HBC attempted to lure permanent settlers from its Red River colony to the land surrounding Fort Nisqually.

1841 The United States Exploring Expedition, headed by Charles Wilkes, began its surveys of Oregon and Washington, using Fort Nisqually as a base of operations in the Puget Sound region.

1844 Joseph Heath, a Scot, settled near Chambers (Steilacoom) Creek north of Fort Nisqually. He farmed and raised sheep until his death in 1849.

1846 The Oregon Treaty between the United States and Great Britain established the boundary between the two countries at the 49th parallel.

1849 HBC officers at Fort Nisqually agreed to lease Joseph Heath's farm to the U.S. Army for what became Fort Steilacoom. Company M, First Artillery under the command of Captain Bennett H. Hill arrived in July. It remained a military fort until 1868.

1850 Donation Land Act passed by Congress.

1852
- Steilacoom post office established.
- Nicholas Delin established a mill at the head of Commencement Bay.

1853
- The Oregon Territorial Legislature established Pierce County.
- Congress created Washington Territory.
- The Longmire-Byles wagon train entered Pierce County over Naches Pass.
- Peter Judson established a claim on the future Tacoma site.
- John M. Chapman and Lafayette Balch platted the two separate plats that became Steilacoom.

1854
- Isaac I. Stevens, as Territorial Superintendent of Indian Affairs, negotiated the Medicine Creek Treaty with the Nisqually, Steilacoom, Puyallup and Muckleshoot tribes.
- Town of Steilacoom incorporated.

1855 Local dissatisfaction among the Native Americans throughout Washington Territory lead to Indian wars in Puget Sound which continued to 1856.

1858 The Washington Territorial Volunteers, under orders from Isaac I. Stevens and following a period of martial law in Pierce County, hanged Nisqually Chief Leschi at a site east of Fort Steilacoom.

1862 Homestead Act passed by Congress.

1864
- Congress incorporated the Northern Pacific Railroad Company
- Job Carr selected his claim at present-day Old Tacoma.

1868 M.M. McCarver acquired a portion of Job Carr's claim.

1869
- Janet Steele opened the Steele Hotel in Tacoma City.
- Tacoma post office and voting precinct established.
- Jay Cooke became the financier for the Northern Pacific Railroad.
- (November) Anthony Carr filed his Tacoma plat.
- (December) McCarver filed his Tacoma City plat.
- First lumber sawed at the Hanson-Ackerson Mill.

1870
- Construction of the NPRR line began.
- Jay Emmon Smith and John Swan offer their land on McNeil Island for a territorial prison.

1871
- NPRR began laying track from Kalama to Puget Sound.
- William Creviston became the first settler at Lakebay on the Longbranch Peninsula.

1873
- (July) Tacoma selected as the NPRR terminus.
- (August) James Tilton began to create a town plat for the terminus.
- (September) M.M. McCarver, John S. Hill and D.B. Hannah completed the McCarver Street wharf.
- (September) Tacoma Land Company formed.
- (September) Frederick Law Olmsted hired to develop a town plat for the terminus.
- (September) Jay Cooke's financial empire collapsed.
- (December) Last spike driven for Kalama to Tacoma line.
- (December) Olmsted plan delivered and rejected by the Tacoma Land Company.
- Tacoma City residents completed construction of St. Peter's on Starr Street as the city's first church.

1874
- Survey for New Tacoma plat completed.
- (June) Tacoma City government formed.
- (June) First recorded burial at Oakwood cemetery.
- (July) New Tacoma post office established.
- Patrons of Husbandry, or Grange, organizations first appeared at Puyallup and Steilacoom.
- Robert Fiander filed a claim in the Ohop Valley.

1876 Miles B. Hunt became the first settler on Wollochet Bay on the Gig Harbor Peninsula.

1877
- NPRR construction was completed to the coal fields of Wilkeson. The railroad also moved its construction and repair shops from Kalama to Tacoma.
- Construction of coal bunkers along Tacoma shoreline began.
- Hatch Mill became Tacoma's second lumber mill.
- Ezra Meeker platted Puyallup.

1880
- (February) New Tacoma government established.
- (November) County seat moved from Steilacoom to New Tacoma.
- The Carbon Hill coal mine opened at Carbonado.

1881 South Prairie Coal Company began operations.

1883
- Filling of portions of the south shore of Commencement Bay for the Half Moon yard began.
- NPRR transcontinental main line completed.
- Clinton P. Ferry is the first to dedicate platted land for a public park.

- The Fannie C. Paddock Memorial Hospital, located on Starr Street, was dedicated.
- J.W. Sprague, Robert Wingate and J.H. Houghton organized the Tacoma Gas and Light Company.
- Tacoma City and New Tacoma governments consolidated with General J.W. Sprague the first mayor.
- Whitworth Academy was incorporated at Sumner and remained there until 1899 when it was moved to Tacoma.
- Tacoma Typographical Union 170 organized as the first union in the city.
- George H. Ryan and John F. Kincaid platted Sumner.

1884
- The collapse of Henry Villard's economic empire made Charles B. Wright president of both the Northern Pacific and Tacoma Land Companies.
- Tacoma Hotel opened on A Street.
- The Tacoma Chamber of Commerce organized.
- James M. McNaught platted the town of Roy.

1885
- Northern Pacific board decided to complete the rail road line across the Cascades. The work included the construction of a tunnel through Stampede Pass, a project contracted to Nelson Bennett.
- Knights of Labor organized in Tacoma.
- (November) Expulsion of the Chinese from Tacoma.

1886
- Construction began on the Northern Pacific Headquarters building prior to the company's move from Portland, Oregon to Tacoma.
- The Tacoma Land Company deeded Wright Park to the City of Tacoma.

1887
- The railroad switchback was completed across Stampede Pass marking the completion of the Cascade Division line.
- The Dawes Act allowed the selling of Indian reservation lands. The measure when implemented in Pierce County began a process whereby many Puyallup Indians would lose their land to real estate speculators.
- F.E. Eldridge platted Orting.

1888
- Nelson Bennett's Stampede Tunnel replaced the rail road switchback.
- Streetcar construction began in Tacoma.
- The St. Paul and Tacoma Lumber Company and the Tacoma Milling and Smelting Company located in Tacoma.
- Congress authorized the use of Point Defiance for a city park.
- Lake Park (Spanaway) was platted.
- Alfred M. Burnham platted Gig Harbor.
- Francis Bisson platted South Prairie.
- Alexander and James Wickersham platted Buckley.

1889
- Washington became a state.
- The town of Orting incorporated.
- Samuel Wilkeson, Jr. platted Wilkeson.

1890
- The town of Buckley incorporated.
- The city of Puyallup incorporated.
- Electric power supplanted horse-driven streetcars in Tacoma.
- George Francis Train undertook a trip around the world to promote Tacoma.
- The Northern Pacific Railroad moved its repair shops from the downtown area to South Tacoma.
- Tacoma's new city charter included the provision for a Board of Park Commissioners. The largest annexation in the city's history occurred the following year.
- Formation of the Tacoma Trades Council.
- Old and New Tacoma school districts were united.
- William Wilson platted Parkland.
- Frank D. Nash platted Brookdale.
- John S. McMillin platted Lime Kiln (McMillin).
- Thomas C. Van Eaton platted Eatonville.

1891
- The town of Sumner incorporated.
- St. Joseph's Hospital was dedicated.
- The Washington State Legislature created the Western Washington Experimental Station located near Puyallup.
- Washington Soldiers' Home and Colony, located out side of Orting, was dedicated.
- The Tacoma Smelter and Refining Company platted a portion of what would become Ruston. The firm filed a second plat in 1901.

1893
- World depression signaled the end to Tacoma's economic boom.
- Public utilities were introduced to Tacoma when the citizens agreed to purchase Charles B. Wright's Tacoma Light and Water Company.

1894
- Members of Coxey's army — Civil War soldiers petitioning for their Congressionally-approved pensions — converged at Puyallup to begin their "march on Washington."
- Pacific Lutheran University was founded at Parkland.

1895
- The University Land Company platted University Place as a possible site for the University of Puget Sound.
- The Ohop Ladies Aid organized as the first women's organization in southeastern Pierce County.

1897
- Beginning of the Klondike Gold Rush.
- George Allen, O.A. Verity and L.F. O'Dell established the utopian colony of Home on Von Geldern Cove on the Longbranch Peninsula.

1898 The Spanish-American War led to the federalization of Washington National Guard units. Most Tacomans were sent to the Philippines.

1899 Congress created Mount Rainier National Park.

1900
- (January) Weyerhaeuser Timber Company incorporated.
- Whitworth College moved from Sumner and opened in Allen C. Mason's mansion and library in Tacoma's north end. It remained at this site until 1913, when the college moved to Spokane, Washington.
- Puyallup Valley businessmen and farmers hold the first Western Washington Fair.

1901
- (February) Pierce County Commissioners annexed Puyallup Indian Reservation lands originally located in King County, thus expanding the county boundary eastward.
- The Northern Pacific Railroad completed the ware houses which lined the south shore of Commencement Bay.
- Tacoma Eastern railroad began operations to Mount Rainier.

1902
- (September) The Interurban between Tacoma and Seattle started running. It lasted until 1928.
- Congress authorized the use of federal funds to dredge the Thea Foss Waterway. The work was completed in 1905.
- The Puyallup and Sumner Fruit Growers Association organized as the county's first farmer's cooperative.
- Henry Lutkins platted Elbe.

1903 •The Tacoma Chamber of Commerce submitted the first of many plans to the Army Corps of Engineers for the development of the Tacoma harbor.
•The Puget Sound Power and Light Company (Puget Sound Energy) completed its hydroelectric power plant at Electron.

1904 •Congressional legislation allowed the Puyallup Indians to sell their land allotments to whites setting in motion the development of Tacoma's harbor east of the Puyallup River.
•In the Northern Securities Case the U.S. Supreme Court outlawed the monopolistic practices of Pacific Northwest railroads. The decision ultimately led to the arrival of all the major transcontinental lines into Tacoma.
•Walter Ashford platted Ashford.

1905 •Following the organization of the Booster's Club, Tacoma's advertising slogan became "Watch Tacoma Grow."
•William Rust sold the Tacoma Smelter to the American Smelting and Refining Company.
•The Pacific National Lumber Company platted National.
•Martin Hotes platted Alder.
•The Milton Land Company platted Milton.
•1906 The town of Ruston incorporated.
•Land developers began platting the Lakewood area.
•The beginning of major floods along the upper Puyallup and White Rivers led to the temporary abandonment of Corps of Engineers work on the Puyallup Waterway.
•Edward Huggins sold Fort Nisqually to the DuPont Company. The firm constructed the Village of DuPont between 1909 and 1916.

1907 •The Narrows Land Company platted Regents Park (now Fircrest).
•(June) Voters approved the creation of the Metropolitan Park District.
•(August) The Tacoma City Council approved the annexation of East Tacoma carved from former Puyallup Indian Reservation lands.
•The town of Milton incorporated.

1908 •The town of Roy incorporated.
•The McKenna Lumber Company established a company town south of Roy.

1909 •The Alaska-Yukon-Pacific Exposition was held in Seattle.
•(May) The Great Northern Railway began Tacoma service.
•Tacomans voted to change its government to a commissioner form. Parts of South Tacoma were also annexed at this time.
•The town of Eatonville incorporated.
•The town of South Prairie incorporated.
•The town of Wilkeson incorporated.
•Tacoma's National Guard Armory on South Yakima Avenue was opened to the public for the first time.
•Tacoma's President's Council of Women's Organizations formed to unite all the female groups in existence at the time.

1910 •The Union Pacific railroad began Tacoma service.
•Washington's State Constitution was amended to allow women's suffrage.

1911 •The Tacoma Chamber of Commerce began a "Greater Tacoma" campaign.
•Union Station was completed.
•Virgil Bogue designed a Tacoma harbor plan.
•(May) The Chicago, Milwaukee and St. Paul railway completed its transcontinental line to Tacoma.
•The Municipal Dock opened on the Thea Foss Waterway.

1912 •The Northern Pacific Railway began rerouting its mainline, one that included the construction of the Point Defiance tunnel.
•Completion of Tacoma's LaGrande hydroelectric power dam on the Nisqually River.
•Voters failed to approve the creation of the Port of Tacoma.
•The town of DuPont incorporated.

1913 •Nettie Asberry organized the Tacoma branch of the National Association for the Advancement of Colored People.
•Completion of the 11th Street (Murray Morgan) Bridge.
•Green River gravity system providing water to Tacoma began service.

1914 •Formation of Commercial Waterway District #1 and the beginning of the dredging for the Hylebos Waterway.
•Auto racing at the newly completed 2-mile wood track at the Tacoma Speedway drew up to 25,000 spectators.

1916 •Paradise Inn at Mount Rainier National Park opened.
•National Guard troops are sent to the Mexican border in an attempt to capture Pancho Villa.

1917 •Tacomans obtain a memorial from the Washington State Legislature directing the National Board on Geographic Names to change the name of Mount Rainier to Mount Tacoma.
•(July) Construction began at Camp Lewis.

1918 •(November) Voters approve the creation of the Port of Tacoma.
•The Tacoma City Council passed the first zoning ordinance.

1919 •(February) The first Red Scare came to Tacoma when local unions initiated a general strike.
•The Service Aviation and Transportation Company made a request to the Tacoma City Council to provide a landing field for airplanes. The Mueller-Harkins Field became the municipal airport sometime after the firm located on the Tacoma Speedway grounds.

1920 (February) The Tacoma City Council created the Planning Commission.

1921 •(March) The first Port of Tacoma dock was put to use.
•Striking miners were forced out of their company housing at Wilkeson.
•The Carbon River bridge was completed.

1922 The Northern Pacific Railroad completed its move to Seattle.

1923 The University of Puget Sound moved its campus to Tacoma's north end.

1924 Tacomans failed to get Congress to officially change the name of Mount Rainier to Mount Tacoma.

1925 The town of Fircrest incorporated.

1926 •(May) Tacoma's hydroelectric power plant on Lake Cushman in Mason County was completed.
•Camp Lewis was renamed Fort Lewis.
•The University of Washington dedicated the Charles Lathrop Pack Demonstration Forest near Eatonville.

1927 •Tacoma businessmen proposed the construction of a bridge across the Narrows.
•Property owners approved the annexation of the Port of Tacoma, the Hylebos Waterway and parts of Northeast Tacoma.

1928 •Marcus Nalley incorporated his potato chip business.
•DuPont Company platted DuPont Village.

1929 •W.L. McCredie developed the first "Greater Tacoma" map.
•(December) The aircraft carrier U.S.S. Lexington was brought to Tacoma to provide power to the city during a drought.

1930 The former Northern Pacific headquarters building became the city jail.

1932 (February) Tacoman Bobby Short was shot down by the Japanese in China becoming the first American to die in World War II.

1933 The new concrete Browns Point lighthouse began operations in Northeast Tacoma.

1934 •The Young Men's Business Club moved the remains of Fort Nisqually from DuPont to Point Defiance Park.
•(April) The Daffodil Festival was held for the first time.
•A 12-week longshore strike blankets the Pacific Coast.

1935 •National Guard and state patrol troops were sent to Tacoma to control a strike by timber workers.
•(October) A fire destroyed the Tacoma Hotel, built in 1884.

1936 The federal Department of Justice completed its pur chase of McNeil Island.

1937 •Lakewood Center, conceived by Norton Clapp, opened.
•The Carbon Hill Coal Company platted Carbonado.

1938 •Construction began on the first Tacoma Narrows Bridge.
•Tacoma's airport was sold to the U.S. Army beginning the construction of McChord Field.
•(April) The end of cable cars in Tacoma.
•(June) Trolleys were replaced by buses in downtown Tacoma.

1939 The Port of Tacoma created an Industrial Development District and began a program of land-fill to reclaim potential building sites.

1940 •(July) McChord Field and the Tacoma Narrows Bridge were formally dedicated.
•(November) The Tacoma Narrows Bridge collapsed.

1941 (June) Dwight D. Eisenhower, then Chief of Staff at Fort Lewis, was transferred to San Antonio, Texas.

1942 (February) Executive Order #9066 initiated the internment of Japanese Americans. The Puyallup Fairgrounds, renamed Camp Harmony, became the embarkation point for all Puget Sound Japanese residents.

1943 Tacoma utility officials began moving Alder residents as a preliminary to flooding the original settlement. Alder Lake dam and reservoir were completed in 1947.

1945 (August) The day after President Harry S Truman announced the end of World War II more than 20,000 people crowded downtown Tacoma for a ticker-tape parade.

1946 •The Top of the Ocean opened for business on Tacoma's waterfront.
•The town of Gig Harbor incorporated.

1947 McChord Field became McChord Air Force Base following the establishment of a separate service for air defense.

1948 •The town of Carbonado incorporated.
•The Port of Tacoma completed the development of industrial sites around the Wapato Waterway.
•An annexation in Northeast Tacoma became the last major addition to the city.

1949 •(April) A 7.1 earthquake caused millions of dollars in damages in Tacoma and killed Marvin Kliegman, a student at Lowell Elementary School.
•(July) The Seattle-Tacoma International Airport at Bow Lake in King County was dedicated.
•The town of Bonney Lake incorporated.

1950 (October) The second Tacoma Narrows Bridge was dedicated.

1952 (November) Tacomans voted to change city government to a Council-Manager form.

Index

See following page for Partners & Web Site Index

Partners & Web Site Index